Praise for *Big Girls Don't Cry*

"I didn't know what I didn't know about the 2008 election until reading Rebecca Traister's smart, entertaining take on it. Well researched, well written, provocative and insightful, *Big Girls Don't Cry* is a high spirited salute to feminism in its many forms."
—Curtis Sittenfeld, author of *American Wife*

"In this riveting account of the 2008 election, Rebecca Traister negotiates the shoals of race and gender with exceptional grace and skill and establishes herself as one of the major younger journalists working today."
—Katha Pollitt, poet, essayist and columnist for the *Nation*

"Traister brings her elegant prose and unique perspective—thoroughly feminist but never doctrinaire—to this absorbing personal exploration of the meaning of gender in the last election."
—Ariel Levy, author of *Female Chauvinist Pigs*

BIG GIRLS DON'T CRY

The Election That Changed Everything
for American Women

REBECCA TRAISTER

FREE PRESS
New York   London   Toronto   Sydney

*f*P

FREE PRESS
A Division of Simon & Schuster, Inc.
1230 Avenue of the Americas
New York, NY 10020

First Free Press hardcover edition September 2010

FREE PRESS and colophon are trademarks of Simon & Schuster, Inc.

For information about special discounts for bulk purchases,
please contact Simon & Schuster Special Sales at 1-866-506-1949
or business@simonandschuster.com.

The Simon & Schuster Speakers Bureau can bring authors to your live event.
For more information or to book an event, contact the Simon & Schuster
Speakers Bureau at 1-866-248-3049 or visit our website
at www.simonspeakers.com.

Designed by Mspace/Maura Fadden Rosenthal

Manufactured in the United States of America

1   3   5   7   9   10   8   6   4   2

Library of Congress Cataloging-in-Publication Data
Traister, Rebecca.
Big girls don't cry : the election that changed everything
for American women / Rebecca Traister.
p. cm.
1. Presidents—United States—Election—2008. 2. Women in politics—
United States. 3. Women—Political activity—United States.
4. Feminism—Political aspects. 5. Clinton, Hillary Rodham.
6. Palin, Sarah, 1964– 7. Obama, Michelle, 1964– I. Title.
JK2762008 .T73 2010
324.973'0931—dc22
2010009631

ISBN 978–1–4391–5028–3
ISBN 978–1–4391–5487–8 (ebook)

"Obama Girl" lyrics by Ben Relles and Leah Kauffman

For two women
born before the 19th Amendment:
Eleanor Howard,
who always voted for Republicans,
and Betty Traister,
who often voted (in protest) for her cat

CONTENTS

Yesterday, a beautiful day . . . I was talking to [an older] woman who said that she wouldn't want to be me for anything in the world. She wouldn't want to live today and look ahead to what it is she sees because she's afraid. Fear is always with us but we just don't have time for it. Not now.

HILLARY RODHAM, Wellesley
commencement speech, 1969

The United States was said not to be ready to elect a Catholic to the Presidency when Al Smith ran in the 1920's. But Smith's nomination may have helped pave the way for the successful campaign John F. Kennedy waged in 1960. Who can tell? What I hope most is that now there will be others who will feel themselves as capable of running for high political office as any wealthy, good-looking white male.

SHIRLEY CHISHOLM, *The Good Fight*, 1973

I think we can all agree that it's a great time to be a lady in America.

TINA FEY, *Saturday Night Live*, 2008

BIG
GIRLS
DON'T
CRY

INTRODUCTION

THE FIRST TIME I entered a voting booth I was nine years old. It was 1984, and my parents had brought me with them so that I could pull the lever for the first woman ever to run on a major party ticket for vice president of the United States. I remember walking proudly with my father and mother and younger brother into the suburban Philadelphia firehouse five blocks from the house in which I grew up, where the poll watchers knew my parents by name because they were two of the very few registered Democrats in our district.

I remember the weight of the curtain closing behind me and my father lifting me up to turn the black lever to make the X appear next to Walter Mondale's and Geraldine Ferraro's names. I remember him putting me back down so that he could turn the buttons for the other Democrats, and then telling me to pull the rubber-covered metal bar back as hard as I could, until the machine made a clanging noise that meant my vote had been counted.

When we left the fire station my brother and I climbed into the back seat of our car and my mother turned to make sure our seat belts were fastened; my father looked at us through the rearview mirror. "I hope that someday you'll have the chance to vote for a woman at the top of a presidential ticket," he said before starting the car and driving us home.

Almost twenty-four years later, on Super Tuesday in February 2008, I walked into a cavernous school gymnasium in Brooklyn to cast my primary vote on Super Tuesday, for the first time in my voting life unsure of which lever to turn. It was the moment that could bring me closest to fulfilling my father's wish: I could put the X next to the name of a woman and bring her closer to the top spot on the Democratic ticket. But I had spent months saying that I would never vote for her, that she was not my kind of candidate, not my kind of woman. Even though I was beginning to change my mind, my distaste for her felt entrenched, and perhaps self-defining.

I spent fifteen minutes behind the curtain, shoving levers back and forth. I considered the other name on the ballot, a man who was also not exactly my kind of candidate, but whose potential place at the top of the Democratic ticket would put him close to becoming the first African American president, a possibility just as thrilling as that of electing a woman. I wished that I didn't have to choose between them. I wished that I could vote for them both. I wished that I could vote for someone else altogether. I mostly wished that it was a different woman's name in front of me, one that didn't fill me with ambivalence and vague foreboding.

I would never have imagined, as I stalled and fidgeted in that booth while a line of voters formed behind me, that four months later I would be ducking out of a cordoned-off press section in the National Building Museum in Washington, D.C., pushing my way through throngs of people in search of a place where I could cry in private. Behind a soaring column I gulped out sobs of exhaustion and disappointment at the end of the campaign of the woman for whom I had not been sure I could vote, even seconds before pulling the rubber-covered bar to seal my choice.

This book is an attempt to tell a story of change, change that came to me, yes, but also to the country, to the Democratic and Republican parties, to the women's movement, and to the White House. Over a period of just a few years, it seemed, the United States, its assumptions, its prejudices, its colors, shapes, sizes and vocabulary, had cracked open.

A woman, Hillary Clinton, won a state presidential primary contest for the first time in this nation's history. Less than a year later a candidate for vice president of the United States concluded her appearance in a national debate by reaching for her newborn baby. Whatever else there is to say about Sarah Palin or the reasons that her youngest son was on stage that night, that maternal reach was a roaring first in presidential politics. We have seen it once now. That means it is possible to see it again. In the first month of 2009 an African American woman moved into the White House, which was built in part by slaves, as the first lady of the United States. Michelle Obama is only the third first lady, though notably the third in a row, to have a postgraduate degree; she met her husband when she was assigned to mentor him at the law firm where she worked. He is now our first African American president.

These are not small things. These are changes that have piled up fast, creating a world that our grandmothers could barely have dreamed of, that many of our mothers thought they'd never live to see. They're also changes that our grandmothers and mothers made possible and that will in turn alter the landscape for coming generations. The events of the past few years provided a prism through which both past and future became briefly clearer.

Though a presidential election is by definition a political event, the cultural shifts made visible and made possible in 2008 took place well beyond the scope of purely presidential history. For a time it was very droll to credit Tina Fey with changing the course of the election and sealing John McCain's electoral fate with her deadly impersonation of his running mate. But Fey, who had made history some years earlier by becoming the first female head writer of *Saturday Night Live*, would never have had the opportunity to make this impact had there not been a woman running for vice president. Fey's most cutting sketches would not have been possible if another woman, Katie Couric, who had made history by becoming the first solo female anchor of a nightly news broadcast, had not been in a position to elicit unintentionally comedic material from Sarah Palin. And Palin, who had made history by becoming Alaska's first female governor, would not have wound up as a mark for Fey and Couric had she not been hired to sop up the tears and the votes of those who had supported Hillary Clinton's run for the presidency.

Political breakthroughs begat cultural breakthroughs begat comedy breakthroughs begat political breakthroughs. The country was in a steady revisionist conversation with itself, with voters, with candidates, with pundits, with entertainers. It was a wild, dizzying ride.

It is a poetic injustice that the drawn-out political marathon of 2008, a contest that at times seemed to drag on for decades rather than months, actually took place at breakneck media speed, and that it was narrated to us faster than we could absorb it. Once it would have taken years of retrospective investigative journalism to inform the American public of everything that had happened during a presidential election. In 2008 twenty-four-hour cable networks and the Internet offered hastily crafted daily tomes. We were fed sloppy synopses and cartoonish characters at rat-a-tat pace. Many of us, struggling to keep up, were happy to just get the Cliffs Notes version. But in the ceaseless cycle of revelation and analysis we lost depth, clarity and perspective on the story that was unfolding around us, as well as on how that story was itself changing and reshaping us.

My goal here is to tell the story of women and the 2008 presidential election, though not exactly the stories of the key women themselves. There are far better political reporters than I who have already begun to fill in the details surrounding why Hillary Clinton didn't fire Mark Penn in January, why Michelle Obama thought it was a good idea to be honest about *everything,* why Sarah Palin didn't just admit that she read the *New York Times* and move on. These women are at the heart of this tale, but insider campaign rehash is neither my talent nor my particular concern. The story I aim to tell is the one about the country and its culture, how we all reacted to the arrival of these surprising new figures on the presidential stage and what they showed us about how far we had come and how far we had yet to go.

Yes, there was misogyny, and I will describe some of it, but that is not the revelation of this book. To say that Hillary Clinton faced sexism is practically meaningless. She was the first woman in American history to get within spitting distance of a nomination for president; of course she faced sexism. It's far more interesting to examine the sometimes unlikely directions from which that sexism sprang, as well as the racism and classism that were often in high relief and aimed at other candidates, and why the manifestations of these prejudices still surprised us.

How ready were American voters for these women, and how ready were the women themselves? How prepared was the media to talk about them? How prepared were their political parties? What did their presence teach us about America's female voters—those who were hounded for supporting women candidates, those who were hounded for not doing so, those who reported on them and those who were still trying to sort out what feminism meant some ninety years after American women gained the right to vote?

In that last regard this book is not simply a narrative history but an argument, one that will not be popular with many who consider the 2008 presidential election as proof that feminism has failed. The political reporter Anne Kornblut has written that the contest was "a severe letdown, with damaging consequences" for women, and that it "set back the cause of equality in the political sphere by decades." And one particularly dour blogger proclaimed in the summer of 2009 that "2008 was when feminism, the women's liberation movement, ended up crashing." I believe the opposite, that this was the year—the years, really—in which what was once called the women's liberation movement found thrilling new life.

The impulse to declare social movements dead is as old as social movements themselves; the term *postfeminist* was used as early as 1919, a year before women gained the right to vote. The movement to increase liberties for women survived its first obit but has never lacked for premature mourners, or for critics eager to hold its wake. When people spoke, as they often did, about the state of feminism during the 2008 election, they mostly fell into one of two camps. One asserted that the women's movement of the 1970s was dead because its goals had been more than accomplished, and that modern women, no longer troubled by inequity, did not assign any larger symbolic value to the election of a female president. The other wailed at the expiration of a feminist dream, averring that the mixed fortunes of 2008's political women were emblematic of the unabated subjugation of women, and that not only had we not come very far at all, baby, but that perhaps we had slid backward.

Reality lay somewhere between, but also well beyond, these two diagnoses. The notion that we live in a world in which gender inequity has been satisfactorily redressed is about as persuasive as the proposition that Barack Obama's election proved that racism was a stage through which the country had successfully passed. But failing to recognize the vast distances women have traveled in the past half-century, let alone the past several centuries, was just as dishonest.

Progress does not happen in a straight line, as any historian of America's founding and revolutionary rupture, the abolition and suffrage campaigns, and the social movements of the 1960s can attest. The path toward perfecting our union has long been marked by semicircles and switchbacks, regress, tragedy and surprising forward bounds. Small advances spark resistance, resistance that in return provokes propellant bursts of reactive fury. The 2008 presidential contest electrified and enraged, radicalized and engaged us; it opened old wounds, and in doing so created new investments in the struggle toward equality. It recharged conversations—some ugly, some hopeful—that were perhaps in danger of going unfinished. The events surrounding the election did not provide a static snapshot of where women or feminism or America was; the events themselves were formative, catalytic, changing the positions and shaping the consciousness of American women and men at every turn.

The campaigns of Hillary Clinton and Sarah Palin, flawed and unsuccessful though they may have been, the arrival of Michelle Obama on Pennsylvania Avenue, the cultural shifts and uncomfortable exchanges these women prompted, the eye-opening revelations about the progress of women in early twenty-first-century America were in fact the most rejuvenating things to happen to the feminist conversation in many, many decades. They created and nourished a new generation of politically engaged Americans and left us with a story worth telling, hopefully far into the future.

★ ★ ★

I am a feminist journalist allied neither with the generations of second-wave (or third-wave) activists that preceded me, nor with the online rabble of younger women who are revivifying and redefining the movement as I type. I was born in 1975 to a mother who taught me not by instruction but by example that it was not only possible for a woman to participate fully in academic, professional and economic spheres, but pretty much expected. She did not go to marches or talk to me about the patriarchy; her political activism had been forged during the civil rights movement and she spent more time telling me how she used to drive to Chicago to listen to Jesse Jackson preach on Sundays. An English professor, my mother worked throughout my childhood, but also did all the cooking, cleaning, laundry and child care in our house. My father believed fervently in the intellectual and political parity of women, but not so much in doing the dishes.

In adolescence I found a few friends with mothers whose consciousness had been raised more directly by the second wave; with them I attended the March for Women's Lives in Washington in 1992; I wore pro-choice buttons on my coat. In college I studied eighteenth-century literature from a feminist perspective and listened to the Indigo Girls.

But having been a teenager in the backlash 1980s and 1990s, when even the girls at my crunchy Quaker high school prefaced their feminist observations with the defensive caveat "I'm not a feminist, but . . ." and having held my first journalism job at a gloriously musty boys' club newspaper where any story pitch that smacked of gendered discontent would have been laughed out of the room, I assumed that although my interest in women's issues might shape my personal life, it would not find a public, let alone professional outlet.

By the time the 2008 election season kicked off, I was not only earning my living writing about gender, but I was doing so in an atmosphere in which looking at the world from a feminist perspective had, improbably, become hot. When I was hired by *Salon* in 2003 it was as a staff writer for the "Life" section, a squishy category that included stories about relationships, sex, children, religion, health: girl stuff. A few of my early pieces touched on gender politics. To my surprise and that of my editors, these pieces generated attention, page views and lots of florid comments. I wrote more about feminism; the comments and traffic kept rolling in. And so I had a new beat, a lens through which I could examine politics, the media, entertainment, and social and sexual conventions.

My approach was not doctrinaire. After covering a thirtieth-anniversary discussion of Erica Jong's *Fear of Flying* in 2003, I wrote a bratty review headlined "The Feminine Antiques." I played with verboten words like *battle-axe* and *bitch*; I dubbed Florida politician Katherine Harris a "chad harpy" and Ann Coulter a "thin political pundit." Fascinated by the often ham-handed attempts of second-wavers to make their movement meaningful to a younger generation, I wrote critically about the 2004 March for Women's Lives in Washington, where older leaders of big feminist groups were unable or unwilling to engage the thousands of eager young women who had shown up to march with them, as well as about the troubled history and shaky future of the word *feminism*. While reporting a story about incorporating questions of morality into the abortion debate, a piece that questioned the bland language of "choice" to which a generation of activists clung, I found myself on the receiving end of a tirade from Feminist Majority Foundation president Eleanor Smeal; she screamed at me over the phone, asking why I would write something so superficial and divisive when women around the world were dying of fistula.

Women around the world *were* dying of fistula, but I didn't believe that that should prevent young people from reassessing signifiers of what had become a badly dated movement. I didn't want to water down feminism or sex it up or dumb it down or sell it out. But I did believe that in order to be taken seriously by serious young women, the conversation had to be drained of some of its earnest piety. Talking about gender in the new millennium required us, I thought, to get over ourselves a little bit, to dispense with the sacred cows, to question power and cultivate new ideas and leaders.

My early tenure at *Salon* coincided with the development of a few online sites created by young women anxious to form a modern feminist community, women whose ideas echoed my own. The most prominent of these was *Feministing,* founded by a twenty-five-year-old Queens native, Jessica Valenti, who was busting her chops to reach people her age whom she believed were hungry for more coverage about women, power and politics. She was right. As the online world exploded in many directions, each month seemed to bring a new site with feminist content, with names like *Feministe, Shakespeare's Sister, Pandagon, Echidne of the Snakes, Angry Black Bitch, Angry Brown Butch, I Blame the Patriarchy, Writes Like She Talks, Majikthise, Pam's House Blend, Shapely Prose, Racialicious, Brownfemipower, Bitch PhD, Feminist Law Professors* and *Womanist Musings.* At various points there were about six publications calling themselves *The F Word.* My musty boys' club newspaper hired a writer who began to cover business and media through an unapologetically feminist lens. In 2004 the Center for

New Words hosted the Women, Action & the Media Conference for feminist journalists, which in its first year drew a hundred people, and five years later six hundred.

Funnily enough, as my youthful commentariat company got broader I found myself becoming a shade less irreverent toward my elders, nodding in agreement with some of the more traditionally old-school feminist figures, the ones whom younger activists sometimes railed against, among them Linda Hirshman and Leslie Bennetts, who exhorted wealthy, educated women to stop dropping out of the workforce to care for their kids, and Ariel Levy, a writer of my vintage whose book *Female Chauvinist Pigs* questioned the purported sexual empowerment of a "Girls Gone Wild" generation. In 2008 I gave an appreciative talk at the thirty-fifth-anniversary celebration of Erica Jong's *Fear of Flying*.

That's where I was when Hillary Clinton announced her campaign for the presidency: a feminist caught between old and new, senior and junior, retro and nouveau, wanting to poke my elders with a stick even as I found myself agreeing with them, and wanting to celebrate the achievements of my younger peers, even when I found some of their commentary short-sighted and overly self-celebratory.

The prospect of a Clinton candidacy was exciting to those of us who wrote about women and power, not least because it promised to be good copy: the story of a much loathed but highly competent woman boarding the presidential roller-coaster and making an unprecedented grab for the brass ring.

But I could not have predicted the kind of electoral rapture that was about to overtake us all. If I foresaw the fury Clinton would provoke, I had no idea of the loyalty she would rouse or the way her campaign would open so many eyes to the realities of sexism. I had no inkling that there would be both Obamas to consider, that the contest between two candidates vying to be the first woman or the first African American nominee would obsess the nation for the better part of a year. I could not have summoned Sarah Palin from my worst nightmare, nor imagined the way she would inspire women on the right to lay claim to what they saw as their share of the feminist legacy. I could never have guessed how many of the questions that bedeviled the feminist world—questions of generational difference, race, class, sex, sexism, abortion, choice, the place of feminism in a Democratic agenda and humor in a feminist agenda—would get so widely aired to an electorate that may never have considered these issues before.

Whether you were a devoted Hillaryite or a Feminist for Barack, a Republican who wore a "Kiss My Lipstick!" button or a self-identified patriot who could not believe that Michelle Obama wouldn't be proud of her country, you were thinking about women and power and perception. If you put an "I Wish Hillary Had Married O.J." bumper sticker on your car or wore a "Sarah Palin Is a Cunt" T-shirt, you were broadcasting messages about gender. If you hugged Michelle in a church basement in Indiana, lined up for a Palin rally in Pennsylvania, voted for Hillary in Guam; if you loved Rachel Maddow's commentary about the election or thought that Chris Matthews was kind of a prick; if you cheered when Campbell Brown defended Palin's expensive wardrobe or snarfed your beer when Samantha Bee forced Republican conventioneers to describe Bristol Palin's decision to keep her baby as a "choice"; if you were a young progressive guy who wished the Hillary supporters would shut up, a Hillary supporter who wished the PUMAs would go away or a PUMA who wished that everyone would just choke on it already, then you were talking and thinking about and making women's history in America.

1 HILLARY IS US

IT'S EASY TO forget that at the start it was feminists who weren't wild about Hillary Clinton.

I don't mean at the start of Hillary. Back in 1993, when she marched into the White House with her ill-tended hair, barren cookie trays and big ideas about health care, feminists thought her the bee's knees, the elephant's instep, the best thing to happen to the executive branch since Eleanor Roosevelt.

I'm talking about more than a decade later, when it was clear that Hillary was locked and loaded to do what Eleanor could not have done: she was the one who was going to make a go at the presidency, the one they'd been waiting for. You'd have thought that women who had dedicated their lives to improving professional and political prospects for themselves and their daughters would have been beside themselves at the prospect of a solid Democratic female presidential candidate. But the intervening thirteen years had made things between feminists and Hillary Clinton considerably more fraught.

In 2006 the country was fired up for midterms that would halt

Republican control of Congress and bring us one election cycle closer to a new Democratic ticket. As the possibility that Clinton was going to jump into the 2008 presidential race became increasingly distinct, it often seemed as though feminists were more distraught about it than the right-wing louts who'd been pressing their "Iron My Shirt" shirts since 2001.

That spring I attended a benefit for the Women's Campaign Forum, a nonpartisan organization dedicated to putting prochoice women in political office. It was a crowd of monied, Botoxed, electorally enthralled dames who, in the popular imagination of the time, should have had "Hillary '08" mown into their Hamptons house topiary, if not their bikini lines. But on that night, a few months before the election that would secure Clinton her second term as the junior senator from New York, discussion of her future beyond New York was as cool as the evening breeze. "I like her a lot more than my wife does!" an affable WCF supporter was telling me, mock sotto voce. His wife heard him and sidled up, eyeballing my reporter's notepad. "We *both* love Hillary," the woman corrected with crisp dishonesty. "I just hope she can *catch fire*."

It seemed a neat summation of how many politically engaged women were feeling about the woman poised to come closer than any before her to gaining Oval Office entrance. Clinton was on the brink, and though many of her would-be cheerleaders weren't eager to say it out loud, they were secretly hoping she would just catch fire. Literally.

Though it is often cited as the period during which Clinton's self-assuredness created the resentments that would later provoke lusty axe wielding, it remains remarkable, miraculous really, that there was a span of months, nestled between two centuries of uninterrupted white male presidential power and one long Democratic primary tussle, during which the nomination of Hillary Rodham Clinton to the Democratic ticket seemed inevitable. Not just possible or probable: inevitable. One of the strangest things about this moment, for which Clinton would pay dearly, was that when her victory was presumptive many American feminists did not cheer her on, but shrugged their shoulders, curled their lips in distaste, or simply kept their distance.

★ ★ ★

In my years writing for *Salon* I had witnessed the feminist hunger for a female president when it was still comparatively abstract. In 2005 I covered a premiere party for *Commander in Chief,* the short-lived network television show in which Geena Davis played the president. The program was a cliché-studded mess, chock-full of menopause jokes and aphorisms most frequently found in forwarded emails. ("If Moses had been a woman leading the Jews in the desert, she'd have stopped and asked for directions. They'd have been in Israel in a week!") The party for the show, hosted by the White House Project at Caroline's Comedy Club, left no Girl Power signifier unturned; chocolate bars were handed out while Shania Twain's "Man! I Feel Like a Woman!" played. The hokeyness of the affair made it all the more embarrassing that, at the moment in the otherwise dreadful pilot when the heroine entered the House Chamber to the familiar words "Mr. Speaker, the President of the United States" and the imposing Geena Davis—Thelma!—walked through the door, an unironic chill shot through the crowd.

Looking around at the gathering of mostly over-fifty women, some of whom had begun to sniffle, it dawned on me that some probably hadn't been sure they'd live long enough to see this, even on television. Gloria Steinem confirmed this realization later in the evening, when she took the stage and asserted, "One of the advantages of being an old person is that you see how far we've come." Steinem also hit on the thing that gave the evening its undeniable frisson: part of what made this silly program moving was the unspoken awareness that women were, for the first time, within striking distance. "We are so ready," Steinem told the crowd.

A year and a half later it was clear that although feminists may have been ready for the *idea* of a female president, they were not so ready for the candidate who was actually going to run. Even Steinem wasn't exactly throwing herself behind Clinton. In early 2007 she announced in a *New York Times* op-ed that she was supporting *both* Clinton and her newly hatched competitor, Barack Obama. The op-ed was very warm toward Clinton, but not a ringing endorsement. Far more damning were critics like Susan Douglas, who described the mood in a piece for *In These Times*: "We sat around the dinner table, a group of 50-something progressive feminists, talking to a friend from England about presidential politics. We were all for Hillary, weren't we, he asked. Hillary? We hated Hillary. He was taken aback. Weren't we her base? Wasn't she one of us? Why did we hate Hillary?"

Why did they hate Hillary? How had the candidate contracted this social disease, and why was it manifesting symptoms at such a crucial historical moment?

Perhaps women demanded authenticity from Clinton in a way that they might not have in another candidate, male or female. Ann Douglas, a Columbia University cultural historian who had profiled Clinton for *Vogue* in 1998, told me in 2006 that because of Hillary's long time in the public eye and her history as a flashpoint for issues political and personal, women saw—or more to the point, didn't see—in her what they wanted to see in themselves. She referred to an old Tony Curtis anecdote about a fan who approached him and asked, "Are you who I think I am?" It was the same with Clinton, Douglas said. "We say, 'I want her to hold up my own ideals of myself. I want her to be who I think I am.'"

Here was a woman who had been vastly overqualified for the traditional role of first lady, making feminist fantasy flesh by attempting a return to the White House as president. She wasn't the kind of woman you'd have guessed might be the first, some shellacked Republican whose politics made Margaret Thatcher look like Barbara Jordan. No, Clinton was a Democrat, with a lifetime of advocating on behalf of children's welfare, women's equality and universal health care; she was a woman whom her spirited conservative detractors had made the standard-bearer for feminism. To hear right-wing men tell the story, left-leaning women were already running through the streets, burning Bella Abzug's bra in ecstasy!

But they were not. By 2006 the discontent that some establishment feminists felt about Clinton's impending run had become the undercurrent of many political conversations. At a September awards reception for the Center for the Advancement of Women, I asked a smiling Jane Fonda what she thought of the idea of Hillary running for president. Fonda tensed; her grin faded. It was a celebratory, lady-happy night at the Waldorf Astoria; later the Washington comedy troupe The Capitol Steps would perform a *My Fair Lady* parody called "Wouldn't It Be Hillary?" Here were all these women celebrating advancement. And here was this unpleasant question. "I don't put so much importance on candidates," Fonda said, though two days later she would travel to Sweden to stump for female parliamentary contenders. "I want to spend my time and energy getting women to the polls. I would never vote for a candidate just because she was a woman, because we have had plenty of female presidents and prime ministers where I would rather have had a male feminist." A few months later Fonda would refine this point in an interview with *LA Weekly,* allowing, "It may be that a feminist, progressive man would do better in the White House than a ventriloquist for the patriarchy with a skirt and a vagina." (She later insisted that she hadn't been referring to Hillary specifically.)

☆ ☆ ☆

When America first met her in 1992 Hillary Rodham Clinton looked like what she was: a working mother. She had recently chucked her Coke-bottle glasses but still sported headbands and weird amounts of ineptly applied makeup. Why should it have been otherwise? Clinton was a busy woman when her husband ran for president. Mind-bogglingly she would be the first first lady in American history to have maintained a full-time career outside her husband's political life prior to his presidency. In short, Clinton was the first candidate for the job of first lady to have a life that reflected post-second-wave America and the many working women who made their careers and raised their families here.

"I suppose I could have stayed home and baked cookies and had teas, but what I decided to do was fulfill my profession, which I entered before my husband was in public life," she famously said. She was responding to reporters at a Chicago diner who pressed her about Jerry Brown's charges that her law profits conflicted with her husband's political career. Her penitent follow-up was never as widely remembered. "I'm a big believer in women making the choices that are right for them," she told the reporters who'd been herded out of the diner as soon as she dropped the cookie bomb. "The work that I have done as a professional, as a public advocate, has been aimed at trying to assure that women can make the choices they should make—whether it's full-time career, full-time mother-hood, or some combination. . . . [That] is a generational change."

Amy Wilentz wrote about that famous remark, "What's wrong with baking cookies, Hillary, huh? Are you too good for that? But she did think she was too good for that, and so did hundreds of thousands of us. We were made for things that were better than baking." Hillary's statement wasn't radical for a certain class of professional women who had built careers in the 1970s and 1980s. But it was radical to hear it expressed by a woman whose task it was to win the hearts of American voters, some of whom had not yet adjusted to the idea of a woman who didn't consider tending home and hearth her highest calling.

"I got hundreds of letters about 'cookies and tea,'" Clinton wrote in her memoir, *Living History.* "One letter referred to me as the Antichrist, and another said I was an insult to American mother-hood." Clinton understood her position: "While Bill talked about social change, I embodied it. I had my own opinions, interests and profession. For better or worse, I was outspoken. I represented a fundamental change in the way women functioned in our society." Alluding to the many times during that 1992 campaign that she was called a Rorschach test for the American people, Clinton main-tained that neither the devotion nor the virulent rage she inspired was about her, but rather was about the still recent rupture in the American social fabric that she represented: "I had been turned into a symbol for women of my generation."

Everyone soon learned that Clinton had not changed her name after marrying her big-pawed law school swain, at least not until 1982, when advisors determined that her refusal to add her hus-band's last name to her own had cost Bill Clinton his second term in the Arkansas governor's mansion two years earlier. The sacrifice of her maiden name in the interest of her husband's political future always seemed to me to shed valuable light on Hillary and what she would eventually become. Whenever people claimed that she was a born shape-shifter, that political chameleonism was written into her genetic code, I would think of that last name and her pro-tracted insistence on keeping it independent. She hadn't wanted to be Hillary Clinton; she wanted to be Hillary Rodham. When faced with the assertion that doing it her way would result in her husband's loss, or at least blame for her husband's loss, she made the change. But it was a compromise, not a concession: she became Hillary Rodham Clinton. The question of her name would return, and on the campaign trail in 1992 it forced her to begin to grasp that although she "had worked full-time during [her] marriage to Bill and valued the independence and identity that work provided," she was now "solely 'the wife of,' an odd experience." Clinton described opening a box of stationery she'd ordered; embossed across the top was "Hillary Clinton." "Evidently someone on Bill's staff decided that it was more politically expedient to drop 'Rodham,' as if it were no longer part of my identity," she wrote, adding that she quickly ordered new stationery. But by that point, hers was a lost name.

There were still plenty of ways Clinton asserted her independence from hoary *femme couverte* practices, including her 1992 campaign trail claim, "[I'm not] some little woman standing by my man like Tammy Wynette." This was a gutsy thing to say. The fury with which the comment was greeted reflected a country unused to the idea that women are not obligated to stay in bad marriages and support their mates. It was the kind of statement that made millions of women, who may never before have identified with a political wife, look up at the television and take notice.

To many of those women Hillary Clinton was the real deal: smart and driven, with good politics. A Goldwater Republican kid who'd turned left at Wellesley, she gave a graduation speech so feisty that she received a seven-minute standing ovation and was featured in *Life* magazine as a student leader. She went to Yale Law School and worked for abused kids at Yale-New Haven Hospital, did research related to Walter Mondale's senate investigation into the treatment of migrant workers, and campaigned for George McGovern in Texas. She spent a summer working for the radical lawyer Robert Treuhaft, monitored the Black Panther trials for civil rights abuses and was one of a handful of young women on the impeachment inquiry staff that advised the House Judiciary Committee during its Watergate investigation. Clinton specialized in children's rights and in 1974 famously compared kids' legal rights to other unjust "dependency relationships," citing "marriage, slavery and the Indian reservation system." She would later be raked over the coals for aligning the institutions of marriage and slavery, but her point was legally and historically dead-on. Clinton was a rigorous social and political thinker.

In 1974 she made the loaded choice to give up her promising career in Washington to follow her boyfriend back to his Arkansas home, where he was planning to run for the U.S. House of Representatives. Her friend Sara Ehrman recalled the road trip the two women took together from Washington to Arkansas, during which Ehrman tried to persuade Hillary that she was making a terrible error; when they entered Fayetteville, Arkansas, they saw football fans hanging from lampposts making Razorback hog calls. A *Washington Post Magazine* piece from 1999 described Ehrman's realization "that her beloved Hillary Rodham, her high-powered hope for the future, was about to settle in a town full of frat boys wearing pig hats." "That," Ehrman told the *Post,* "is when I started to cry."

Clinton found a way not only to live her life in Arkansas, but to make herself heard over the "Woo Pig Sooie!" chorus. She became the second female faculty member at the law school of the University of Arkansas at Fayetteville. She cofounded Arkansas Advocates for Children and Families and was appointed by Jimmy Carter to the board of directors for the Legal Services Corporation, which she was the first woman to chair. Garry Wills would write in 1992 that Hillary Rodham was "one of the more important scholar-activists of the last two decades." As the first female partner at the Rose Law Firm in the years preceding her husband's run for the presidency she was twice rated one of America's most influential lawyers by the *National Law Journal.* Chelsea Clinton was born in 1980, and Hillary scored an Arkansas Mother of the Year award in 1984, an honor that might have surprised those who deemed her the cookie-eschewing Antichrist eight years later.

Hillary Rodham Clinton was a boomer lady of the left, successfully balancing work and life, and many women just plain admired her. As the late great columnist Molly Ivins joked when Bill Clinton was traversing the campaign trail in May 1992, "What this country needs is a candidate half as good as his wife." The filmmaker and feminist writer Nora Ephron, who had covered the nomination of Shirley Chisholm for president in 1972 and had attended Wellesley a few years before Hillary, marveled to *Newsday* in 1993, "Did you ever think that anybody like us would be in that job? . . . She has a career and a child and a husband, and she's doing it." In the same interview Ephron said, "I love her so completely that, honestly, she would have to burn down the White House before I would say anything bad about her."

Hillary didn't burn down the White House, though tabloids claimed that she broke a lamp or two in fights with her husband. But her tenure on Pennsylvania Avenue did not seal her place in the hearts of the American public. People who liked her liked her *a lot*. When she entered the White House her favorability ratings were higher than those of either Laura or Barbara Bush. But those who didn't like her really *hated* her. Bill Clinton had crowed about giving the nation a "two for the price of one" presidency, but the nation was not grateful. For those women who saw in Hillary a reflection of their own values and achievements, it was startling to witness the contempt that she inspired.

The hammering of Hillary was unrelenting. She was a bitch, a witch; she had big thighs, fat ankles. She was Shillary, Shrillary, Hellary Rotten Clinton. Together she and her husband were "Billary." Republicans sifted through her every business deal, tried to nail her on Whitewater and tie her to the death of deputy White House counsel Vince Foster. She was mocked bitterly after reports that she was having imaginary conversations with the spirit of Eleanor Roosevelt. By 1996 Nora Ephron was telling a graduating class at Wellesley, "Don't underestimate how much antagonism there is toward women and how many people wish we could turn the clock back. . . . Understand: every attack on Hillary Clinton for not knowing her place is an attack on you."

What juiced many of the most damaging early attacks on Hillary was her role in the failed effort to pass a well-intentioned and dismally received plan for universal health care. She and her husband, like many before them, understood that America's health care system was broken and needed to be rebuilt. Just after taking office in 1993, Bill announced that Hillary, who had led a successful effort to reform Arkansas's education system, would lead a task force to overhaul the national health system. Although her appointment provoked some early grumbling, her work initially earned positive reviews. Her lengthy testimony before five congressional committees in September 1993, weeks before the legislation was formally presented to Congress, was widely hailed as brilliant, though she would later write that she suspected the accolades were the product of "talking dog syndrome," a riff on Samuel Johnson's comment that a woman preaching was like a dog walking on its hind legs. "Some people are still amazed that any woman . . . can hold her own under pressure and be articulate and knowledgeable," Clinton wrote. "The dog can talk!"

Regardless, Hillary's barking testimony was soon forgotten; the Health Security Act was a political disaster. The reasons for Clinton's health care belly flop were varied and depended on who you asked. Many felt that the complex plan reached too far and too left, pushing for limits on spending and coverage requirements that the public and business employers were not ready to accept. Republicans knew that they could not afford to let health care pass and hand middle-class voters to the Democrats for generations; Republican strategist Bill Kristol had told them as much in a memo that urged them to kill the bill in any form. Both Clintons suffered from a hunted-animal, anti-Beltway complex; their early work on health care was done mostly in secret with their friend and business consultant Ira Magaziner, who did not have many Washington ties. By the time the Clintons trotted out the package they had a Congress full of Democrats who had been rubbed the wrong way and Republicans ready to pounce. Some have reported that it was Hillary's unwillingness to sacrifice the "universal" aspect of her plan, even when her husband was open to doing so, that helped seal the project's fate. Others, such as former White House senior health policy advisor Paul Starr, who worked under Magaziner, have written that Hillary's role in the plan's drafting was never as great as her husband, or history, led us to believe. But it didn't matter; she was too enticing a target for Republicans to resist. The plan was promptly dubbed "Hillarycare," linking her name with policy debacle, and its failure helped provide some of the fuel her husband's opponents needed to retake Congress in 1994, under the leadership of Newt Gingrich. Hillary's history-making role in the West Wing had been a fiasco.

She wasn't completely abashed. In 1995 she went to the United Nations Fourth World Conference on Women in Beijing and made the mundane but revolutionary statement that "Women's rights are human rights." At home she partnered with Janet Reno to support the creation of the Violence Against Women Office at the Department of Justice and told the United Nations in 1997, "In too many places, the suffering of women is defined as trivial, explained away as a cultural phenomenon; perhaps it is for this reason that women do not receive proper healthcare, including access to family planning." In a 1999 speech about pay equity she observed, "We know that women who walk into the grocery store are not asked to pay 25 percent less for milk. . . . It's not just a gap in wages, it's a gap in our nation's principles and promises."

But she did begin to tone it down, to smooth the unruly spikes of her personality. The hair, the makeup, the clothing: they all got fixed, patted down into some inoffensive template of first lady presentability. She also began to tame some of her political cowlicks, minimizing her role in her husband's administration and fulfilling more pro forma first lady obligations. (See *Dear Socks, Dear Buddy: Kids' Letters to the First Pets,* Hillary Rodham Clinton, Simon & Schuster, 1998.) Deducing that she was perhaps too much, too soon for the United States, Clinton took her show on the road, focusing on areas in Africa, Asia and the Middle East where she could talk about women's rights, child welfare and health care, often taking teenage Chelsea with her.

Clinton was seeking a middle path, where she could be heard and not reviled. But some of the directions in which she was willing to bend frustrated even her most devoted supporters. Gloria Feldt, who was president of the Planned Parenthood Federation of America during the second half of the Clinton administration and who would eventually become one of Hillary's most dedicated backers for the presidency, conceded retrospectively that at the start of Clinton's 2008 campaign she was unsure whether or not to support her. "I had had my ups and downs with her," said Feldt. "Knowing where her heart was, knowing where her intellectual understanding of things was. There were just so many times that she tried to appease people who would never be appeased anyway." Appeasing was a habit Clinton shared with her husband, a president whose hope-infused victory had filled the heads of his Democratic supporters with dreams of an energetic and progressive America, and then woke them rudely with "don't ask, don't tell," welfare reform, NAFTA and a second term lost to a blow job and a thong. For Hillary's army of early female adherents the let-downs were hard to take.

Feldt had been in Beijing for the women's conference. "I was in the room when she made that speech," she said, "and I was totally taken with her at that point." But when it came to reproductive rights in the Clinton White House, Hillary was best known as the rumored architect of Bill Clinton's famous assertion, anathema to pro-choice activists, that abortion should be "safe, legal, and rare," a formulation that cast abortion not as an integral component of women's rights and health, but as a regrettable last resort. In 2006 one of Feldt's predecessors at Planned Parenthood and later the head of the Center for the Advancement of Women, Faye Wattleton, told me with deliberate care that she hoped that as a presidential candidate Clinton would advance the notion that "unintended pregnancy should be rare and that abortion should be safe and legal."

As a team, the Clintons had often forced feminists to bob and weave. How many foreheads hit the desks at the National Organization for Women and the Feminist Majority when, less than three years after hammering the term *sexual harassment* into the American lexicon with their vocal support of Anita Hill's claims against Clarence Thomas, these organizations were being called on to respond to Paula Jones's accusations that Bill Clinton, the Democratic president supposed to be on their side, had committed the very same offense against her?

Feldt remembered with some horror the twenty-fifth anniversary of *Roe v. Wade* in 1998, which women's groups were marking together in a show of solidarity. Tipper Gore was scheduled to speak at a brunch for which President Clinton had been persuaded to make a video. In that video, recalled Feldt, Bill Clinton "was literally speaking from the playbook about the importance of family planning, connecting it to women's abilities to live their lives and be free. It was magnificent." At eleven thirty the night before the party someone called Feldt to say that Gore had the flu. "I knew something was wrong," Feldt said. At six the next morning she turned on the news, "and there was Monica." The video of Bill Clinton talking about family planning was never shown. "It was just devastating," said Feldt, "and kind of a metaphor for how the Clinton administration was for reproductive rights: your friends can do you in faster than your enemies."

★ ★ ★

It was fallout from the Lewinsky scandal that did Hillary in with some feminists, at the same time that it made her history-making future a possibility. Throughout the endless rehash of White House intern Monica Lewinsky's relations with her husband, Hillary Clinton allowed the president to play her for a fool. She attacked the media for their prurience, described a vast right-wing conspiracy, stood by her man. She did *not* do what many women yearned for her to do: throw him out. In 2009 Gloria Steinem wondered if some of those women weren't angry at their own husbands, yearning for Hillary to be the better versions of themselves. "They wanted her to punish Bill on their behalf," she said, "in the way that they were unable to punish their own husbands." Some of them simply wanted her to put her money where that anti-Wynette mouth had been; some perceived a more complex feminist betrayal. Melissa Harris-Lacewell, a professor of politics and African American studies at Princeton, told me in 2009 that she thought Clinton made "an appalling choice as a feminist—not that she stayed with her husband, but that she did not speak out in defense of a barely-older-than-teenage girl who was harassed by her husband. . . . And then she used that experience to create sympathy for herself."

Suddenly Clinton was more palatable to those Americans who had previously despised her. What had made her so unlikable for so long was her power, but it turned out that she hadn't had any power over her partner's itinerant pecker. For some it was comforting to see mighty Hillary brought low; for others the scandal provided an antifeminist moral about professional women unable to keep their men satisfied. Some argued that America just prefers its women prostrate and suffering. Whatever the explanation, the Lewinsky scandal made people who had always hated Hillary love her, which made the people who had always loved her nuts.

Some steadfast Hillary defenders, such as Ann Douglas, tried to put a positive spin on the situation, arguing that Clinton's refusal to defenestrate Bill was a rejection of the Victorian notion that "women's real business was punishing masculine immorality" and a sign that she had more important things to do than fret over her horn-dog husband. But this was the kind of rhetorical high-wire act that feminists had been performing on behalf of the Clintons for years, and it was frankly exhausting. Especially when Hillary was watching her own approval ratings skyrocket and pursuing a spot in the Senate. All it took was a little martyrdom and a lot of humiliation to make the widely loathed Clinton politically viable herself. According to the columnist Maureen Dowd, the equation was depressingly direct: "She couldn't move up until she was pushed down." Suddenly it looked like Hillary's political boost had been leveraged by her husband's presidency, and by its damaging scandal, rather than by her own dynamism, calling into question the notion of her feminist accomplishment and offering instead the distinctly unprogressive whiff of dynastic privilege.

In January 2001, before her husband had even vacated the White House, Hillary Rodham Clinton was sworn in as the junior senator from New York, a state in which she had resided for just one year.

☆ ☆ ☆

As she set about becoming the most popular girl on the Senate floor, Clinton was buoyed by startlingly high approval ratings and buzz about where her political career might go next. It went directly toward the center. Clinton's youthful work on behalf of migrant workers was replaced by her assertion on the radio in 2003 that she was "adamantly against illegal immigrants." Where she once fell on the sword of universal health care she now partnered on a health care compromise with Newt Gingrich himself. Where she once advocated passionately on behalf of children's rights she now pressed the reactionary Family Entertainment Protection Act, ostensibly protecting hapless kids from the dangerous effects of video games. Her positions shifted rapidly. She bid adieu to her longtime support of Palestine with a final wanton embrace of Suha Arafat in 1999. In its place was an unctuous devotion to Israel, embodied by the introduction of one of those convenient lost Jewish relatives. In 2005 she cosponsored a bill to ban flag burning.

After the 2004 election Clinton gave reproductive rights leaders worse heartburn than ever by joining the herd of Democrats distancing themselves from the pro-choice plank in the Democratic platform. Calling abortion a "sad, even tragic choice" for some, she told an Albany audience of family planning activists in January 2005, "I, for one, respect those who believe with all their hearts and conscience that there are no circumstances under which any abortion should ever be available." In the same speech she urged activists to shift their emphasis from abortion to prevention. "She's telling the people who invented prevention that they should get involved in prevention," Gloria Feldt said of the speech in 2009. "Honest to god!"

These gaffes were no longer the kind you could forgive or cheer, all knees and elbows and Tammy Wynette. They seemed not to be gaffes at all, but a preemptive shedding of her enlightened, liberal, populist impulses in favor of centrist agreeability. Clinton's political contortions radiated not independence or even a grim fuck-you attitude toward patriarchal, conventional wisdom, but a surrender to that wisdom. Unfortunately she had little of the ambrosial panache that her husband deployed to distract from his own obsession with likability. In January 2006, speaking at a black Baptist church, Hillary compared the House of Representatives to a plantation, adding with tone-deaf infelicity, "And you know what I'm talking about."

Most egregious for progressives, of course, was that not only had Clinton voted to authorize the use of force in Iraq, but she steadfastly refused to apologize for her vote and was late in condemning George W. Bush and his administration for taking the nation into a conflict as misguided as any since Vietnam, the war that had so obsessed her in her college years. Clinton voted for the Patriot Act, a bill that stripped away the kinds of civil liberties she had been so keen to protect as a law student. She resisted the idea of designing a timetable for troop withdrawal. She voted to categorize the Iranian Revolutionary Guard as a terrorist organization. She played it both ways in a crucial Connecticut senate race, backing her buddy Joe Lieberman in the primary and later lending his opponent, Ned Lamont, her communications director Howard Wolfson.

The galling thing was that it worked. Many predicted that Clinton would be a pariah in the Senate: an entitled, carpetbagging celebrity, a health care vampire whom no self-respecting moderate would come near without a garlic necklace and whom hard-right Mississippi Republican Trent Lott had publicly speculated might be struck by lightning before she set foot in the Capitol rotunda. Six years later Clinton and Lott were introducing legislation together.

In certain unexpected Washington venues Clinton went over like gangbusters. She became the first New York senator to sit on the Armed Services Committee. In New York she applied workmanlike hustle to addressing issues faced by her rural, conservative, upstate constituents. Her approval ratings in the state remained high, and she won reelection without breaking a sweat.

A cover story about Clinton in the *Atlantic Monthly* in 2006 opened with a scene from a 2001 Washington prayer breakfast, where she had become a regular as soon as she'd joined the Senate, during which anti-abortion, antigay Kansas Republican Sam Brownback asked her forgiveness for having hated her in the past. She and Brownback went on to cosponsor a bill calling for a study of violent television shows and video games. It was her willingness to play well with others, not simply by compromising with them politically, but by sitting respectfully at their knee, abiding by the hidebound traditions of seniority and spectacle that had long supported the Senate power structure, that paved her path to popularity.

As Joshua Green reported in his *Atlantic* piece, upon her arrival on the Hill, Clinton sought counsel from Robert Byrd, the aged West Virginia senator who had been in Congress for more than four decades and who had played a major part in blocking her health care plan seven years earlier. She asked him to lead classes for freshman senators on parliamentary rules and procedures. She brought her mother to meet him. Byrd told Green in 2006, "I guess I'm blowing myself up a little . . . but I think of her as a pupil of mine." Green reported that many prominent Republicans, including foresworn Clinton foes Gingrich and South Carolina Senator Lindsey Graham, warmed to Clinton in similar ways, and colleagues offered glowing reports of her willingness to move aside deferentially in photographs and to pour coffee for her (mostly male) colleagues, who approved of her efforts to be "a workhorse, not a show horse."

Clinton's curtseying was partly simple professionalism. Her reputation for being strident and chilly had been born mostly of sexist assumptions about powerful femininity, not reality. Expectations were upended easily when her archest of enemies actually worked with the woman most people agree is funny, warm, diligent and immensely likable in person. Clinton got major traction from a story about a trip to Estonia, during which she and John McCain threw back shots of vodka in a drinking contest. McCain told the *Atlantic,* "She can really hold her liquor."

Clinton was benefiting from the reverse of her "talking dog" formulation. The very fact that she was polite and civilized, that she was even kind of fun, was enough to impress her conservative male colleagues. The talking dog could heel! But the success of her ego-stroking strategy provided a disheartening lesson about how easily a powerful woman can change the minds of men if only she's willing to conform to power models that reassure rather than threaten them. Clinton was willing to do it, mirroring the process of abasement she underwent during the Lewinsky nightmare, to get what she needed. It was great for her presidential prospects, this comforting of feminist-frightened conservatives who had made her destruction their goal in the early 1990s. But it didn't put a spring in the step of the women who should have been her base, the ones whose initial admiration had been won by her refusal to kowtow to assholes.

Through an orchestrated willingness to manipulate parts of her belief system, Hillary Clinton became the world's most unlikely poster child for bipartisan cooperation and presidential potential. In the process she alienated many of the people who should have been cheering her on. She had become a one-size-fits-all likability machine who, in the minds of her detractors—the ones who used to be her supporters—would suck up to the bad guys, juggling freedom and flag burning if it meant winning the talent show.

☆ ☆ ☆

This was the baggage weighing down those American women who had worked their whole lives to amend the single-sex history of the U.S. presidency but who no longer saw themselves or their political beliefs reflected in Hillary Clinton. As they headed into the 2008 presidential cycle they struggled with the question of whether to turn their backs on the disillusionment that was Clinton, or whether the rare, flawed opportunity she presented them was a better shot at progress than no shot at all.

Thirteen years after wishing in print that it were Clinton, and not her husband, battling for the White House in 1992, Molly Ivins wrote a column titled "I Will Not Support Hillary Clinton for President." "Sen. Clinton is apparently incapable of taking a clear stand on the war in Iraq, and that alone is enough to disqualify her," Ivins wrote. "Her failure to speak out on Terri Schiavo [an autonomic patient at the center of a political battle over the removal of her feeding tube], not to mention that gross pandering on flag-burning, are just contemptible little dodges." Ivins would not live to see Clinton compete in the primaries. Nora Ephron, who had sworn that Clinton would have to burn down the White House in order to earn her ire, wrote in 2006 that Clinton had "as much authenticity as Naugahyde."

The Pulitzer Prize–winning journalist Margo Jefferson recalled listening to Clinton's attempts to distance herself from feminist politics, even while counting on the support of feminists, and thinking, "'Bullshit! We're all feminists. What the hell are you talking about?' This would drive me mad. It enraged me. She seemed to have this way—all politicians do it, but I wanted more from her—of taking advantage with one group of being the embattled, patronized, terribly intelligent and competent woman, and with another group, being the loyal partner and wife. I found this very galling."

It seemed as if the strength of identification, idealization and self-idealization that many feminists had first directed at Clinton amplified the degree of discontent they felt as she developed as a political animal. Medea Benjamin, cofounder of the feminist pacifist group Code Pink, told the *Nation* that the group's anti-Hillary stance was born of the fact that people "expect more of a woman." Susan Douglas, who wrote that all her feminist friends hated Clinton, went on to point out, "We don't want the first female president to be Joe Lieberman in drag. . . . We expect something better." The actress and activist Susan Sarandon flayed Clinton as "a great disappointment." "[She is] not worse than other politicians," Sarandon said, "but I hoped she would be better."

So that was it, in part: women hoped she would be better. Perhaps her failure to hold fast her positions through political gales made them doubt their own strength. Or maybe it just made them sad, the recognition that someone so like them could never have gotten as far as someone who was willing to become unlike them.

The tragedy of stratospheric hopes destined to go unmet was one that no one would have understood better than a young Hillary Rodham. As she told her Wellesley classmates almost four decades before she ran for president, "We arrived not yet knowing what was not possible. Consequently, we expected a lot." She was referring to the high-minded dreams of young women who had come of age in a time when people walked on the moon, joined the Peace Corps, led the civil rights movement. But when these young women arrived at buttoned-down Wellesley, she said, they found "a gap between expectation and realities." What she argued for, even as a disruptive liberal student, was a kind of compromise: although Wellesley's strictures inhibited the progressive ambitions of its students, they would not abandon the school, but try to change it as best they could from within.

There were many who didn't question Clinton's slip-'n'-slide centrism, but appreciated it as her political career progressed. One was her longtime supporter and friend Ellen Chesler, who told me in 2006 that Clinton "has clearly shown herself to be a candidate who can carry the banner of women without making it offensive." This jibed with an anecdote reported by Joshua Green in the *Atlantic*. Many right-wing women on the Hill, he noted, had at first dutifully despised Clinton. "But many eventually went on to confess a grudging admiration for her, for reasons that initially struck me as bizarre. 'She wore slacks to her swearing-in ceremony,'" wrote Green, recounting the reaction of one Republican staffer. "'I mean, you just don't *do* that in the Senate.'" The staffer's point "was that Clinton has flourished in the male-dominated milieu without making the normal concessions demanded of women, and has done so—this is important if you're a Republican—without making a big feminist stink about it."

But—and this was important if you weren't a Republican—feminist victory was supposed to involve offense and stink making, wasn't it? As Anna Quindlen wrote, "The fantasy was that the first woman President would be someone who would turn the whole

lousy system inside out and upside down. Instead the first significant woman contender is someone who seems to have the system
down to a fine art." Then again, no true agitator would ever have
made it as far as Clinton had. That, as Quindlen herself called it,
was fantasy, not American reality. For some Clinton defenders it
was time to dig in, butch up and stop being so damn picky. "The
days of believing in any leader with your whole heart are over," the
literary agent Sarah Burnes told me in 2006, fuming about liberal
women who were turning up their noses at Hillary. Burnes suggested that it was "a political responsibility" for left-leaning women
to support Clinton and stop wringing their hands about the authenticity of her feminism.

As she warmed up for her White House bid, Clinton regained
some political ground with reproductive rights activists by pushing
over-the-counter emergency contraception Plan B through the gluti-
nous bureaucracy at the FDA. In the fall of 2006 she appeased some
who had been disgusted by her refusal to support gay marriage by
signing on to a bill that would provide insurance benefits for same-
sex partners. These moves—late and somewhat limp, but good for
women, good for underrepresented Americans, good for civil liberties—appeared to encompass the best of what Hillary Clinton had
to offer the American left going into a presidential election: unreliable but intermittently effective action on behalf of the good guys.

"I see enormous progress right now," Faye Wattleton told me
after expressing her hesitation about Clinton's abortion waffling.
"We are a long way from Pat Schroeder, who was run off in tears
because of pressure and ridicule." Schroeder, the former congresswoman from Colorado who had attempted a run for the presidency
in 1987, was far from ambivalent; in 2006 she told me that she was
delighted at the prospect of a run by Clinton, or even Republican
Secretary of State Condoleezza Rice. Schroeder believed it was time
to storm the White House bearing the slogan "We couldn't mess it
up any more!" She understood better than anyone that women were
a lot closer to the executive branch of government than they'd ever
been. To her that was good news. But to others it meant the blighted
prospect of Clintonian compromise.

By the time Clinton entered true front-runner territory for the
nomination, some doubters, such as Feldt, were considering where

they stood. "I still had reservations about her," Feldt said retrospectively, "but from a philosophical position, I knew that she would be the person I would be supporting because I did not believe there would be another opportunity like this coming for quite a while."

There had always been utopian visions of female leadership, perfect because they could not, until this point, have been real. There were the hopes, the dreams, the bumper stickers declaring that if women ran the world there'd be no war. But as Hillary Clinton became the first to close in on the fantasy, she was voting for wars and her journey was laying bare just how a woman's position on the inside of the power structure could result in, or more chillingly, could be made possible only by a paralysis of political idealism. As Clinton's longtime political advisor Ann Lewis told me in 2010, "There has always been a tension in the women's movement between the extent to which you can get things done and the purity of your issues." Lewis made reference to suffragist Carrie Chapman Catt, who as president of the National American Woman Suffrage Association supported Woodrow Wilson's entry into World War I and was denounced by her pacifist colleagues, but whose actions allowed NAWSA to retain influence with the U.S. government, greasing the passage of the Nineteenth Amendment in 1919.

Clinton was forcing women to ask themselves, *What did we have to give up to get inside? Did we have to bastardize our beliefs to do it? And were bastardized beliefs better than the alternative?* If Clinton could balance her political ambitions with the principles that motivated her to invest in politics in the first place, then she still had something in common with feminists: they were balancing their ambitions for her, and themselves, with the ideals that first motivated them to invest in her.

☆ ☆ ☆

I was not among those who had ever invested anything meaningful in Hillary Clinton going into election season. It's not that I didn't care about her at all. I was seventeen when Bill Clinton won the White House, and to my teenage mind he and his wife were superheroes. Too young to remember a Democratic president, I believed that the Clintons' arrival in Washington was going to change everything: we were going to have a new New Deal; education was going to be reworked from the ground up; everyone would get health care. I cheered when Bill and Hillary got out of their car at the 1992 inauguration; they were going to govern us benevolently and brilliantly. I believed the Fleetwood Mac song: I didn't stop thinking about tomorrow. I opened my eyes and looked at the day, and I saw things in a different way.

I was the perfect age for getting my political heart broken. Just as in young romance, the letdown—of welfare reform, "don't ask, don't tell," centrism—didn't make me any less likely to fall for the guy again four years later. All those compromises were just so he could get reelected, I reassured myself, so he could give us the new New Deal in his second term!

The political disillusionment of our youth casts particularly long shadows. I guess it can make some people very angry and cynical. It wrought in me a perpetual state of hopeful resignation. In my memory the Clinton years were two brief periods of high-octane campaign optimism bookmarking eight years of feeling like Charlie Brown on his back in the grass, trying to remember why it was that he'd believed Lucy this time.

I wish I could say that I ever truly got over Bill Clinton. But I fear he was imprinted on me as the president I would fall for again and again. I remember staring at him as he boarded the helicopter to fly away from the White House on the day that George W. Bush moved in. I couldn't believe that I wouldn't see my emotionally abusive, constantly disappointing, dissembling, philandering leader every day anymore. I was going to miss him so much! I have since wondered if I took out my steely fury, which I seemed constitutionally incapable of truly aiming at Bill, on his wife, who was beguiling but ultimately resistible in a way her husband never had been. Perhaps I chose to blame her for all the things I couldn't really stay mad at her husband about.

I admired Hillary well enough, but twenty-eight years her junior, I had none of the visceral reactions to her that my elders had. I saw in her no reflection of myself or my experiences, though I surely saw echoes of my mother: hard working, uncoiffed, practical, smart and reassuringly competent.

I understood that she was important, but for me her import was literally academic. In 1997, my senior year of college, I went with my roommate, who was writing an honors thesis on Hillary, to see her speak with Jesse Jackson in Chicago. I was mostly there to see Jackson, my mother's longtime oratorical hero, but nonetheless found Clinton impressive. I marveled at how awkward she was when she shook hands at the rope line afterward. It was like shaking hands with a textbook, a person we had already studied, considered, argued about and were perhaps a little bored by.

As she moved through the White House and into her own political career, I actually tried not to think about her. It was embarrassing, how everyone expected women to have such strong feelings about her. That wasn't me. It's not that I had completely tuned out; I just managed to remain cool about her. I took reasonable offense to the epithets hurled at her without ever becoming passionately interested in defending her. I noticed that her popularity rose after she was cuckolded, but I was not particularly bothered by it. I was appalled by her Iraq vote but not surprised by her unwillingness to play a lady dove. I certainly hoped that she would apologize for that vote but was perfectly aware that apologia and self-recrimination were signs of feminine fallibility she was not likely to flash. I got it. I understood what she was doing, the binds she was in, the deals she'd had to make. I just didn't have any intention of voting for her. For me, Hillary Clinton was Darth Vader, a candidate who might once have been skin and bone and female empowerment, but who was now practically mechanical, who didn't have anything to do with me or my women's movement.

In those languorous inevitability days, when there seemed no question that she would be the candidate, my Clinton disavowal was not exactly symptomatic of the attitude that would later be caricatured and attributed to young female Clinton-resisters. I was not beyond feminism. I was not over it. I was not immune to caring whether or not we had a woman president. In fact I really wished, to the tips of my toes, that there were a female candidate for whom I could cheer loudly and lustily, in part because she was a woman. Clinton just wasn't that person. But my distaste did not come without cost. I was sad that I couldn't enthusiastically get behind her, and many young women shared my melancholy. The journalist Allison Hantschel wrote in the fall of 2006 that although she was "unexcited" and "indifferent" about Clinton, she was "nagged by the feeling that this [made her] a bad feminist. . . . After all, a woman president, any woman president, is a victory for womankind, right?" Was it? I didn't know. Should gender have trumped political ambivalence?

Before Clinton announced her candidacy, Kate Michelman, the former president of the National Abortion & Reproductive Rights Action League (now NARAL Pro-Choice America), told me, "If she runs, it will have been a long journey." But, she cautioned, "even though it will be historic, women want to be assured that they have a candidate who will represent them." Me, I agreed with Faye Wattleton, who before anyone had officially entered the race told me presciently, "Often, the pioneers who clear the paths do not have the honor or privilege of running along them. If it's not Mrs. Clinton who becomes our first [female] president, she will have made an enormous contribution."

2   SPOUSAL SUPPORTS

ALTHOUGH HILLARY'S BIG mouth and independent career were idiosyncratic departures when the Clintons hit the White House in 1993, the vision of the political wife was even more radically transformed by the brief presidential foray of North Carolina Senator Elizabeth Dole in 2000, and then by wives like Judith Steinberg Dean (who insisted that even if husband Howard became president she would not abandon her medical practice in Vermont) and Teresa Heinz Kerry (who listened to her husband's stump speeches with all the focus of a distracted tabby and greeted the Democratic convention in the five languages in which she was fluent). As the candidates geared up for the 2008 campaign America was greeted by Michelle Obama, who had met her husband when he was a summer associate and she his mentor at the corporate law firm where they both worked, and Bill Clinton, who was not a wife at all. The *Family Circle* cookie contest was not extinct, but when, in 2004, Heinz Kerry blithely admitted that a staffer had submitted a recipe in her stead, it was clear that the multicentury reign of happy first hausfraus was petering out.

The conga line of 2008's potential presidential partners reflected the broadly changed educational, professional, social and economic circumstances of women, especially American women of the class most likely to marry future presidents. In addition to the spouse who had already been commander-in-chief, there was Judith Giuliani, a divorced former Bristol-Myers sales manager, whose husband suggested that she might sit in on cabinet meetings; Cindy McCain, the founder of an international medical aid nonprofit, beer heiress, and recovering drug addict; and tongue-pierced sylph Elizabeth Kucinich, who had a master's degree in conflict analysis.

Elizabeth Edwards, an attorney and health care expert, copped one of the race's more traditional poses, as John's devoted spouse, unwavering in her adoration for him. That stance did not quite convey the centrality of her role, both within her husband's campaign and for the women deciding whether to support her husband.

Coming out of the 2004 election John Edwards did not appear to be going places. John Kerry had brought him on as a charismatic running mate and charged him with charming the pants off voters. Instead he was successfully tagged by the Bush campaign as a blood-sucking malpractice lawyer. As a vice-presidential candidate he had projected no coherent agenda and presented a résumé of slick and slightly dodgy jobs that only got dodgier when in 2005 he took a position at a firm with hedge funds incorporated in the Cayman Islands. The idea of Edwards attracting a following for a presidential run of his own seemed unlikely, especially with a Democratic field filled to bursting with female, African American, and Latino candidates.

But perhaps in part because he *was* a Caucasian guy who didn't have to worry about scaring other Caucasian guys with his difference, in competition with candidates who might attract their own progressive followings by dint of their history-making identities, Edwards had more freedom and more incentive to develop a broadly progressive agenda. When he wasn't working with the hedge fund, he was reinventing himself by talking about issues that no one else on the left would touch: poverty and the class divide in America. Edwards was rich; revelations about the size of his mansion and the price of his haircuts scratched his populist shell. But, as he was keen to remind anyone who asked, and everyone who didn't, he had grown up poor, the son of a mill worker. To those who believed in him, what mattered was that he was giving voice to a usually unspoken truth: that there were two Americas, one living above the poverty line and one below it, and that they offered their inhabitants starkly different scales of possibility. In this, Edwards was talking more about both race and gender than anyone else. Implicit in his calls for health care for every man, woman, and child, his insistence on better schools and on raising the minimum wage, were the facts that in 2007, 34.5 percent of African American children, 24.5 percent of all African Americans, and 21.5 percent of Hispanics were living in poverty, and that women were more likely than men to live below the poverty line.

I supported John Edwards going into the 2008 election because I agreed with him about the crucial place of poverty and class difference in the problems that ailed the nation. I liked what he said about the minimum wage and about rebuilding our education system. I believed that he had the most realistically progressive ideas about making the country a better place. And I really liked his wife, even if her earliest flirtation with women voters was not feminist-friendly.

In October 2006 Elizabeth was promoting her memoir, *Saving Graces,* which recounted her childhood as an army brat, the death of her sixteen-year-old son, Wade, in a car accident, the subsequent births of two children when she was close to 50 and her fight against breast cancer, which had been diagnosed days before the 2004 election and was then in remission. At a *Ladies' Home Journal* lunch she noted that she and Hillary Clinton were from the same generation of women: "We both went to law school and married other lawyers. But after that, we made other choices. I think my choices have made me happier. I think I'm more joyful than she is." The Edwards camp would later claim that her remarks had been inaccurately elided, but the rebuttal was not convincing, particularly because in her public apology to Clinton she reiterated a version of her earlier sentiments: "[Senator Clinton] holds a serious and demanding public office, while I am largely home, joyfully I must admit, with two lovely children."

Elizabeth Edwards had charged headlong into the battle royal referred to as the Mommy Wars. One of the most hotly debated subjects among well-off, highly educated feminists in the years leading up to the election was the purported Opt-Out Revolution, in which privileged heirs to the second wave had supposedly chucked their degrees (and their paychecks) in order to stay home with their kids. Studies would later demonstrate that the trend was largely invented, yet at the heart of the conversation was the concern that although feminism had created opportunities for some lucky women, it had not effectively redistributed or reimagined domestic expectations, leaving working mothers, still expected to cook, clean and manage children, to either take on the punishing "second shift" or leave the workforce altogether. On the other side were stay-at-home mothers who felt attacked and argued that feminism's goal was to give women choices, not dictums about how they must spend their days in order to qualify as feminists.

These brawls played out in magazines, newspapers and books about the pros and cons of working or staying at home: David Brooks's op-ed column in the *New York Times,* Caitlin Flanagan's pieces for the *Atlantic* and *The New Yorker,* Linda Hirshman's *Get to Work* and Leslie Bennetts's *The Feminine Mistake*. Mostly, however, invectives were slung in the mushrooming world of parenting and feminism blogs, where feminists, stay-at-home moms, working mothers and stay-at-home dads hashed and clashed until everyone's ears bled.

Well-known for the time she spent engaging in online debate, Edwards would have been acquainted with the hyper-self-righteous exchanges that took place on both sides of this discussion. Addressing a group of ladies who were literally lunching, Edwards chose to highlight one of the only discernible differences between her own professional history and that of her husband's prospective competition: that after the death of her son she had chosen to leave her law practice. She was sending a bat signal to mothers who might feel they had nothing in common with Hillary Clinton, a woman who not only had worked through motherhood, but was now fulfilling every conceivable dimension of her academic and professional promise by seeking the presidency of the United States.

Edwards's comments were, if technically true, wildly disingenuous. The "different choices" she and Clinton made after law school had come *a long time* after law school. Elizabeth had worked at the

North Carolina attorney general's office and then for a firm. During her cancer battle she had become an expert on the health care system and was one of its most zealous and inspiring public critics. She remained Elizabeth Anania until Wade's death, in 1996, when she became Elizabeth Edwards. But as she informed *Ms.* magazine in 2004, "I took my son's name; I didn't take my husband's name." In many respects the distancing of herself from Clinton was more performance than authentic self-expression. As dismaying as her Donna Reed feint was, it demonstrated that she understood something about the upcoming election: that in part it was going to hinge on women, and how they felt about other women. Even as she made digs at Clinton's less joyful choices, Edwards admitted that she remembered her congressional testimony on health care and that "as a woman, you couldn't help cheering from the sidelines." Edwards knew that there were others who would share her memories, and she was trying to figure out how to woo them to her husband's campaign. "That will be a factor for John," Elizabeth conceded. "She will be a formidable opponent."

Perhaps Elizabeth was so focused on Hillary not because of the differences she strained to manufacture, but because of how alike they were. Elizabeth Edwards was nothing if not formidable, another woman you couldn't help cheering from the sidelines. Her brains, her passion for policy and her brassy ability to endure hardship allowed women who were conflicted about turning away from Hillary the opportunity to invest in another dynamic political partner.

When the Princeton professor Melissa Harris-Lacewell, who would go on to be a vocal supporter of Barack Obama in 2008, initially said publicly that she thought he would make an excellent *vice*-presidential candidate, people assumed she meant as a running mate to Hillary Clinton. "I absolutely meant John Edwards," she told me in 2009. As a student in North Carolina, Harris-Lacewell had worked as an envelope stuffer for Edwards's 1998 Senate campaign. "I was just so impressed with him," she said in retrospect, "and with Elizabeth." She liked that John was a white southern Democrat, a profile she associated with Carter and Clintonesque coalition building. She liked in Elizabeth that, aside from her feminist credentials, she had a remarkable tale. "A fat woman married to a good-looking man is always a good story," said Harris-Lacewell, "particularly if she is a breast cancer survivor who has lost a child. There were so many different categories of women who could relate to those things and see themselves in her. When John Edwards looked at her lovingly, it was a way of valuing a whole group of women who are not typically valued in a public sphere."

In January 2007, just a week after Edwards declared his candidacy, Kate Michelman, former chief of NARAL Pro-Choice America, announced that she would be coming onboard as a senior advisor to the Edwards campaign. Michelman had spent her professional life fighting for reproductive rights, including running NARAL from 1985 to 2004. By 2007 she was struggling through a family health care crisis and needed a job, badly. Looking to work as an advisor to a presidential campaign, she would have been an obvious match for Clinton. But Clinton, trying her damnedest to pretend there was nothing unusual about her candidacy, certainly wasn't hiring feminists. John and Elizabeth Edwards were.

"It's rather unusual to have someone like me at a high level as a part of a campaign," Michelman told me soon after taking the job. Apart from Al Gore's depressing campaign dalliance with Naomi Wolf in 1999—*The Beauty Myth* author had famously advised him to wear "earth tones"—there was not an extensive history of presidential candidates taking on feminist advisors. Walter Mondale had solicited advice from the National Organization for Women, but that was because he was running the first female vice-presidential candidate, Geraldine Ferraro. Edwards had hired Michelman early, a full year before the Iowa caucus would kick off primary season. "It says a lot about his seriousness and commitment to addressing the experiences of women in society," Michelman said at the time. It also said something that he had not chosen just any old women's leader, but one who had specifically devoted herself to reproductive rights, one of the socially explosive issues away from which so many Democrats had swerved after the 2004 election. Her professional history, Michelman allowed, "could make a candidate feel somewhat reluctant or questioning. But it didn't with John and Elizabeth."

Michelman fielded questions from people who had assumed, or hoped, that she would work for Hillary. "I have three daughters and a granddaughter; I've been working for women's rights for nearly thirty years," she told me at the time. "Hillary's run is historic. . . . Part of me said, 'How could you not be a part of this given all you've worked for?' . . . But John's vision was very compelling." As Gloria Feldt later reminded me, "Kate had to live through the Clinton administration like I did, and it was not fun. They sold us down the river any number of times once Newt Gingrich had taken over Congress. And to get a budget through they'd sell their mothers."

What interested me more than Michelman's choice to work for Edwards was Edwards's choice to hire Michelman. Here was a male candidate's campaign preparing to tackle the challenges of facing a history-making female candidate by doing what she herself could not: making gender a centerpiece of his candidacy.

The month after Michelman signed on, the Edwardses added two even more surprising women to their staff, young denizens of the rowdy feminist blogosphere. Melissa McEwan, then thirty-two, was the founder of the online feminist site *Shakespeare's Sister* (later renamed *Shakesville*) and had written positively about Edwards on her blog; the campaign hired her as an Internet outreach consultant. McEwan supported Edwards because she was an economy voter, because she believed that Edwards was the most progressive candidate and because she loved Elizabeth. Though she would eventually move into the Clinton camp, she had a host of reasons for not initially supporting Hillary. "I bought into narratives about her that are just flatly untrue," McEwan told me in 2009. "Somehow I didn't think she was a great politician and was too focused on video games and flag burning—and she was. But those are little things. I wasn't careful enough to question things I normally question because the narratives about her are so pervasively negative." Despite the retrospective self-flagellation, McEwan maintained that she still would have been an Edwards supporter. "He had a good message that was prescient," she said.

Amanda Marcotte, then twenty-nine, had been writing about politics from a feminist perspective at the popular liberal site *Pandagon* since 2005. The Edwardses hired her as their campaign blogmaster. Marcotte, who would eventually become an Obama supporter, shared none of McEwan's self-recrimination about her decision not to support Clinton, a decision that many of the young liberal women at the forefront of online feminism would also make. "I always respected Hillary Clinton and thought she was kind of awesome," Marcotte said in 2009, but she added, "Hillary Clinton's flaw, at the end of the day, was that she voted for the Iraq war." Edwards had also voted for the war in Iraq but had bent over backward to assert that his vote had been a mistake. Marcotte liked Edwards because she believed he dragged his competitors to the left; she was also drawn to the campaign because they were drawn to her. "When they reached out to me, I thought, 'Here is a campaign that is trying to ground themselves in the netroots, and that obviously thinks feminism is viable and important.' The other campaigns struck me as play-it-safe types."

Hiring McEwan and Marcotte was anything but playing it safe. Though they had different writing styles, both were combatants in the skirmishes increasingly fought in the coarse vortex of the political blogosphere. For lefties and feminists furious at a warmongering and torture-condoning administration and incursions on reproductive rights and civil liberties, the unedited Internet meant no polite limits on discourse. Marcotte's and McEwan's posts on everything from birth control to popular culture often dripped with cynicism and outrage; they engaged in heated arguments with their readership and were profane with regard to institutions—the Catholic Church, the Bush administration, the right-wing media—about which many people still felt it inexcusable to be profane. Male-dominated liberal blogs tended to be wonky and politically aspirational, but feminist sites, dealing as they did with reproduction and body issues, were often raunchy and raucous in their embrace of carnal liberation and their rejection of sexual censure; feminist bloggers often made incisive but indelicate connections between sexual and other kinds of politics. Among the things Marcotte had written prior to joining the Edwards camp was a caption mocking the Catholic Church's position on birth control, posing the imagined rhetorical exchange, "Q: What if Mary had taken Plan B after the Lord filled her with his hot, white, sticky Holy Spirit? A: You'd have to justify your misogyny with another ancient mythology." McEwan, for her part, had a thoughtful and sharp-edged online persona and mostly engaged in old-fashioned cussing. She titled a 2006 post about a conservative Christian group's movement to ban gay adoption, "What don't you lousy motherfuckers understand about keeping your noses out of our britches, our beds, and our families?"

The choice to hire Marcotte and McEwan revealed either the campaign's prescient instinct that the election might lie in the hands of the young and the logged-on, or its short-sightedness with regard to some very old, creaky conservative machinery. The creaker in question was Bill Donohue, since 1993 the leader of the Catholic League (a league that may have included only Bill Donohue) and the erstwhile protester of every movie with questionably Catholic credentials since *The Last Temptation of Christ*. Donohue went to town on Marcotte and McEwan as soon as their hirings were announced, calling them "anti-Catholic vulgar trash-talking bigots" and stirring up easily purchased sympathy from conservative pundits like Michelle Malkin and Kathryn Jean Lopez. Even the *New York Times* dutifully reported Donohue's outsized ire against the bloggers, but failed to put it in the context of his history of outsized ire against *Dogma, South Park,* pop singer Joan Osborne and a 2005 episode of *CSI: Crime Scene Investigations.*

"It was Elizabeth Edwards who called to fire me," McEwan told me two years later. "That was the first time that I talked to her, and it broke my heart. It was so devastating that the first time I ever spoke to this woman whom I had so admired, I was getting fired." *Salon* was the first to report that McEwan and Marcotte had been discharged in stories I wrote with my colleague Alex Koppelman; our posts on their dismissals caused the liberal blogosphere to erupt. "I'm looking for a candidate who won't throw allies under the bus to appease opponents. Are you that candidate, John Edwards?" wrote Zuzu at *Feministe*. "Faithful flock of bitchitude, please take the time to contact the John Edwards Campaign in support of my blog sisters . . . who are currently dealing with all manner of bullshit because they had the audacity to be critical of the Catholic church," was the plea from Shark-fu at *Angry Black Bitch*. The respected liberal writer Ezra Klein blogged, "This will be a choice for the campaign. [Whose] respect do they care more about retaining? The netroots'? Or Bill Donohue's?"

In firing McEwan and Marcotte the Edwards campaign had affronted the online political community, the very progressives—young, brash and potentially influential—they had correctly surmised they needed to seduce. Scrambling to do damage control, the campaign denied to *Salon* (and every other media outlet) that the women had been fired; then they rehired both, though only after Edwards himself told them they needed to publicly apologize, which they did. Days later Marcotte included religious commentary in a film review on *Pandagon*; Donohue went ballistic and Fox News's Bill O'Reilly picked up the story, calling Marcotte and McEwan "Christian-haters." Marcotte resigned from the Edwards campaign first and McEwan left soon after. The Edwardses' great experiment in reaching the netroots had failed. But not before ensuring that one of the first campaign scandals of the election cycle involved young feminists.

About a month after McEwan and Marcotte quit, Elizabeth Edwards felt a pain in her ribcage and went to her doctor for X-rays. Within a few days the Edwardses stood next to each other for a press conference about Elizabeth's diagnosis. John talked in very matter-of-fact terms. She had gone to the doctor; there were further tests, a bone study. "The thing that is true is that her cancer will not be cured now. Elizabeth will have this as long as she's alive." They were both dry-eyed. No, they said, they would not suspend the campaign. "I expect to do next week all the things I did last week," said Elizabeth.

I found Elizabeth's commitment to chin-up fortitude almost chilling, but deeply admirable. To deal with a son's death by making two more children at fifty, to put off treatment of breast cancer until after a presidential election, not to let its return get in the way of continuing that quest—these weren't choices that many of us would likely have made, and I understood that perhaps they weren't all good ones. But the kind of person who would make them? To my mind, she was extraordinary. The next day, when I read Elizabeth's statement in the *New York Times* that she hoped to give her children wings so that they might "stand by themselves in a stiff wind," I felt as though a brisk, cold wind had just blown through me. It was an arresting image of what it means to survive and move forward.

As I watched the press conference it struck me that John Edwards did not look like a man who wanted to be running for president, but that Elizabeth Edwards looked like a woman who wanted to be doing nothing other than plowing toward the White House. It seemed clear that it was Elizabeth who was driving this, who herself might have been the candidate had she been born just a few years later, or perhaps if she were given more years than she likely had left. In my mind she was the motor, the candidate manquée. I was imposing a Clintonian model on the Edwardses, but it was not so outlandish: Hillary and Elizabeth were of a generation in which the only conceivable road to the presidency for a woman with political ambition was through a man. Hillary had maneuvered her way into her own political career, but her fortunes remained lashed to her preeminently powerful mate. Elizabeth was still steering the only vessel available to her—one later revealed to be terribly unseaworthy—with all her might.

Two years after the campaign McEwan recalled how much she had loved Elizabeth, before and even after she had called to dismiss her from her job. "I liked Elizabeth even more than John," she said, mentioning the most obvious comparison: "The two of them together—[John] would talk about the economy, and [Elizabeth] would talk about health care—in a weird way, it was Bill and Hillary all over again, wasn't it? It was two for one. God, the irony." She paused, and I assumed that she was referring to what would become John Edwards's own turgid sex scandal. But she was talking about something else: "I suspected that Elizabeth was the brains of the operation, and I'd thought the same thing about Hillary. But when I had the chance to support the brains of the operation, I chose the partnership. I literally went for the team that still had the dude on it."

★ ★ ★

Not every presidential spouse was thrilled about being on the road to Pennsylvania Avenue.

The tip-off that the lady sitting in the alcove of the Monticello Public Library in November 2007 would soon become a cultural lightning rod was that even in the dull safety of this standard-issue Iowa campaign setting, she was neither safe nor dull. Michelle Obama, the forty-three-year-old mother of two girls, was reading *Olivia . . . and the Missing Toy.* "Do you guys know Olivia?" she asked the rapt gaggle of children at her feet. "She's a pig. She's quite the personality." Told that there was time for one more story, Obama glanced at the preselected options. One was a hardback edition of *Our National Anthem,* the sort of starred-and-striped book that an aspiring first lady should read. "Not that one," said Obama quickly, discarding the patriotic pablum in favor of *Skippyjon Jones,* the story of a Siamese kitten who, for reasons too murky to convey, used "his very best Spanish accent" to say things like, "My ears are too beeg for my head. My head ees too beeg for my body. I am not a Siamese cat. . . . I AM A CHIHUAHUA!"

The tale of Skippyjon Jones's trippy quest for beans (or something) required an increasingly incredulous Obama to utter lots of awkwardly accented Spanglish things like "Yip Yippee Yippito! It's the end of Alfredo Buzzito! Skippito is here, we have nothing to fear. Adios to the bad Bumblebeeto!" As she persevered, the kids went *loco,* rolling off their beanbags with belly-busting laughter. The wife of presidential candidate Barack Obama was laughing pretty hard herself, but on she forged, hollering "Holy Frijoles!" with great gusto. The next day one of Michelle's staffers overheard a photographer and me laughingly recall her rejection of the patriotic for the politically incorrect Mexican accent; the staffer half-jokingly, half-pleadingly said to me, "That was off the record."

The decision to read *Skippyjon Jones* was a minuscule one. But in Iowa in the months before the caucus the minutest of actions carried weight. Given that Michelle's husband had just been caught in a preposterous flap over his failure to put his hand on his heart during the "Star Spangled Banner" at Senator Tom Harkin's steak fry, the sound choice would have been the book about the anthem. But Michelle Obama, a Princeton and Harvard Law School graduate from Chicago's South Side, a woman who had quit a fancy law firm job to work instead for the city in which she was raised, a wife who had made known her reticence about jumping into the presidential fray, could not help but choose the book that was untested over one that was boring.

Michelle Obama, who was still working part time as the vice president of community and external affairs at the University of Chicago Medical Center, appeared determined to temper the near messianic expectations that greeted her husband's candidacy. In this she was, worryingly for some, reminiscent of Teresa Heinz Kerry, the troublemaker who had insisted on keeping the country's (already rather dim) appraisal of her mate in check. "I don't want to give [John] more [due] than he deserves," Heinz Kerry once informed *Hardball*'s Chris Matthews, a sentiment that Michelle echoed in 2005 when she rolled her eyes at the entourage trailing her husband at his Senate swearing-in and said to a reporter, "Maybe one day he will do something to warrant all this attention."

Michelle Obama's particular impulse was to reject the mush of helpmate hokum in favor of candor and a good laugh. In the year-long windup to the Iowa caucus she had told various audiences about Barack's shortcomings when it came to putting the butter away and making the bed; that he was "snore-y and stinky" when he woke up in the morning; that she agreed to his presidential run only if he promised to kick his smoking habit. Perhaps most memorably, she had said, "He's a gifted man, but in the end, he's just a man." It wasn't like she was kneecapping the guy, whom she met at the Chicago law firm Sidley Austin in 1989. But so accustomed were we to hearing political mates in reverential mode that her remarks earned her an early reputation. The *New York Times* columnist Maureen Dowd wrote an April column in which she referred to Michelle, via an unnamed interlocutor, as "emasculating" and chided her for casting Barack "as an undisciplined child." Why, Dowd asked herself, if she liked the snap and twinkle of "a cheeky woman puncturing the ego of a cocky guy" in 1940s romantic comedies, did she not like it when the pinpricks were inflicted by Michelle, whom she referred to as a "princess of South Chicago," unwilling, in Dowd's colorful parlance, to polish her husband's pedestal?

It was hard to imagine that the theme of Obama as threatening to her husband's masculinity was born entirely of her cute jokes about putting away butter. But it was just as hard to discern whether its roots lay also with her height (five-foot-eleven), strength (her muscular arms would later become the subject of national obsession), or some combination of popular apprehensions of black femininity as angry, dominating and ultimately emasculating. Dowd's longtime specialty was making political figures into cartoons, but that proposition became problematic when political figures emerged from populations that historically existed in the white cultural imagination as cartoons to begin with.

Dowd's loopy characterization of Michelle was one of the first to depict her as perilously close to a stereotype of sassy, nagging, castrating black femininity, often referred to as a "Sapphire," in reference to one of its early popular iterations, the belittling wife on *Amos 'n Andy*. But Dowd wasn't alone in her concerns. The cultural critic Margo Jefferson told me in 2009, "There was a huge amount of discussion among black women, white women, all women, about [Michelle's approach]: 'Is this too much?' . . . Certainly some black women felt [she] was . . . not as extreme as a Sapphire, but a little too much 'Mmmm, hmmmm' and 'I'm gonna put you in your place!'"

Whether the anxiety Michelle produced in circles both black and white consciously or unconsciously had to do with her race, it was often expressed as concern that she might be hobbling her husband's presidential chances by making him either less of a man or too much of a black man. Barack Obama's mixed racial heritage, along with his Hawaiian upbringing and Kansas roots, helped to mitigate some of the racist assumptions about American blackness that might otherwise have been directed at him. But Michelle—darker skinned than her husband, descended like most African Americans from slaves, raised in a black neighborhood—was a reminder of all that was different and possibly scary about Barack. Melissa Harris-Lacewell told me in 2009, "Michelle is a representation of Barack Obama's choice to aggressively move toward blackness. He went to Harvard. He was editor of the *Law Review*. He could have actively made a choice to move toward whiteness or something else."

In a post on the women's pop culture blog *Jezebel* the writer Moe Tkacik counted among Obama's sins against her husband's reputation the time that she'd called him "the brother" even though "she knows it makes the white folks uneasy." In fact the reference to her husband as "the brother" was made not in front of white folks, but in a speech to a mostly black audience in Iowa, in which she had assured them, "This brother is smart!" Ironically this was also part of Michelle's job. For those Americans worried that Barack was not being black enough, she served as a reminder that he too was African American.

Marrying Michelle, who had strong ties to Chicago's black political community, had smoothed Barack's entrance into the circle from which he would build his career. According to her biographer, Liza Mundy, Michelle was clear about her role as his black credential in an interview with a Chicago public television reporter who asked about her husband's blackness in 1999, during his ill-starred congressional campaign against the African American incumbent Bobby Rush. "I'm as black as it gets," said Michelle. "I was born on the South Side. . . . We weren't rich, you know. I put my blackness up against anybody's blackness in the state, okay? And Barack is a black man. And he's done more in terms of meeting his commitments and sticking his neck out for this community than many people who criticize him. . . . And I can say that . . . because I'm black."

Eight years later she was taking a more subtle approach but hammering home a similar point. She told Steve Kroft of *60 Minutes* that she didn't stay up worrying about her husband's being assassinated because "the realities are, as a black man, Barack can get shot going to the gas station." In response, *RaceWire*'s Malena Amusa wrote that Michelle was "the saving grace" of the Obama campaign, both required and able "to be the typical Strong Black Woman," and thus present "a well-engineered counter to Barack's Black masculinity that has been attacked for being diluted."

An identification with Michelle was especially acute for black women, some of whom responded to her with the kind of intense recognition that some women had felt for Hillary Clinton a decade and a half earlier. Paula Giddings, an African American studies professor at Smith College, would later write in *Essence*, "Many of us [black women] began to take him [Barack Obama] seriously only after we saw and heard Michelle. . . . That Barack Obama would choose for his life partner a nearly six-foot-tall, incredibly smart, loquacious lioness of a woman told us virtually all we needed to know about his fundamental character—and the way he felt about us." Harris-Lacewell, who shifted her allegiance from Edwards to Obama in late 2007, echoed this sentiment: "[Obama's] open adoration for Michelle, a strong woman and a smart woman and a challenging woman and a tall woman [went] a long way toward generating a sense [among women] that 'We'll give Barack a chance.'"

Like Hillary before her, Michelle was walking smack into the high expectations of women who saw in her an independent woman with an education and professional history comparable to her presidential-caliber mate, a woman who was once his mentor and whom he often credited as being smarter than he. Harris-Lacewell explained that she became a professor at the University of Chicago in 1999 just as Obama was running against Bobby Rush. "He was smart, and terribly awkward at that point," she said. "I thought, here was a guy who was not terribly savvy. He picked a race he couldn't really win, he tried to intellectualize the whole race question, he tried to run against an incumbent, for god's sake!" Barack's political future might be maxed out, she thought at the time, but the one to watch was his wife. "The person who did have political acumen, who was capable of negotiating multiple communities, was Michelle. I don't mean as an elected official. But I thought to the extent that some-one was really going to be the superstar, it would be Michelle, and Barack would be her competent partner. She was fabulous."

For Margo Jefferson, recognition of the Obamas' shifting balance of marital power explained some of Michelle's attempts to suck the air out of her husband's mythos. "It was not unlike what Hillary was faced with," said Jefferson, "a woman in an equitable intellectual relationship who was suddenly finding a huge divide of power. In Michelle's case, she did not consider herself a person who loved politics and saw nothing possibly to gain from it. I think this was really hard for her. What woman, including Maureen Dowd, wouldn't understand that?"

Some leaped in on her behalf, cranking expectations even higher. Upon learning that Michelle had reduced her workload at the University of Chicago Medical Center to devote more time to her husband's campaign, Debra Dickerson wrote in *Salon* about her "feminist fury" at seeing a successful and independent woman reined in: "She's traded in her solid gold résumé [and] high octane talent . . . to be a professional wife and hostess. Any day now, Michelle Obama's handlers will have her glued into one of those Sunday-go-to-meeting Baptist grandma crown hats while smiling vapidly for hours at a time. . . . I hate to add to Michelle's load, but . . . I hope she'll keep her role in women's history in mind." More specifically Dickerson hoped that Michelle would "confront dysfunction in the black community, . . . help America understand that black progress is American progress [and] . . . bring feminism to black women."

It was a colossal amount of pressure on a woman who hadn't wanted her husband to run for president in the first place. And yet, whatever competing or contradictory demands weighed on Michelle, they seemed in the early days of the campaign neither to slow her down nor dim her personality. "You've never seen anyone like us before, and that's a little freaky, isn't it?" she asked the crowd of grown-ups assembled at the Monticello Library after the *bangito* conclusion of *Skippyjon Jones*. "It's like, 'They're real!' Well, guess what? Real people can be politicians too. We as a country have grown suspicious of real. We take the fake."

Michelle Obama was aggressively not fake. Over burgers between events, she and four staffers reminisced about the Iowa State Fair. "All the candidates go to the fair," said Peter Weeks, Barack's staffer who was traveling with Michelle on this trip, but "we *went to the fair.*" What I gathered from this locution was that the Obama family had not attended the fair as a piece of presidential performance art: milk a cow, eat a corndog, pin a ribbon on a pig, and other assorted photo ops. Rather, they had stuffed their faces and ridden the rides like nonpresidential people whose lives had not been made into a camera-friendly tableau of fun, but were in fact *real fun.* As staffers recalled Barack and elder daughter Malia riding everything on the fairway, I asked Michelle why she hadn't been on the amusements herself. Was she scared? "Oh no, I love the rides," she said, explaining that she had to stay on the ground with six-year-old Sasha, having scared the bejesus out of her a year earlier by taking her on the Tower of Terror at Disneyland. One of Obama's aides, a mother, looked at Michelle reproachfully. "I know, bad mommy," conceded Obama. "Now I can't persuade her to go on any rides. She's like, 'You don't have good judgment.'"

Michelle hadn't completely laid off the "Take my husband, please" domestic complaints since her run-in with Dowd, telling one Iowa crowd, "I didn't marry [Barack] for all his degrees. Certainly he's made less money over the years, as my mother has pointed out."

But she seemed to be winning over Iowans, who in six short weeks would gather to caucus. It wasn't a given that Michelle, with her advanced degrees, her height, her grace, her killer Jimmy Choo boots and impeccably tailored bell-sleeved tunics, would connect so completely to the comparatively pale, squat groups of people who crowded restaurants and theater lobbies to hear her speak. But she did. As Margaret Blake, an eighty-one-year-old white woman, told me plainly in the back of a movie theater–cum–pizza parlor in Wau-kon, "I think she's one of our own. Our different heritage probably doesn't matter so much if her experience leads her to understand us." Forty-two-year-old Laura Hubka, an ultrasound technician, cried after embracing Michelle in a church basement in Cresco. She had never voted before but had become a precinct captain because of her belief in the Obamas. When I asked what she loved about Michelle, she said, "The strength that she has as a black woman married to a black man, running for president. The trust in the American people, that we can look past that, is such a courageous act. I would vote for *her* for president." At an old opera house in De Witt, Peter Weeks waited as Michelle embraced nearly every woman who approached her. "She's a hugger," he said, with weary appreciation.

The hugging, the smart speeches, the impact she had on people, the no-bullshit authenticity—it was all part of what led me, at some point during the three days I followed her around the rural towns of eastern and northern Iowa, to get on the phone with my *Salon* editor and confess to him that I was a goner. "She's too awesome to be objective about," I told him, voicing a sentiment that critics would later hear in the press's coverage of her husband.

I did not feel that way about Barack Obama. Like others, I'd been captivated by the Illinois senator candidate's keynote address at the 2004 Democratic convention, in which he had spoken of one America. And while reporting on the midterm elections in subur-ban Philadelphia, a year before I traveled to Iowa to write about his wife, I had heard him speak as part of a Democratic all-star tour that included Nancy Pelosi and Al Gore. Waiting in a six-block line in my hometown, the former blood-red suburb where my parents had once been among the only Democrats, I'd been blown away by the thirteen hundred people gathered outside the Keswick Theater. Some had been there for hours and come from great distances, just to see him.

I had wanted to love him as much as the long line of adherents did, but had been surprised and disappointed when his speech that day underwhelmed me; I found it derivative and thought that he lacked the charisma for which he was already being celebrated. But I was struck as I'd watched the crowd around me—old, young, black, white—practically levitate with joy. They were not underwhelmed; they were inspired by him. I felt like one of those people genetically incapable of tasting the deliciousness of cilantro. My first brush with Obamamania was also my first experience feeling immune to its thrilling energies.

His wife was a different story. I saw her on fire in Dubuque, giving a speech in which she said the United Auto Workers guys with whom she'd just shared a beer downstairs were like her city-worker father. Ron Hughes, a small-business owner, told me before her speech that he was a Joe Biden supporter and that his wife was apathetic about the political process. "She just comes for the socializing," Hughes assured me. By the time Michelle got to the part about how fear is used to bully and divide us, Hughes's supposedly apathetic wife, Suzette, a fifty-nine-year-old retired physical therapist, was nodding in assent. At the end of Michelle's address Suzette told me, "I think I found my candidate. . . . I hadn't been moved until tonight."

Part of what moved people, oddly enough, was what critics had been griping about: Michelle's gimlet-eyed view of her husband and the steady drumbeat of discontent about the process she was living through. "I'm not doing this because I'm married to him," she said again and again. "Because truly, this process is painful. If you have a choice, America, don't do this! Teach! Do something else. I tried to [tell] Barack—there are so many ways to change the world. Let's do them!" In another version, she said, "I [didn't] want to run for president! Life was comfortable! It was safe! Nobody was taking pictures of us!" This refrain went over well, in part because everyone in her audience could relate to it. Who among them would want to give up privacy, security, routine, all in a bid to watch their mate get verbally attacked and take on the most high-pressure, all-consuming job on the planet? She was telling the crowd, "You do what you say you're going to do in this life. Your word really matters. You put your *best* into everything you do." At the word *best,* emphasized through gritted teeth, eyes squeezed, it was all laid out for me: she had not wanted to do this; it sucked. But this woman who grew up on the South Side and went to Princeton and Harvard did not do anything halfway. So as long as she was here, she was going to sell it, and make clear that her exertions must be shared. "Don't ask if Barack Obama is ready," Michelle said, "because he is ready. The question is: are *we* ready?"

Watching Michelle reminded me of the chill I got from reading about Elizabeth Edwards teaching her kids to stand in a stiff wind. Running beneath the presidential foot-dragging, the perforation of her husband's hype, her calls to readiness, was an arresting sense of caution and realism. She might have been the only one making the sober estimate of how hard this was going to be, of what a leap people would need to take to make this happen. "Change is scary," she told the Iowans. "It was scary for me to say yes to this. So I know." It seemed to me that she was carrying many of the burdens for her husband. He had the hope, she had the fear; he had the enthusiasm, she had the reluctance; he had the high expectations, she lived on planet Earth. In many ways, for those who doubted a black man's ability to run successfully for president, be they cynic or racist, Michelle worked as an interlocutor, as a stand-in for what she presumed would be the larger national experience: she doubted, shook her head, said no. But then her experience and the country's became further aligned: she took a chance on the guy with the funny name and slim prospects for success, because, frankly, she fell for him, just as the country was beginning to.

Fifteen years after Bill Clinton promised a two-for-one presidency, Michelle hit a similar note on her own behalf: "[If you elect Barack] not only will you get to hang out with me—because I'll be there; I'll go to the White House with him—but we have a chance to fundamentally change this country." She was unapologetic about the fact that she, like Hillary, was not a housewife but a working mother. "I've felt so disconnected from Washington. You don't know me! As a mother, as a professional, as a wife, you can't represent me!" she said. Here was an unfussy assertion that her identity was multifaceted, and that in that formulation at least, her wifeliness came third to children and career. Over coffee in Monticello she told me her BlackBerry was the only thing that kept her connected to her job. "The one that *pays* me," she added, eyebrow arched.

As I left Michelle's Dubuque speech I spied hand-lettered signs advertising John Edwards's appearance that night at a bar where he would be visiting with the UAW members Michelle had greeted earlier. I followed the arrows. It was late, and Edwards was not part of my assignment, but I was a reporter and a voter curious to see my candidate up close. As I watched Edwards enter the teeming bar and moved as close as I could to address some questions to him, I felt my desire to speak with him evaporate. He was shiny and syrupy, pounding guys on the back and swigging beer, but somehow not really talking with anyone, and certainly not listening. He was tired, I told myself. It was past midnight. But I had spent two days watching a woman who, no matter how wiped out or disenchanted with her task, appeared to focus on every person who approached her. I slunk out of the bar, disgusted by Edwards, and then disgusted by myself. I was not someone who cared, or ever wanted to care, whether or not a candidate was someone I'd like to have a beer with. I liked John Edwards because of his platform, his policies. But, boy, did I not want to have a beer with him.

The next morning Michelle was an hour north of Dubuque, speaking to a crowd in a restaurant overlooking a broad stretch of the sinuous Mississippi River. While she was hugging after the speech, I overheard a group of four women gossiping about the Clintons, speculating rather ungenerously about why Hillary might be running for president. One, who was wearing a precinct captain button, boiled down the differences between the former first family and the Obamas: "Michelle and Barack are like us," she said.

It was this comment that provoked in me the reaction that is etched most clearly in my memory of this trip. Michelle and her team packed into their van, I got in my rental car, the photographer got into hers. It was November in rural Iowa, and between the Hopperesque towns in which we were stopping we drove through farmland, and brittle leaves blew across the road. I had thrown some CDs into my bag, and at some point on the drive to Michelle's next stump stop, on a crisp bright day following this crisp, bright woman, Bob Dylan's "The Times They Are A-Changin'" began to play. I was thirty-three years old; I had no memories of the 1960s, in which the modern civil rights movement took hold, or of the 1970s, in which second-wave feminism bloomed. But I felt for a few minutes as though, on some small highway east of everything urban in Iowa, I was living in the most powerful historic moment of my lifetime, as if the country I'd grown up in, with its rules and limitations and assumptions about who can do what and who can be what, was finally beginning to fulfill Dylan's decades-old promise. Elderly white women in Iowa felt they had more in common with Michelle Obama than they did with Hillary Clinton. Inhabitants of towns like the conservative rural Maine hamlet my mother had fled and the Republican Pennsylvania suburb where I'd been raised were crowding into church basements to listen to a black woman with advanced degrees tell them to elect her husband president. Mawkish as it may have been, I felt sure in that moment that everything was different. Anything was possible.

Though I would go on to feel great respect and appreciation for her husband, that trip with Michelle—the experience of watching one crowd after another fall head over heels for her, my own feelings of connection with and admiration for this powerful working mother who twenty years earlier might well have been a figment of our imagination—was the closest I would come, until November of the next year, to experiencing the optimistic fever caught by so many of my compatriots during Obama's campaign. And it felt fantastic.

⋆ ⋆ ⋆

During the Iowa trip I stopped with Team Michelle at a Hardee's restaurant in Allamakee County. As Michelle filled her medium soda cup, she was approached by an elderly couple, the woman wearing an American flag sweat suit. They were on their way to see her speak down the road and were beside themselves at their luck at catching her here first. "We just love you," they told her. When I told Michelle over lunch that I was surprised so many people who apparently had nothing in common with her managed to see themselves reflected in her, she looked unsurprised. She nodded, swallowing her bite of cheeseburger before saying, "They see beyond the surface to the core. We are so close to each other." It was campaign-issue political sentiment, but as she said it she made a small gesture with her thumb and forefinger that reminded me, in tone and content, of another political sentimentalist, and the other spouse on the campaign trail who was helping to turn history inside out.

For years Bill Clinton had been holding forth on genetic research showing us how much biology all human beings have in common, in spite of their outward diversity. While covering the former president's summer 2007 trip to Africa, I'd seen him make that thumb and forefinger gesture many times, in reference to exactly the same thing: how close we all are to each other regardless of our race, regardless of our sex.

Bill Clinton's wife was about to do something that no American woman had done before, and her efforts would involve asking Americans to rethink ingrained ideas about gender and power. That meant not only expanding the imagined bounds of traditional femininity to include authority (often coded as masculine and thereby monstrous when exhibited by women), but also stretching our ideas about masculinity to include subordination (coded as feminine and thereby pathetic when exhibited by men). The notion of a "first man" had always been seen as inherently comical. Television's *Commander in Chief* had eked knee-slappers from the fate of the female president's husband, played by Kyle Secor. In one episode a chipper amanuensis shows him around his new, pink East Wing office, asking him how big a staff he'd like and noting, "Mrs. Clinton had twenty. . . . That didn't go over very well." Would he like to confer on daily menus? "Mrs. Clinton, of course, shunned that. . . . That didn't go over very well." The humor was derived not only from the pathos of the neutered first man, but from the aberrations of a real-life former first lady.

For many, the suggestion that Bill Clinton could ever play second banana to his wife was ridiculous; he was the ultimate alpha male when it came to political achievement, charisma and sexuality. After the heart problems and memoir writing that took up his immediate post-administration years, Clinton had emerged from his presidential husk and established the William J. Clinton Foundation, a web of international projects that combined humanitarian interests with profitable enterprise. In this role he had persuaded pharmaceutical companies to lower the costs of medicines and provide drugs to a million people; his Clinton-Hunter Development initiative promoted sustainable growth in Africa, expanding access to clean water, fertilizer and irrigation systems. The Clinton Climate Initiative worked with banks to finance the reduction of carbon emissions in some of the world's biggest cities, and in the United States he had been bargaining with snack and beverage companies to get healthier food into schools.

Shuttling between hospitals and schools, hearing from rape victims and HIV patients, investing in education and training for women and girls, holding babies and watching schoolchildren skip rope, in the fall of 2007 Clinton published *Giving,* a book about his humanitarian work. Dana Milbank at the *Washington Post* sniggered that Clinton was "auditioning for two quite different honors: following Jimmy Carter to Stockholm as a Nobel Peace Prize recipient, and following Hillary Clinton to the White House as the first first gentleman." But the two paths were far from divergent. Whether by design or by accident, the work that Clinton had taken on dovetailed rather elegantly with his new role as campaign spouse. By plying the traditionally feminine art of giving, he appeared to be seeking an outlet for his immense ambitions and an angle from which his light could flatter Hillary rather than outshine her. As he told an audience at the Nelson Mandela Foundation in Johannesburg, "She helped me in every race I ran from 1974 to 2000. . . . I've got about twenty years to go before we're even."

"Even" was a tricky proposition if you were Bill Clinton, the former leader of the free world, one of the most recognizable people on the planet, a man who would joke to Jon Stewart after he returned from Africa, "I may slit my throat," when Stewart asked if he could handle trading places with his wife. "A First [Lady's] . . . power is derivative, not independent, of the President's," Hillary wrote in *Living History.* No matter how Bill contorted himself, his power was never going to fully derive from Hillary's. Persuading her ambitious and cocksure husband to curate a collection of letters to the White House family pets seemed about as likely as turning one of the lions we saw at the Ngorongoro Crater in Tanzania into the first house cat. In Ngorongoro the lionesses were the killers. Clinton watched one of them rub out a warthog in a neat metaphor for what he hoped might happen in November 2008. As he excitedly described the lioness kill over lunch in the crater, with zebras grazing in the near distance, he seemed to be gearing up to play his part in a social evolution—electing a woman president— that should have been tiny in comparison to the miraculous trek out of Africa and around the globe, but that had been unthinkable throughout American history. Perhaps Clinton's dominance was a boon, I thought as I watched him. Maybe only a man so sure of his power would be comfortable enough to give his wife a turn at the most public kind of supremacy. Or at least put on a show of it.

One day at the midpoint of the trip Clinton boarded the private plane that was flying the press from Malawi to Zambia and settled himself in a captain's chair. We reporters gathered on couches and at his feet, as if he were our favorite professor at the University of I Can't Believe I'm on a Private Plane with Bill Clinton, and he began to talk. He talked about ecofriendly bricks, ATM cards that could be activated by thumbprints, the aggregate impact of the Grameen Bank in Bangladesh and eBay philanthropy. He discussed his Middle East peace plan, explained why the Nigerian organized crime network was probably the most sophisticated in the world after the Mafia and the Russian mob and recounted the kidnapping and murder of Colombia's former culture minister Consuelo Araújo. The man appeared to remember every conversation he had ever had as president, and every conversation he had ever had *about* his presidency; his narratives looped and trailed back to his accomplishments, his regrets, his mistakes, his victories. It was easy to see why Bill Clinton might consider himself the most fascinating person in a room. I was gobsmacked by the sheer volume of words, his ability to nimbly and cogently jump from subject to subject. When his gaze swept his audience and caught mine, it felt as though my brain had been X-rayed, the flabbiness of my cerebrum exposed; I was overcome by a desire to please the whirring brain, to nod in sage agreement and chuckle wryly at his declamations about the expiration of the Multifibre Arrangement. I also could not help but wonder how this guy was ever going to stop talking long enough to let his spouse run for president.

Bill Clinton was made of words, and in the summer of 2007, though he was being held at arm's length by a Hillary campaign skittish about his rumored post-presidential peccadilloes, he was spilling a lot of them on the subject of his wife. Bill liked to talk politics and Hillary was the politician to talk about, but many of his references were also in the vein of easy camaraderie born of long-term partnership: "Hillary always tells me . . ."; "Hillary and I once knew these women . . ."; "Hillary thinks I'm nuts, but . . ." They spoke several times a day. An American raised on lurid speculation (and revelation) about the Clintons' marriage, I was taken aback by the apparently tight weave of the couple's dynamic. On our last night in Africa, in a small hotel in Arusha, with a 4:30 a.m. wake-up call ahead of him, Clinton and his aides stayed up all night so that he could call to wish Hillary luck and then watch her in one of the earliest Democratic debates. They seemed an almost spookily well-matched pair. In *Living History* she wrote, "Bill Clinton and I started a conversation in the spring of 1971, and more than 30 years later we're still talking." They sure were. Clinton fantasists had spent years unspooling conspiracy theories about the couple's power-mad pacts and dual presidential plans; a week in Africa offered a less malevolent and more persuasively affectionate vision of the couple's bond. But Bill was locked in on two subjects, his legacy and his wife, and I wondered whether he would be able to let go of the former in order that the latter might go it on her own. At the time I believed that he was giving it a thoughtful, studied try.

Clinton was spending his days holding babies, visiting sick kids, listening to stories of sexual assault, worrying about maternal health—work that had historically been marked as soft, feminized. "I never believed that those so-called soft power issues were unimportant," he said to me. "I always thought that [it was important] when Hillary did it; and Eleanor Roosevelt did the same thing all during the Depression." His favorite first ladies extended the reach of the Oval Office, tending to the international relationships that their husbands did not have time to focus on. "I didn't want Africa or India to believe I didn't care about them just because I couldn't physically go there in my first term," he said. So he sent his wife in his stead. In some ways he was still catching up to her. The reason we went to Ngorongoro was because Hillary and Chelsea had loved it back in 1997; Bill had been wanting to get there ever since, perhaps for reasons that were not simply geographic. When I asked Senator Clinton if she saw any of her own duties as first lady mirrored in her husband's foundation work, she replied, "I do, and he's even said that on a few occasions." When he finally traveled to Africa himself in 1998, the first American president to make an extended visit to the continent, Bill reaped the benefits of having dispatched an earlier avatar. He described meeting with Senegalese women who had previously talked with Hillary about their opposition to genital mutilation. "They saw America as actually caring about what happened to people like them, because Hillary had been there and met with them," he said. "Derivatively, they loved me and America." He also recalled the "brave men" who accompanied the women to their meeting with him. Shaking his head with remembered admiration, he said, "These few hardy guys there were so proud of themselves that they had been sticking up for these women and taking all this crap from the other guys, you know?" Taking crap from other guys was a position with which the former president was becoming familiar.

Two of Hillary's presumptive Republican opponents, Mitt Romney and Fred Thompson, got their jollies in 2007 with sissifying cracks about their wives making prettier, better first ladies than Bill. On Playboy.com's "Battle of the Sexiest" Bill Clinton had beaten Ann Romney; it was not meant as a compliment. A fall 2007 *New York* magazine cover story featured an image of the former president in drag, proving that the biggest hoots still came from putting a powerful man in women's clothes. The accompanying story opened with the question of whether Bill would hold the Bible at his wife's inauguration. It was a ludicrous query. Why on earth wouldn't he? In *Living History* Hillary described how moving this precise moment of role reversal felt at her Senate inauguration.

The leering speculation amplified how embarrassingly inconceivable such reversals remained—and how hard a time we were going to give the people trying to make them happen. A skeptical Barbara Walters later asked Bill, "If your wife becomes president, I don't suppose that you're going to participate in the Easter egg hunt or the Christmas decorations." "You know, I'd actually like doing that," Clinton assured her. "You're gonna do the Easter egg hunt?" asked a faintly mocking Walters. "If I'm asked to do it. I would love to do that," he replied. Walters still felt the need to ask, "Mr. President, is your wife really smarter than you are?" Yes, in some ways she is, he replied calmly, adding, "I'd rather spend the night talking to her than anybody I can think of." Hillary, predictably, told me she was not perturbed by the prospect of her husband's inevitable spaying. "We've been at this for a pretty long time," she said drily. "I don't believe that anything that is said will come as a surprise."

One of the great ironies of Bill Clinton, given his galling history with women, was that he appeared to be making an effort to stand apart from many men on the American left who talked the talk but would not walk the walk next to broads more powerful than they. When I asked Hillary if she thought Bill would have a difficult time adjusting to secondary power, she said, "I can't imagine a better partner. Obviously, this is my campaign and this would be my presidency. Neither of us would expect it to be any different. But I will count on him to be there for me just as I was there for him." He convinced me, in Africa, that he was genuinely unthreatened by the idea. I asked if he could conceive of inheriting the legacy of Hillary and Eleanor. "Yeah!" he replied. "And I wouldn't be ashamed to do it, either. I'd be proud of it."

In the months leading to the primaries, the question of whether he could follow through seemed less pressing than the question Michelle Obama was asking as she too dove into the breach of American history and prejudice on behalf of her history-making partner: Were the rest of us ready to follow their leads?

3 CAMPAIGNING WHILE FEMALE

HILLARY CLINTON MUST have been as aware as anyone that by entering the presidential race she was kicking off a long-awaited social experiment. In 220 years of American presidential politics there had been no serious female major party contenders, though women had been campaigning for the presidency since before they could vote, starting with Victoria Woodhull in 1872 and Belva Lockwood in 1884.

In 1964 Maine's Republican senator and former congresswoman Margaret Chase Smith became the first woman to have her name placed in nomination and receive more than one vote at a major party convention. At the Cow Palace arena in Daly City, California, Chase Smith came in just behind Barry Goldwater, William Scranton, Nelson Rockefeller and George Romney on the first ballot, taking 27 of 1,308 votes.

Eight years later, New York's Democratic congresswoman Shirley Chisholm became the first African American woman to run for the Democratic nomination, and the first black major party candidate to run for the presidency (Frederick Douglass received one vote during the roll call at the Republican convention in 1888; the minister and civil rights leader Channing Phillips's name was placed in nomination at the 1968 Democratic convention). Chisholm, who in 1969 became the first black woman to serve in Congress, was a founding member of the Congressional Black Caucus and the National Women's Political Caucus and the honorary president of the newly formed National Association for the Repeal of Abortion Laws (which became the National Abortion Rights Action League, or NARAL). Chisholm won a nonbinding preference primary in New Jersey, though competitors George McGovern, Edmund Muskie, Hubert Humphrey and Eugene McCarthy were not on the ballot. Her run was more symbolic than realistic, and activists who might otherwise have backed her were anxious to curry favor with more powerful candidates. At a truly eccentric convention in Miami Beach, Humphrey released his black delegates to vote for Chisholm, helping her win 151.95 votes on the first ballot and ensuring that she would address the gathering at which McGovern and Thomas Eagleton received their party's nomination.

In 1984, when Minnesota Senator Walter Mondale chose another New York congresswoman, Geraldine Ferraro, to be his running mate, the idea was so exotic that Ferraro was treated more like a zoo animal than a politician. During a prenomination interview, Barbara Walters, a woman not known for her own professional timidity, noted that Ferraro had missed weekends with her kids because of her political career and wondered why she'd kept her maiden name. She also asked with wide-eyed incredulity, "Vice president, okay, fine. But do you think you're equipped to be *president*?" After her place on the ticket was official Ferraro met equally disbelieving interrogators, including one who asked during the vice presidential debate, "Do you think . . . the Soviets might be tempted to take advantage of you simply because you are a woman?" Her vice-presidential competitor, George H. W. Bush, offered in the same debate, "Let me help you with the difference, Mrs. Ferraro, between Iran and the embassy in Lebanon." Losing to Bush and Ronald Reagan in spectacular fashion, Mondale and Ferraro walked away from the election having won only Minnesota and the District of Columbia.

Recent elections had included marginalized runs by Pat Schroeder, Carol Moseley Braun and Elizabeth Dole. Had any of these women come into a race with the profile, momentum or money that Hillary Clinton had going into 2008, they might have been the ones to face the full-bore resistance of a white male establishment. Any plausible female candidate for the presidency was not simply offering herself up as a double-x interruption in the circle of white male faces that ring commemorative presidential plates. She was also presenting herself for cultural dissection, as a prism through which the country's attitudes about sex, power and the place of women in society were going to be projected. It was impossible for Hillary Clinton to have chosen a path to the White House that bypassed the loathing, jeering derision and gendered stereotyping built on two centuries of male power. What was interesting was how hard she tried to do just that.

As Clinton got closer to the race, a widely anticipated wave of resistance began to make itself apparent. This was the easy-bake misogyny of anti-Hillary men, but also of women eager to advertise their solidarity with and enthusiasm for traditional gender roles, like the one who entered a John McCain rally in Hilton Head Island, South Carolina, in November 2007 and asked the presumptive Republican candidate, "How do we beat the bitch?" McCain looked only momentarily uncomfortable before congratulating her on her "excellent question" and trotting out his most recent poll numbers against Hillary Clinton. He hadn't needed a proper noun to know to which bitch his supporter was referring.

Ideas about how to beat her came via truckloads of T-shirts, bumper stickers and urinal targets bearing Hillary's image—the crude calling cards of her most predictable foes: right-wing bullies. These guys had been spoiling to express their animus toward Clinton, whom they, if no one else, saw as a symbol of left-wing feminist politics. What better way to simultaneously neutralize her menace than by mocking, belittling, desexualizing and demonizing her while peeing on her likeness?

This population of Hillary antagonists produced a dizzying array of paraphernalia. Among the favorites were T-shirts from a group with a clever acronym, Citizens United Not Timid, and a related "I Love Country Music" rebus involving images of Hillary and of a tree. Anything that stood still long enough to be silkscreened bore lines like "Life's a Bitch So Don't Vote for Her," "Fuck Hillary: God Knows She Needs It," "Anyone But Her '08," "Even Bill Doesn't Want Me," "Stop Mad Cow" and "KFC Hillary Meal Deal: Two Fat Thighs, Two Small Breasts and a Bunch of Left Wings." More naked expressions of loathing included "I Wish Hillary Had Married O.J." and "Wanna See Hillary Run? Throw Rocks at Her." This brand of misogynist aggression was bracing, yes, but it also felt like the death rattle of a patriarchal culture, the last gasps from critics who had been spewing anti-Hillary bile for decades yet had failed to impede her rise to political power.

The most widely celebrated anti-Clinton effigy was a nutcracker. On the website that sold the implement (later to be joined by the Bill Clinton corkscrew) a thought balloon was attached to the Hillary figurine; it read, "I don't bake cookies. I crack nuts." After hearing Gloria Feldt complain about the nutcracker on television, its creator, Gibson Carothers, wrote her an email defending its production and sale. He concluded with the antifeminist chestnut, "Don't sell short the value of showing a sense of humor." Blogger Melissa McEwan, still an Edwards supporter, unknowingly took his advice, inaugurating a "Hillary Clinton Sexism Watch" on *Shakesville* (a series that would eventually comprise 114 posts). The September 6, 2007, entry showed the nutcracker with the hypothetical "Q: What's the going rate for indisputably proving to the world that you are a tiny little man who is profoundly afraid of women? A: $19.95."

Some men on television were antsy to get the Clinton bonfire started. One was Tucker Carlson, who seemed fixated on the possibility that the candidate might geld him. First he claimed, "Something about her feels castrating"; then "[When Clinton] comes on television, I involuntarily cross my legs"; finally he suggested, "The one thing we learned from the Lorena Bobbitt case . . . [is that] women are angry at men in a lot of ways." In one interview with Carlson, Cliff May, president of the Foundation for Defense of Democracies, called Clinton "a vaginal-American," prompting Carlson to ask, "Do you think that people who are voting on the basis of gender solidarity ought to be allowed to vote in a perfect world?" He seemed unaware that his gyno-obsession with Clinton, alongside his castration anxiety, revealed his very own commitment to gender solidarity.

In December, when a *CNN Headline News* guest observed to the conservative host Glenn Beck that most senators see a president in the mirror when they shave, Beck replied, "Does that include Hillary?" Then he mimed her shaving her chin and growling, "Gimme a pack of Kool cigarettes, will ya?'"

I was almost glad for this first, coarse wave of Hillary-hate; I practically wanted to buy a Hillary nutcracker myself. As someone who had written for years about the ambient antipathy toward ambitious women, I was more attuned to it than those who had been lulled by the myth of a peachy postfeminist world and were now aghast. These brazen expressions of threatened masculinity were gratifying, in part because they did not seem particularly effective, but also because they were loud, bright, incontrovertible consciousness-raisers. This stuff wasn't new, and it wasn't unearthed just for Hillary. For young women and men who had never seen blatant misogyny before, who had never heard a woman called a "cunt" or seen the size of a senator's thighs referred to on a T-shirt, these in-your-face examples of gender-based resistance to Hillary were eye-opening. They would later prove to be powerful talismans, tangible examples on which to call when the misogyny got more insidious, more complicated, more difficult to parse or name.

Far more curious, in the year of preprimary campaigning, was the unwillingness on the part of everyone *except* the bumper-sticker louts and right-wing windbags to address the thing that made Hillary different from the rest of the presidential candidates.

☆ ☆ ☆

From the start, advertising the historic nature of Hillary's run was not high on the agenda of her campaign strategist, Mark Penn. A pollster and CEO of the public relations firm Burson-Marstellar, Penn had advised political candidates from New York City mayor Ed Koch to Israeli prime minister Menachem Begin and had become Bill Clinton's *consigliere* in the mid-1990s. Penn was the architect of one of the most irritating aspects of Clintonian politics: the overpolling, people-pleasing approach that was a hallmark of Bill's reelection and Hillary's campaigns for the Senate, on which he advised her. Months before she was to make her presidential bid official in January 2007 Hillary hired Penn as her chief strategist and pollster, to the consternation of many who had worked closely with her in the past. The socially inept Penn took a bloodless approach to the race. In an October 2006 memo outlining basic requirements for Hillary's upcoming launch, and later published in the *Atlantic,* he recommended that she develop such fundamentals as a "basic message," a "fundraising operation," policy outlines and a press strategy. He added one final and furtive reference to an "fwp (first woman president plan)." Although the memo went into some detail about the other requirements, Penn did not expand on the "fwp."

A month before Clinton officially declared her intentions, Penn offered further thoughts in another memo. He seemed to believe that she led "a movement of women looking to achieve the true promise of America—that a qualified woman could be president of this country." But three paragraphs later he advised, "Most voters in essence see the presidents as the 'father' of the country. They do not want someone who would be the first mama, especially in this kind of world. But . . . they are open to the first father being a woman." The model for which Clinton should aim, Penn believed, was Margaret Thatcher: "The adjectives that were used about her (Iron Lady) were not of good humor or warmth, they were of smart, tough leadership." He pointed out that the national press wanted to be kingmakers but that "Hillary [was] already the king."

Penn was the pollster who popularized the term *soccer moms* during Bill Clinton's reelection campaign in 1996. Alongside its descendants—*security moms, SUV moms* and *Sex and the City voters*—the phrase was one of many that pollsters had invented to describe large groups of women who they presumed would vote as a giant, ovarian bloc if they could just be convinced to go to the polls. In the months immediately preceding modern presidential elections, women were bombarded by politicians suddenly eager to talk about things they thought chicks dug—Day care! Work-life balance! Peace!—at least until the election was over and they could go back to gradually eroding reproductive rights. In recent campaigns the wooing had been particularly egregious, with both major parties and their boosters bombarding electoral quarry with preschool-reading-level slogans like "W is for women" (George Bush) and "V is for Vote" (Eve Ensler), a tactic that made most thinking women want to "S for self-immolate."

Penn assured Hillary that internal polling showed that 94 percent of young women would automatically vote for the first female president. It was perhaps this confidence that led him to shrug off concerns about reaching them. In one eleven-page memo he wrote just a few sentences advising Clinton to look into "set[ting] up separate fwp (first woman president) internet site and subgroup organizations as place to stimulate that vote. Check whether their [*sic*] can even be legally separate movement. Understand the life issues of young women." With strategies like this—act like their father, assume you're already king, set up a subgroup to stimulate their vote, and understand their "life issues"—it was not unjust to suggest that one serious problem with Clinton campaign leadership was that it did not think much of the women with whom it was supposed to be making history.

Hillary had traveled a lot of road with a group of bright, loyal, mostly female staffers, dubbed "Hillaryland" back when they'd helped her establish the first lady's office in the West Wing. These women knew her inside and out and many of them were deeply invested in her presidential prospects. But when it came time to run, first for the Senate and then for the presidency, she turned to an abrasive and contentious group of male advisors borrowed largely from her husband, installing only two Hillaryland veterans in powerful positions: Patti Solis Doyle as her campaign manager and Mandy Grunwald as her ad maker. Although many Hillaryland denizens—including Huma Abedin, Lissa Muscatine, Capricia Marshall, Cheryl Mills, Melanne Verveer and Maggie Williams—would ultimately work for Hillary's presidential campaign, they were initially placed in marginalized roles, a factor that may have accounted for the campaign's early disengagement with the question of how to present Hillary as a woman.

In charge of women's outreach was longtime Hillary advisor Ann Lewis, whom the political reporter Anne Kornblut claimed was not even present on the campaign's morning strategy calls, an account Lewis backed up in 2010, telling me, "They got smaller and earlier, and at some point I realized I was not on them anymore." At the time Lewis was sanguine about being shut out: "I thought, I can insist on getting back on the call and spend more hours in internal decision making, or get out there and do what I know how to do, which is reach women." Others within the campaign told me that Lewis had retrospectively reconsidered her passivity and wondered if she could have made a bigger difference had she worked harder to stay on the inside of Penn's operation. Lewis herself told me that she didn't believe Penn's error was necessarily in undercutting Hillary's feminist credentials. "She was presenting herself as 'I can be president,'" Lewis told me. "Here is where I think the strategy Mark developed missed it: Hillary Clinton has been a change agent all her life, certainly from the days in which she made the speech at Wellesley. Yet she wound up being presented as the candidate of the status quo. . . . What we missed, and what's painful, is that at a time when what the American people really wanted was change we had a candidate who had spent her life making change and we missed it."

Penn's suggestions for the language Clinton might use to address her gender in a kickoff letter to supporters were not electrifying: "Few thought a decade ago, a woman could be president—today we have 16 women senators and if we don't try we will never know if a woman can be president. It is a barrier that can mean a lot for a new generation wondering if we can overcome barriers of this new age, if we can again secure our prosperity and regain our footing in a more dangerous world." Clinton chose to sidestep mention of her gender altogether in both the videotaped announcement of her candidacy and in an email to supporters, in which sex was sucked right out of an oblique call to make history. "We can only break barriers if we dare to confront them," read the letter she signed, failing even to acknowledge what those barriers might be.

It was not crazy to avoid emphasizing womanhood on the road to the presidency. In 1987, when asked repeatedly why she was "running as a woman," Colorado's first congresswoman, Pat Schroeder, had a witty, if slightly baleful answer: "Do I have a choice?" Inasmuch as a female candidate *could* exercise choice in how to present herself, the decision was often to try to pass as masculine. To come across as traditionally female, and thereby not traditionally powerful, was to call into question an ability to command, to defend the nation, to be taken seriously by world leaders. "The conventional wisdom is that a woman cannot get elected president without being really, really tough," said Kim Gandy, former president of the National Organization for Women, in 2009.

This was part of what made untenable the pressure on Clinton to apologize for her war vote. In 2004 John Kerry's willingness to say he'd made a mistake had gotten him labeled a weak-kneed flip-flopper, and John Kerry was a tall, strapping Vietnam veteran. Clinton was a mother, a wife, a chick; the slightest overexposure of that reality put her at risk of ridicule. When she made her video-taped campaign announcement, placidly inviting America to begin a "conversation," Jon Stewart joked, "Look, Hillary, this may not be the most politically correct thing to say, but I don't think that slogan's going to help you with men. . . . You might as well get on your campaign bus, The-I-Think-We-Really-Need-to-Talk Express, to unveil your new Iraq policy: America, Let's Pull Over and Just Ask for Directions." Soon Clinton was emphasizing the bizarre and pugilistic slogan "I'm in it to win it!"

Even her rival's wife, Elizabeth Edwards, understood Hillary's quandary. She told *Salon*'s editor in chief Joan Walsh in a 2007 interview, "I'm sympathetic, because when I worked as a lawyer, I was the only woman in these rooms, too, and you want to reassure them you're as good as a man. And sometimes you feel you have to behave as a man and not talk about women's issues. I'm sympathetic—she wants to be commander in chief. But she's just not as vocal a women's advocate as I want to see." There was the rub: too dainty and she wouldn't have been taken seriously; too burly and she wasn't really running as a woman at all.

Mark Penn's breezy assumption that young female votes belonged to Clinton whether or not she extended a pinky toward them reflected his dismal estimation of young women's electoral impulses (They'll pick the girl!) and allowed him to pursue his plan to convince more discerning (male) voters that Clinton was not only not anomalous, but practically had been president already! Behaving as if he were running a candidate against George W. Bush, Penn was determined to hide Hillary's femininity under a bushel of boxing metaphors. Anyone who had known Hillary Clinton for more than two hours would tell you about her improbably sharp sense of humor, her devotion to her friends and strong relationships with children, her taste for a good drink and her visits to friends' sickbeds. But Penn was firm in his belief that voters did not want humanity and that they had no interest in entering into the inherently stirring covenant of changing American history with a groundbreaking candidate. He argued not only that forging emotional connections with voters should not be Clinton's priority, but that it was an enfeebling strategy to be avoided at all costs. As he wrote in one memo, "The idea that if only you were warmer and nicer so many more people would like you and [you] would be in the White House is wrong. True, more people would like you. Fewer would vote for you."

Occasionally Clinton broke down the wall. At the August 2007 AFL-CIO debate she barreled her way through a self-sell with the delicacy of a Sherman tank. "For fifteen years, I have stood up against the right-wing machine. And I've come out stronger!" she bellowed. "If you want a winner who knows how to take them on, I'm your girl!" At this final locution she looked momentarily surprised and almost pleased with herself, as if she couldn't quite believe she'd just pulled off such a perky line. More often her confessions of femininity came when she was talking to mostly female audiences. In an October appearance on *The View* she said, as she would many times throughout her campaign, "Women in their nineties come to my events. . . . When I'm going around shaking hands, they'll say something like, 'I'm ninety-five years old and I was born before women could vote and I want to live long enough to see a woman in the White House.'" But these moments were always couched safely amid assertions of swaggering brawn. On *The View* Clinton made up for her brief girl-power indulgence by railing against cowboy diplomacy and making a towel-snapping remark about how we "can't be patsies" when dealing with China.

On the stump Clinton would sometimes drop a reference to electing the first woman president, but practically trip over herself to reassure people that she was not running *because* she was a woman, but because she was the best qualified, the most experienced, the most prepared, the closest to an incumbent. Audiences and the media responded in kind: the language they used about her—that she was tough, ready to stand up to Republicans, inevitable, the front-runner, the establishment candidate, a hawk and part of a political dynasty—reinforced the notion that she was a competent masculine norm rather than a nut-cracking or lily-livered feminine exception.

✲ ✲ ✲

What Penn was not counting on was that voters and the media *were* responding to emotion on the stump. In Iowa Barack Obama's campaign was presenting the United States with one of its first African American candidates and trying not to overemphasize his racial difference, much to the reported chagrin of black leaders like Al Sharpton and Jesse Jackson. But Obama was eating Clinton's lunch when it came to feminine appeal. On the stump he was passionate and articulate; he connected and hoped and dreamed. If gender is performance, as disciples of the philosopher Judith Butler have long argued, then both candidates were engaged in some serious cross-dressing.

Obama had help from Oprah Winfrey, an oracular presence for American women, who had endorsed him and was headlining rallies for him that drew tens of thousands of people. "Obama is the woman. . . . He is the warm candidate, self-deprecating, soft, tender, sad eyes, great smile," Clara Oleson, a former labor lawyer, told my colleague Michael Scherer before a Clinton speech in Iowa City. In Oleson's estimation Clinton was "the male candidate—in your face, authoritative, know-it-all." In *Salon*, Scherer described Obama rallies that featured the music of the Indigo Girls and Aretha Franklin and in which Obama promised, in a language spoken most commonly by Oprah-approved gurus, "We can discover the better part of ourselves as a nation. We can dream big dreams." Clinton meanwhile was described by supporters as the candidate who could "stand up to bullies" and would quite often tell audiences, "When you are attacked, you have to deck your opponent."

This surely gratified Mark Penn, who made no secret in his internal memos of his scorn for Obama's hope-y, dream-y speechifying or his assumption that racism and xenophobia would make the Illinois senator "unelectable except perhaps against Attila the Hun." But there were those who believed that Clinton was making a grave error.

Mary C. Kelley, a women's studies professor at the University of Michigan, told the *Los Angeles Times* in December 2007, "I strongly believe that it's feminism that made Hillary Rodham Clinton's presidency plausible. Therefore, I would like a candidate who is not simply running like another man, and that's what I see in her self-presentation again and again." Frances Kissling, the former president of Catholics for a Free Choice, wrote that Clinton had "missed the opportunity to talk about what it really means for women to be equal in this country. . . . A woman candidate who considered her gender a strength (as opposed to something she needed to overcome) would announce a series of measures specifically designed to ensure that women's needs and rights were at the forefront of her agenda. . . . We'd like to see a woman president, but more than anything we want to be able to say . . . that the first woman president did things no man would have done." Some women felt that Penn's insistence on stressing Clinton's toughness was misplaced. After all, it wasn't as if she had entered the race with a reputation for ditzy fragility that she needed to counteract. Ellen Malcolm, the founder of EMILY's List, an organization at the forefront of putting pro-choice Democratic women in political office, told me in 2009, "I understand [Penn's] concern about the credibility, but I don't think there's anybody in the universe who [didn't] think that Hillary Clinton [was] smart and tough, and I think it was clear that it wasn't working and that a pivot was needed, and it took way too long for the pivot."

Elaine Lafferty, a former editor of *Ms.* magazine and a Clinton volunteer, told me in a 2009 interview that when she arrived in Iowa she quickly concluded that the gender reversals were a serious problem. Lafferty believed the Clinton campaign had failed to take Oprah Winfrey's endorsement and coaching of Obama seriously enough as a threat to their base. In a memo, she wrote, "We believe Oprah and her organization has been closely advising Obama in terms of *message, vocabulary, and delivery.* Bottom Line: you are running against a WOMAN candidate. Obama's language and presentation is not just poetry. He employs the vocabulary of femaleness, the vocabulary of emotion that fills women's magazines and daytime television. He speaks endlessly of that which 'is deep inside of me.' (How many men speak that way?) . . . Everyone knows Hillary is a policy ace. They DON'T know she shows up in hospitals for friends."

Lafferty wasn't just hoping to jostle the campaign machinery; she was determined to roust Hillary's would-be female supporters, women who were still dragging their feet, and women's leaders she felt were not taking Hillary's precarious position in Iowa seriously enough. "I jumped up and down and yelled 'The sky is falling' and tried to sound an alarm," she said of her fears that Clinton was going to blow Iowa with no women behind her. Trying to deliver some recognizable feminists to Iowa for the Clinton campaign, Lafferty was not met with an energetic response.

The truth was, Penn's gender-masking strategy just hadn't fulfilled his vision. For the first half of her campaign it allowed women to see Clinton as representative of the masculine norm from whom they could feel distant or antipathetic without guilt. It alleviated pressures on them to either state their loyalties or disavow her. Why should they show up to support a woman who would barely reveal herself as one?

* * *

Despite the best efforts of the campaign to ensure otherwise, by the time Clinton had been on the trail for the better part of a year some people besides Republican T-shirt sloganeers were beginning to notice that she was a lady. It was the Pulitzer Prize–winning fashion critic Robin Givhan who first and most efficiently shattered the illusion of Hillary Clinton's hermaphroditism. In a July 2007 story in the *Washington Post* headlined "Hillary Clinton's Tentative Dip into New Neckline Territory," Givhan pondered the subtleties and political implications of a blouse worn by the senator as she spoke to Congress about the costs of higher education: "The neckline sat low on her chest and had a subtle V-shape. . . . The cleavage registered after only a quick glance. No scrunch-faced scrutiny was necessary. There wasn't an unseemly amount of cleavage showing, but there it was. Undeniable."

A surprised Clinton campaign, hoping perhaps to line the war chest by fanning a chest war, responded with an indignant email to supporters, provocatively titled "Cleavage." Ann Lewis, head of women's outreach, explained the email in 2010: "What became clear to me was that [Givhan's piece] had touched a nerve. I had underestimated the impact, but as the day went on, I started hearing from a lot of women." Lewis signed her name to the message that began, "Can you believe the *Washington Post* wrote a 746-word article on Hillary's cleavage? . . . I've seen some off-topic press coverage—but talking about body parts? That is grossly inappropriate."

I, for one, *could* believe that the *Washington Post* had published an article on Hillary's cleavage, and I thought it was pretty fascinating. There was merit to the campaign's complaints about "body parts" only in that many readers probably did not absorb the story as a nuanced consideration of the sartorial constructs of gender, but rather as a piece about Hillary's ta-tas. Otherwise the Clinton camp's charges were trumped up. Givhan had written an examination of how femininity and character were being communicated through clothes in this historic race. As she pointed out, it was not until the early 1990s that women staffers were permitted to wear pants on the Senate floor. To pretend that there were not questions to be asked about how Clinton was going to dress on a presidential trail was foolish. When Clinton herself found out about the email, she ordered a stop to any further promulgation of outrage.

Fifteen years of public futzing made attention to Clinton's self-presentation a reasonable line of inquiry. Mocking her hair had been one of the chief pastimes of those who wanted to express dislike for her ambition and her independence; her willingness to change that hairstyle was a handy metaphor for those who thought her politics were inconsistent. Her thighs and ankles and pantsuits had been thoroughly examined. In 2006 her Republican opponent for the Senate, John Spencer, allegedly remarked to a reporter, "You ever see a picture of [Clinton] back then? Whew. I don't know why Bill married her." He speculated that she had had "millions of dollars" of plastic surgery.

It's not that male politicians escaped related evaluation. During the primaries several shots of Barack Obama exiting the sea in swim trunks were published in celebrity weeklies. But those photos were admiring. Tellingly, when male politicians were jeered for their physique or their fashion it usually involved feminizing them: John Kerry was rumored to have had Botox injected in his patrician brow; John Edwards's pricey trims had gotten him labeled "the

Breck Girl"; Al Gore had been derided for turning to Naomi Wolf for clothing advice.

The scrutiny was much more intense for Clinton, because for women value is intrinsically tied to desirability and attractiveness. This meant that her advisors and her most vicious detractors had a shared goal: her complete desexualization. Those who supported her had to downplay her feminine attributes lest she be diminished by objectification. For those who hated her the goal was to humiliate her, and at the same time affirm that she held no alluring power over them. As Shirley Chisholm said decades before, "One distressing thing is the way men react to women who assert their equality: their ultimate weapon is to call them unfeminine. They think she is anti-male; they even whisper that she's probably a lesbian . . ." Sure enough, Clinton had long been called frigid, a lesbian, a wife who couldn't satisfy her husband. The *New York Times* had run a story toting up how many times a month she and Bill shared a bed. But now Givhan had destabilized everything by pointing to a garment that had given the impression, by one zillionth of an inch, that Hillary Clinton had breasts.

That same week, in an early YouTube debate between the Democratic contenders, one questioner asked each of the candidates to look to the person on his or her left and say one positive thing and one negative thing about the person. John Edwards cast his eyes on Clinton and said, "I admire what Senator Clinton has done for America, what her husband did for America. . . . I'm not sure about that coat." Barack Obama, dutifully playing Gallant to Edwards's Goofus, replied in turn, "I actually like Hillary's jacket. I don't know what's wrong with it." It was a startling moment: presidential candidates were discussing outfits in the middle of a debate for the Democratic nomination. *Politico*'s Roger Simon instructed in his debate wrap-up, "Write this down, guys: Attack her policies, attack her past votes, attack her personality if you want to, but don't attack what she is wearing. It looks sexist and cheap."

But this, for me, was part of the package, part of the fun, really, of what it was going to feel like to watch a woman run for president. They weren't treating her like the boys? That's because she wasn't a boy! Here at last was some sign of it. As a woman, Clinton had been able to don a coral blazer for the debate. How many other presidential candidates' closets contained a rainbow of jewel-toned jackets? In one sense it actually gave her an advantage: she got to be the pretty flamingo in the sea of navy and gray, the one who drew your eye, whether you liked her or not. On the other hand, she was forced to suffer the indignity of having her clothes picked over by her opponents, to have a positive assessment of her record—or rather, her *husband's* record—lost in tittering over her ensemble. These were not just the costs of being the first serious female contender; these were the realities of a candidacy that could never have been as run-of-the-mill as her handlers were hoping. The awkward revelation that one of these things was not like the others was actually freeing, kind of a hoot. As Helena Andrews wrote in *Politico,* "First off, her coat was fabulous. . . . That color! . . . Clinton's got the same exact coat in electric sky blue. I'm glad she didn't wear that one, because she looks like a space alien in it. . . . [S]he managed to glow even standing next to Edwards. It was a statement without words: I'm a woman; get used to it."

As tongues finally began to loosen on the subject of Clinton's femaleness, some took nastier liberties than others. In December 2007 Matt Drudge posted a photo of Hillary Clinton in Iowa under the headline "The Toll of a Campaign." Rush Limbaugh picked it up in a radio segment titled "Does Our Looks-Obsessed Culture Want to Stare at an Aging Woman?" The photo, taken at the start of the final, grinding slog through Iowa, was simply of Clinton's face. She had crow's feet, bags under her eyes; her brow was furrowed, and some of her neck skin had been pushed up around her chin thanks to the unfortunate convergence of talking and scarf wearing that was unavoidable when campaigning for president in Iowa in December.

Limbaugh's take on the image was couched in oleaginous insincerity, what in Internet parlance is called "concerned trolling." Posing for the moment as a pseudo-feminist, he fretted to his estimated 14 million listeners that the public's thirst for a sexism-fed spring of eternal youth would make it hard for Clinton to grow old in public. "As you age, and . . . women are hardest hit on this . . . America loses interest in you," he said. "Will this country want to actually watch a woman get older before their eyes on a daily basis?"

The radio host's main thrust, that "the appearance of perfection and good health . . . ties into the perception of mental acuity, stamina, being able to hold up to the job," reminded me of a bit of collegiate apocrypha, a legend about sorority sisters who made freshman bids stand on a table in their underwear while older sisters circled their physical flaws in magic marker. What had always struck me about this myth was not the social torture of it, but the idea that it was for the good of the initiates: before they could represent the sorority they had to rid themselves of distracting blemishes, lest their pocks or pimples distract from all their other excellent qualities. How, Limbaugh was innocently wondering, would Hillary Clinton represent the sorority of women? What if Americans never paid attention to her health care plan because they were so distracted by her wattle?

Limbaugh had successfully stirred the pot. The blogger Immodest Proposals asserted, "Whichever photog snapped this photo effectively ended Sen. Hillary Clinton's presidential campaign." The law blogger Ann Althouse wondered, "Did some treatment wear off?" before acknowledging, "A picture like this of a male candidate would barely register. Fred Thompson always looks this bad, and people seem to think he's handsome."

The freakout over Hillary's appearance was extreme; it provoked the kind of anxiety that an octogenarian candidate's senescence or physical infirmity might. This was especially strange because the picture was not that terrible. When it was taken Clinton was sixty years old and was about to commence a tour of all of Iowa's ninety-nine counties. An examination of former presidential candidates at exhausting stretches of a race would have turned up similar pallor, flappy necks and dry skin. In the weeks before Bill Clinton was elected in 1992 he had lost his voice. It was regarded as a mark of how many stump speeches he'd given, how many germy hands he'd clasped. Then there was the toll of the presidency itself: grayed heads and haggard faces on presidents from Abraham Lincoln to George W. Bush had long been evidence that being commander in chief was never a job for anti-aging enthusiasts.

In an age of lifts and injections and implants, and in a culture in which age confers on men authority and wisdom but makes women appear dried up and too lazy to maintain the illusion of youth, we had begun to forget what a sixty-year-old female looks like in nature. Here she was: a woman in late middle age. Wrinkled. Tired. She was getting pulled over for campaigning while female, and we were all witnessing the arrest.

Appearing on several Sunday morning talk shows in September, Clinton had laughed often, prompting a discourse on the sound of what some called her "cackle." Glenn Beck compared the laugh to the Wicked Witch of the West's; Bill O'Reilly's "body language expert" dubbed it "evil," Sean Hannity "frightening"; Frank Rich wrote that it had "all the spontaneity of an alarm clock buzzer." In fact Clinton's laugh, while occasionally overexuberant, was precisely the same breed of stalling tactic deployed for centuries by politicians trying to buy time before answering questions, to appear falsely relaxed or dismissive of criticism. Clinton's laugh sounded different in part because its register, high-pitched and female, was unfamiliar to those who no longer even noticed the low but equally fake rumblings of Bill Clinton, Newt Gingrich or any of Hillary's presidential adversaries. We were used to hearing old men chuckle long and deep while fielding questions from Tim Russert. A woman's voice sounded different, not old-man comfy and cocky, but witchy and crone-y.

None of us were above thinking about how Clinton sounded or looked or what she wore. We were like babies first encountering a new object: a potential president who had breasts and hips and a high voice, who was once pregnant and whose female skin changed as it aged. It was only natural that we were sometimes going to get tripped up and befuddled in how we talked about her. Noticing it, grappling with it, was part of accepting her presence on the stage. The notion that this was going to be easy and smooth and that Clinton's gender was going to go unnoticed had always been a false idea that took as its equally false premise that we were all totally comfortable with women in power.

Just as Clinton was dealing with undermining evaluations of her femininity, so was her opponent faced with criticism linked to his race. In December, former Nebraska governor Bob Kerrey, a Clinton supporter, took pains to emphasize that Barack Obama's middle name was Hussein; later, when defending his remarks on CNN, he said that Obama had "spent a little bit of time in a secular madrassa." Around the same time another Clinton backer,

Billy Shaheen, speculated, Limbaugh-style, that Republicans might ask questions about whether Obama had ever sold drugs. When Mark Penn went on *Hardball*, purportedly to disown Shaheen's aspersions, he instead sharpened them by using the word *cocaine* on air. Obama's youthful dalliance with drugs was not so different from Bill Clinton's half-admitted experimentation or rumors that had long dogged George W. Bush. But Obama's race allowed his opponents to push into the small-minded corners of the American imagination and try to peddle a factually implausible, shadowy suggestion of the candidate as drug dealer. These caricatures of Obama appealed to time-honored racial stereotypes, the still contemporary prejudices that for the previous two hundred years had prevented people with names like his from running for president. Barack Obama's father and paternal grandmothers had been Muslim; he had written openly about his experimentation with drugs in his memoir. These were things that had no presidential precedent, that made him an anomaly in the campaign.

The racist allusions that dogged Obama and the nastiness about Clinton's appearance testified to the endurance of certain stereotypes about black men and women. This was the oddity of both candidacies. They illustrated how far and how quickly the nation had progressed; no one would have appealed to sexist or racist stereotypes had there not been an African American and a woman running for president. At the same time they drove home how far we had to go.

☆ ☆ ☆

As attention to Clinton's womanhood made Penn's gender-free strategy increasingly unwieldy, the campaign began to send out mixed messages. Clinton was still presenting herself as a patsy-decking leader in drag, except when her advisors were making badly aimed attempts to draw the attention of recalcitrant women supporters by portraying her as a victim of sexism. The worst misjudgment came after Clinton's poor performance in a debate in Philadelphia, during which she stumbled on a question about driver's licenses for illegal immigrants and her opponents pounced. Her campaign proceeded to portray her as an injured party, splicing clips of the debate and posting them as a video called *The Politics of Pile-on.* Ann Lewis told me in 2010 that the ad was not intended to play up a gender divide: "The only pile-ons I knew of were in football." But Clinton herself stoked a boys-against-girls reading of the response. Speaking at her alma mater the day after the debate, she said, "In so many ways, this all-women's college prepared me to compete in the all-boys' club of presidential politics."

As soon as she realized the message that she was sending, Clinton pulled back by telling reporters, "I don't think they're piling on because I'm a woman. I think they're piling on because I'm winning." It was true: she was winning in the polls, and this was partly why her opponents were teaming up to take her down. But the campaign could not shake the impression that it had been demanding special treatment for its female candidate by first obscuring her gender and then portraying her as the world's most improbable damsel in distress. At the time of the "pile-on" complaint, Kate Michelman said that Clinton was "disingenuously playing the victim card" and though she was speaking in her capacity as an advisor to one of Clinton's rivals, it was hard to disagree with her.

By and large, feminists seemed to be wary of intervening in this mess. EMILY's List was an exception, one of the only women's organizations to put boots on the ground in support of Clinton in Iowa. The National Organization for Women had issued a lengthy endorsement in March 2007, but was not a particularly visible presence later in the year. In fact, in the weeks before the first caucus, feminists were notable mostly for their absence from Iowa. One person in the Clinton campaign seemed to have noticed.

"Elaine, how are you?" volunteer Elaine Lafferty remembered Hillary Clinton greeting her in an Iowa restaurant a few weeks before the January 3 caucus. Clinton was talking with a lot of nodding eye contact, trying to communicate something but behaving as if someone with a tape recorder might be around any corner. "I'm good, Senator, how are you?" was Lafferty's reply. "I'm fine," said Clinton, pausing. "How's Gloria?" Clinton was referring to Gloria Steinem, the founder of *Ms.* magazine, which Lafferty had edited. "She's good," Lafferty said to Clinton. "Ah," replied Hillary. "*Where* is Gloria?"

"I said, 'She's in Bhutan, Senator.'" Lafferty remembered. "And Hillary said, 'Ah-ha. When is she coming back?'"

It was reasonable that the first woman to launch a realistic campaign for the American presidency might well wonder, as she tromped her way through the frigid Iowa winter, why Gloria Steinem, the most recognizable women's leader in the country, was nowhere in sight. Then again, Clinton could have summoned Steinem if she'd wanted to; she hadn't.

Steinem would later tell me that while she had always supported Clinton, whom she believed to be a strong and competent candidate, her initial reticence about throwing herself behind her campaign had stemmed from the fact that she had never believed that Clinton could win the nomination. Steinem initially endorsed neither Clinton nor Obama because she believed they were comparably great candidates. But she told me, "What was interesting was that white women, and black women . . . didn't think Hillary could win. And black people, men and women, didn't think Obama could win." The doubters, Steinem said, "were responding to the hurts of our lifetimes and assuming that they were going to be definitive."

If some feminists were doubtful that Clinton could win, others felt queasy at the prospect of a primary contest that would pit two histories of marginalization and disenfranchisement against one another. Still others cited the off-putting message they had received from the campaign itself. There was an offended *froideur* provoked by the distance the Clinton camp had put between the candidate and a feminist legacy. When I asked former NOW president Kim Gandy in 2009 whether there was pressure for her to go to Iowa, she responded, "The campaign wasn't pursuing it. . . . You never know who makes the decisions in a campaign like this, but Mark Penn, in my opinion, did not want an active feminist presence in her campaign." So there wasn't one.

4 FIVE DAYS IN JANUARY

HILLARY CLINTON DID not just lose the January 3 Iowa caucus to Barack Obama. She lost Iowa's women to Barack Obama, by a startling 5 percentage points. That night proved to be not simply the opening bell of primary season, but the kickoff to a surreal period between the Iowa and New Hampshire contests. Those five days were disconcerting for anyone who had gotten comfortable with the apparent ease with which America had made room for a female presidential candidate.

I was thrilled on that Thursday night, rushing to a friend's apartment to watch the results. It felt great to put an end to the election season windup, to learn how Americans were going to vote rather than how political prognosticators *thought* they were going to vote. The answer came fast and early: Barack Obama was the winner. I could not wipe the smile off my face.

It's not that I was an Obama supporter. I still planned to vote for Edwards. But the Iowa results were undeniably thrilling. Though he was not the first African American to win a primary or a caucus

(Jesse Jackson had won Louisiana, Washington, D.C., South Carolina and Virginia in 1984 and thirteen contests in 1988), Obama's
Iowa win had the shimmer and vibration of a history-making event;
his speech, which began "They said this day would never come,"
carried the promise of some future rapture.

There was also the invigorating bump of an upset: late polling
had shown Obama ahead of his competitors, but it was a surprise
that Clinton had come in a close third behind Edwards, and it was
big news that only 30 percent of female caucus-goers had supported
her, compared to the 35 percent who had rallied to Obama. Mark
Penn's presumed female constituency, underaddressed and under-
valued by his strategy, had also apparently been underwhelmed,
and supported Clinton's adversaries.

This was a welcome reminder that in politics, as in baseball, anything can happen. If voters were veering away from the stale scripts
of pundits and strategists, I was all for it. I was sick of primaries
decided before Super Tuesday, by campaigns that devoted attention
and resources only to states with early contests. I wanted an election
that would engage voters and candidates beyond Iowa and New
Hampshire; it had never been more important. Here was an opening shot that got everyone's attention and presented a bracing array
of Democratic options.

Obama's triumph was definitive, with 38 percent of the vote,
but the remaining 62 percent had been divided quite neatly, with
Edwards coming in at 30 percent and Clinton at 29. Edwards had
put a lot of eggs in his Iowa basket, but I did not see this upset as his
death knell; similar numbers in 2004 had made him a strong competitor. Nor did I see Clinton's loss as determinative: Iowa, where
Bill Clinton had not campaigned in 1992 and ran unopposed in
1996, had never been a Clinton-friendly contest. Only six months
before the caucus a memo from Hillary's deputy campaign manager, Mike Henry, had been leaked, recommending that she skip
Iowa altogether since it was the campaign's "consistently weakest
state." Clinton had rebuffed the advice and sunk a lot of money into
the state, but it wasn't as though her Iowa showing came as a complete shock. The most exhilarating thing about January 3 was that
220,000 people had come to caucus, compared to 124,000 four
years earlier. That meant that Obama, Edwards and Clinton had

each drawn more supporters than 2004's definitive winner, John Kerry. As far as I was concerned, *this* was an election.

Apparently I wasn't seeing the same results that the men on television were seeing. It was my friend Geraldine who first pointed out how they were talking about Hillary Clinton. Geraldine, a political junkie and former news editor, had an investment in all the candidates; she was an undecided but dedicated Democrat. Her face grew ashen as Chris Matthews offered a mean little metric showing that Hillary's 30 percent share of the Iowa votes meant that seven out of ten caucus-goers had rejected her. Well, yes, that's what it means to get 30 percent of the votes. Seven out of ten voters had also rejected Edwards, six of ten had rejected Obama. "It's hard to call yourself the people's choice if two-thirds of the Democrats are voting against you!" Matthews said.

He was not alone in his glee. Before the caucuses had officially concluded, the *Washington Post*'s Eugene Robinson told us that if Clinton lost Iowa she would probably lose New Hampshire too. And South Carolina! She'd be lucky to scrape by with small states like Nevada, Matthews chimed in. Obama's victory wasn't even official yet when *Newsweek*'s Howard Fineman predicted, "If [Obama] wins this thing, even by one vote in Iowa, then that five-point lead of Hillary's [in New Hampshire] is going to disappear in a second."

On a night when Iowans old and young had come out in droves, on which Barack Obama had given one of his fine speeches, on which three strong Democratic candidates had carved up an unprecedented number of votes fairly evenly, all these people could talk about was throwing Mama from the presidential train. Geraldine was visibly upset. I realized that I'd never seen anyone my age react so strongly to Hillary Clinton, and she wasn't even a Clinton supporter. "I hadn't made up my mind," Geraldine told me in retrospect, "but I remember having a very strong reaction to how she was being treated by those guys on MSNBC. To have her unfairly torn down before I had the opportunity to vote was absolutely infuriating."

By the next morning, and the five mornings after that, what could have been written off as an overcaffeinated blitz on a briefly debilitated Hillary had transformed into a rowdy wake at which pundits were doing jigs on her freshly dug grave, speculating cheerily, practically drunkenly, about when, exactly, Clinton would pack it in. The night after Iowa Matthews proclaimed, "For Clinton, what was once considered inevitable is now barely likely." "Could New Hampshire end the Democratic primary race?" leered Keith Olbermann on January 7, during an hour in which he also speculated that the primary there "could be a blowout" and "the final score for the Democrats." Chuck Todd described for Olbermann the anticipatory certainty of the press in New Hampshire: "It's weird out here. . . . Everybody's already speaking in the past tense . . . about Senator Clinton's attempts to win the first two states."

Most discomfiting was that from my Democratic point of view these were supposed to be the good guys. For years MSNBC had stood up to the right-wing domination of Fox News. But some of its talking heads had long displayed a passionate investment in Hillary's demise. Matthews had made his career as a pundit in that heady era of Clinton bashing, the 1990s. That Hillary's political career had survived his wrath seemed to have incited him further, not just in the months leading up to the 2008 primaries, but for years preceding them. His fetishization of the threat posed by Hillary had led him, often, to imagine her strategy and imaginatively discredit it before it unfolded, or to offer helpful tips to her opponents.

When, in 2000, the Utah financial advisor Howard Ruff had begun taking donations to bring down Hillary, then not yet even a senator, he had appeared on *Hardball* and explained to Matthews that in a battle against Hillary's nascent political power, "it's a lot easier to kill a twelve-inch snake than a twelve-foot cobra." Matthews expanded his metaphorical arsenal: "You want to destroy the missile in its silo, which makes sense to me." The night after the Iowa caucus Matthews spoke to Elizabeth Edwards and coached her directly: "Even if Barack has to win up here [in New Hampshire], it's better to knock Hillary out because if she is knocked out, then you two can fight it out, John Edwards and Barack Obama." As Melissa Harris-Lacewell said in retrospect, "Chris Matthews lost his damn mind. It was not normal, the way that he was talking about Hillary."

Matthews's premature jubilation after Iowa was infectious. So cooked was Clinton's goose that the *Washington Post* reporter Dana Milbank saw fit to make a droll little video called *Fired Up and Ready to Bore,* about how deadly dull her New Hampshire rallies were. Criticized in Iowa for not taking questions from supporters, Clinton had switched gears in New Hampshire by opening up the floor to questions. In a desultory voice-over, Milbank explained that after a "peppy" stump speech Clinton "engaged the crowd in more than an hour of torpid Q and A." The video showed audience members yawning and trickling out. She was *soooo booooring.*

Milbank's little funny was especially cutting next to media reports of the massive, adulatory New Hampshire crowds lined up to hear Obama speak. Never mind that Clinton's purportedly snoozy events were drawing huge and sometimes comparable numbers; Obama's gatherings were for a purpose loftier than outlining policy points or answering voters' questions. Richard Wolffe, an MSNBC political analyst, told Olbermann, "The crowds I see at Obama's events are not just there to pick a winner . . . or even to pick a president. . . . They're really there to be witnesses to what they talk about as being history in the making."

Obama was making history, while Clinton was putting supporters to sleep with her talk of what she'd do as president. This was the narrative that took hold of the media, even as some tried to dispute it. When the *Huffington Post* editor Roy Sekoff appeared on Dan Abrams's MSNBC program on January 7, openly rooting against Clinton and saying that her "product's not selling," fellow guest Rachel Maddow interjected, "I was in New Hampshire this weekend. I know that Hillary Clinton and Barack Obama were turning out similar-sized crowds at a lot of their events. So it's not patently obvious, it's not a factual thing that's necessarily being reported."

Maddow would tell me in an August 2008 interview that she'd been gobsmacked by the press's twisting of the electoral tale in New Hampshire: "I remember thinking, 'I can't believe the media narrative about these guys [compared to] what this is like in person! The difference is a hundred eighty degrees.'" After recalling a John Edwards event, which she described as "so emotional, and small *d* democratic," Maddow then described going to an Obama rally: "It was like, he's talking about himself! And he was three hours late! And there was a mile-long line to get in and now we're going to hear about how inspirational your campaign is? I just listened to John Edwards talk about how inspirational the American people who struggle through adversity and still succeed despite all the forces arrayed against them are, and I'm supposed to be inspired by which guy?"

Joan Walsh, the editor in chief of *Salon*, reported on the primary from New Hampshire after covering a September debate and the Iowa caucus. In the fall she had heard fellow journalists grumble about whether Obama had the fire in his belly, but by the time she got to Iowa covering his rallies from the press section was "like being at a Springsteen concert. It was like he had become the hottest ticket and they were not even trying to cover up their fervor." She particularly remembered two journalists, "sixty-something political veterans, white guys, old enough to know better," rocking back and forth during an Obama speech. "They were literally finishing lines of his speech," she said, "like 'There's that line again, I love it!'"

Three days before the primary Democrats held a debate in Manchester during which Hillary responded to the enthusiasm for Obama's "change" message by outlining her experience with getting things done, tallying, in loud numerical detail, the medical and military programs she'd fought for. The media reaction was that she had lost her cool, an assessment that perplexed some young journalists who didn't agree but were having their eyes opened to how groupthink press spin got made. "It's a bit astonishing to watch the real-time narrative construction that went on at last night's debate," wrote Ezra Klein on the website for the *American Prospect*. "I must have heard the term 'meltdown' in reference to Hillary 65 times. And I talked to reporters who would literally say, 'I thought she did okay, but I just misjudged it.'"

Covering Clinton for the *New Yorker*, George Packer swam against this tide of mutual hallucination, digging deeper at the popular characterizations of the former first lady and her opponent, describing how, at a New Hampshire rally, "whatever question the crowd threw at her, she had an informed answer, often accompanied by a multi-point plan: immigration, health care, global warming, student loans, small business, animal rights, Cuba," but that her answers were delivered in a uniform shout and did not have emotional resonance. As Packer described it, "She wouldn't risk the loss of control that it might take to energize the room with humor or anger or argument, or the sort of spontaneous human touch that everyone who spends private time with her notices and likes."

Hillary was aware of her communicative limitations. "I think that the world is only beginning to recognize that women should be permitted the same range of leadership styles that we permit men," she told Packer. But years of putting her (female) humanity in deep freeze to preserve an aura of (male) impermeability was a seemingly unbreakable habit that was now crippling her: she was unable to simply be herself in public. Meanwhile, Packer described an Obama rally at which the candidate "spoke for only twenty-five minutes and took no questions. . . . I walked outside and found five hundred people standing on the sidewalk and the front steps of the opera house, listening to his last words in silence, as if news of victory in the Pacific were coming over the loudspeakers. Within minutes, I couldn't recall a single thing that he had said, and the speech dissolved into pure feeling, which stayed with me for days."

The tightly wound gender constructions of Clinton and Obama were unraveling quickly. Gone was the image of Clinton as the defending heavyweight champ and Obama as the soft-touched ingénue. In defeat she had been feminized; in victory he had been lionized.

Where once Hillary's competence had made her a prepared and inevitable presidential standard, it was now the thing that made her a particular kind of female archetype. Like Harry Potter's Hermione Granger or Margaret from *Dennis the Menace,* Hillary was being portrayed as the hand-in-the-air, know-it-all girl, grating and unpopular in her determination to prove herself. By broadcasting their disdain for Clinton, pundits like Dana Milbank and Chris Matthews and Roy Sekoff were affirming their own social worth: *nobody* asked women like Hillary to the dance. Obama meanwhile had been cast as the swaggeringly underprepared cool guy, a characterization that may have been intellectually unjust and more than a little bit racially inflected, but that nonetheless won him the popularity contest that was the press's presidential coverage. Everyone wanted to hang out with this guy!

A *Slate* video from later in January summarized these classically gendered views of Clinton and Obama, splicing clips of Reese Witherspoon's Type-A overachiever Tracy Flick from the movie *Election* with clips of Clinton. Both women, whom we were to understand had been preparing for their political victories since they were in diapers, were fuming over the easy ascendency of the prom king, who'd decided on a whim to get into the race and was destined to beat them. The video was very funny, the comparison trenchant enough, but as I watched I realized that the neat overlap of Flick and Clinton was rooted in daunting truths about the avenues open to ambitious women in the wake of the second wave: understanding that being popular wasn't going to get a girl taken seriously, women had spent years toiling to prove their professional mettle, only to get passed over for guys whose masculinity allowed them to take a more relaxed, and thus more appealing approach to achievement.

Jonathan Alter wrote in *Newsweek* that Hillary was "substantive and strong and . . . a better debater so far than Obama." But, he continued, "like most women in politics, she lacks a critical asset. Male candidates can establish a magnetic and often sexual connection to women in the audience." In the New Hampshire debate Scott Spradling, a local news anchor, prefaced a question to Clinton by reporting that voters believed her to be "the most experienced and the most electable" candidate. But, he asked, what could she say to New Hampshire voters who "see a résumé and like it, but are hesitating on the likability issue, where they seem to like Barack Obama more?" Clinton replied with a one-liner—"Well, that hurts my feelings. . . . But I'll try to go on"—and acknowledged that Obama was "very likable." But she added, "I don't think I'm that bad." Obama, looking absently down at his notes, added coolly, "You're likable enough, Hillary," and in his next response made a joke about the Washington Redskins.

Obama was a guy, a history-making guy who delivered addresses so powerful that they caused throngs of people to fall reverentially silent. Clinton, after all that inevitability, was apparently just a girl—and a nerdy, unpopular girl at that. As soon as her femaleness was established, other misogynistic characterizations began to fly: she was desperate, unhinged, melting down, hysterical. On ABC's blog the reporter Jake Tapper described her as "bickering" with Obama during the debate, and reported that Clinton, "well . . . she got angry." Tapper didn't see her as mad "about an issue, so much, as about the fact that Obama is beating her. . . . Pundits will say that her tone made male voters recoil. And led some female voters to sneer." Clinton, whose womanhood had until so recently been kept under wraps, was suddenly an example of femininity on the edge.

The eagerness to trash Clinton had been laid bare, and it reeked of a particular kind of relief: relief from the guys who had thought they were going to have to hold their noses and get pushed around by some dame.

And then she cried. Sort of.

During a question-and-answer session with undecided voters in Portsmouth on the day before the New Hampshire primary, sixty-four-year-old Marianne Pernold Young asked Clinton, "As a woman, I know it's hard to get out of the house and get ready. My question is very personal. How do you do it? How do you keep upbeat and so wonderful? And who does your hair?"

Clinton paused before replying, acknowledging the final query by noting, "Luckily on special days I do have help. . . . If you look on some of the websites and listen to some of the commentators they always find me on the day that I didn't have help." Then she paused again, returning to the more serious question. "It's not easy," she said. "And I couldn't do it if I just didn't passionately believe it was the right thing to do." She hesitated again, stammered briefly, and said in a voice that sounded unusually reflective, "You know, I have so many opportunities from this country." Then came the sound of her voice breaking. "I just don't want to see us fall backwards. You know, this is very personal for me. It's not just political. It's not just public. I see what's happening, and we have to reverse it. And some people think elections are a game. They think it's like 'who's up,' or 'who's down.' It's about our country, it's about our kids' futures, it's really about all of us together." This was what Packer and others had surmised was impossible for her to do: ratchet down the defensive semishout, make the connection with voters. The spell broke, and Clinton returned to politicking as usual, noting that some of us (she) were ready to lead and others (Obama) weren't.

Around New Hampshire and around the country BlackBerrys and emails began to ping. Hillary had cried! She'd *cried*!

Melissa Harris-Lacewell, by now an ardent Obama supporter who had shepherded a group of Princeton undergraduates to New Hampshire to volunteer for a variety of the candidates, was sitting with the students in a restaurant when her phone began to buzz with news that Clinton had broken down: "I was like, 'What? Hillary did *what*?' It didn't sound right to me." The immediate reaction from those around her was, "'It's over. A woman having shown emotions? It's done.' There was a bit of glee on the part of Obama supporters."

The bulletin provoked similar assumptions of finality around the country. At *Salon*'s New York office it was just before lunch when an email arrived from the *Wall Street Journal* headlined "Emotional Moment for Clinton in N.H." The report of Clinton's remarks asserted that she was "softly crying, her voice breaking." My colleagues and I gathered around a computer screen, somber. Whatever we felt about her campaign, none of us wanted to see Clinton go out weeping. We found the clip and played it, staring intently as she discussed the personal, the political, the kids, the future. She sounded drained, her voice shot. We waited for the waterworks. Her voice cracked as if she might be about to lose it. We leaned in, squinted, but did not see a single salty teardrop fall.

That technicality didn't matter to those writing the congested headlines: "Clinton Fights Back Tears," "Clinton Gets Emotional," "Hillary Gets Leaky." She was leaky all right. As far as the media was concerned, she was leaking her feeble, funny femininity all over the place. Either that, or she had manufactured the whole episode, fulfilling yet another misogynistic expectation of manipulative femininity.

"Big news from New Hampshire tonight is, 'It cries,'" crowed Glenn Beck. "After spending decades stripping away all trace of emotion, femininity and humanity, Hillary Clinton actually broke down and actually cried yesterday on the campaign trail." Discussing whether the press was being unfair to Clinton, Dan Abrams asked Roy Sekoff to predict by how many percentage points she would lose New Hampshire. Sekoff sneered, "I give it a nine, and that's very personal to me," pretending to wipe a tear from his eye. John Edwards, the man who had built his candidacy in part on the support of progressive women, got in on the act, telling reporters with toothy opportunism, "I think what we need in a commander in chief is strength and resolve, and presidential campaigns are tough business, but being president of the United States is also tough business."

Such bliss was there at Clinton's journey from the front of the social evolution class back to the primordial stew of high-strung, overwrought femininity that even those who noticed that she had not actually wept could not help but tell the story as if she had. A blubbering Hillary Clinton was just too good an image to abjure. Olbermann opened his show promising coverage of "Senator Clinton . . . not crying at all, but close enough." But later in the hour he reported, "Today, Hillary Clinton, for whom I have the greatest possible respect, gets all emotional, a sentence later, attacking Obama and crying. By the way . . . after Ed Muskie, what Democrat cries in New Hampshire?"

Perhaps, on the verge of predicted electoral immolation, Hillary Clinton had had it. Maybe she felt the end was near and decided that there was little to lose. Maybe she was just too tired to be guarded. Maybe she was rebelling against Mark Penn, whom many speculated would be toast after her predicted loss. Ann Lewis said in 2008 that although Clinton had been conscientiously trying to follow Penn's campaign plan, in New Hampshire "she was true to herself. She forgot the plan and responded to the moment." In those few days, for the first time since the start of her campaign—and for the last time until the end of it—she let herself be Hillary. Answering questions in front of a New Hampshire crowd from a pushy Matthews, Clinton snapped, "I'm not on your show." "Please come on the show," Matthews immediately pleaded. "Yeah, well, right," she responded, getting a big laugh from the audience. Emboldened, she continued, "I don't know what to do with men who are obsessed with me. Honestly, I've never understood it." Matthews responded, "I'm not obsessed." And pinched her cheek.

The next day a man stood up in the middle of a Clinton rally holding a sign reading "Iron My Shirt." The guy and his companion turned out to be radio pranksters, but their presence provoked Hillary to blithely toss off a word she had not dared to utter in the gender-free calm before Iowa. "Ah, the remnants of sexism, alive and well," she said, adding, "As I think has been abundantly demonstrated, I am also running to break through the highest and hardest glass ceiling." She opened the rally to questions by cracking, "If there's anybody still left in the auditorium who wants to learn how to iron his own shirt, I'll talk about that." The crowd stood and roared its support.

Sexism! *That's* what this was! She hadn't whined about it, hadn't sent out a fund-raising letter about it, hadn't tried to capitalize on it. She had simply named it. And women had felt it, without having been directed to.

The night of the imaginary tears, the night before the primary, something changed. Spurred perhaps by the familiarity of Clinton's raw exhaustion, or a grim understanding of how she'd been persecuted for her lack of humanity and was now being jeered for revealing it, or a fury at the media hootenanny over her Iowa loss, or the obvious enthusiasm for embarrassing and degrading her, women began to break. They had had it, too. Suddenly feminists, missing in action for months, were sliding down the fire poles.

On primary day Gloria Steinem, back from Bhutan, published a *New York Times* op-ed provocatively headlined "Women Are Never Front-Runners," in which she laid out a litany of *Free to Be You and Me*–era rhetoric about women, race and politics, and declared her support for Hillary Clinton, concluding with a call to arms: "We have to be able to say: 'I'm supporting her because she'll be a great president and because she's a woman.'" EMILY's List's Ellen Malcolm, in New Hampshire campaigning for Clinton, recalled how the candidate's performance in the face of mortification sealed a personal commitment to what had already been her professional commitment. "She was so phenomenal I couldn't get over it," said Malcolm of the events in the last days before the primary. "She took questions for an hour, she had the audience in the palm of her hand, she so clearly understood what people were talking about. And the press was all *Obama Obama Obama*. I remember saying, 'I don't care, I'm in this now.' She so won me over."

Frustration with the Hillary pile-on was also gripping younger women. The cultural critic Cintra Wilson blogged that the spectacle of Clinton-hate was "a little witch-burny," and *Slate*'s Meghan O'Rourke questioned *USA Today*'s "Iron My Shirt" headline, which read, "Clinton Responds to Seemingly Sexist Shouts." "If these comments were only 'seemingly' sexist," O'Rourke wrote, "I wonder what, exactly, *indubitably* sexist remarks would sound like?" On *Feministing*, until now relatively quiet on Clinton, founder Jessica Valenti wrote that she had been "grossed out" by John Edwards's pouncing on Clinton's purported tears, and later that, "The last few days have really brought out some sexist assholery concerning Sen. Hillary Clinton."

Talking with MSNBC's Abrams the night before New Hampshire, Rachel Maddow said, "I'm not a Clinton partisan. If you had to put me in her camp or out of it, you'd put me out of it. But in doing media appearances talking about politics I have become somebody who praises Hillary Clinton, if only because I feel like I'm up against this scrum against her. I feel like, as a person who's not inclined toward Hillary Clinton's politics, I feel like somebody needs to defend her because it's such an onslaught of attacks on her."

I began to hear sentiments like Maddow's, often preceded by the phrase "I'm not a Hillary supporter, but . . ." uttered by friends and colleagues. Like its cousin, "I'm not a feminist, but . . . ," this utterance was invariably followed by an expression of its inverse truth, in this case, support for Hillary. Those who were "not Hillary supporters, but . . ." were downright horrified by the eagerness with which the media ridiculed her and declared her yesterday's news.

On the weekend preceding the primary I sat silent and surprised as my friend Merideth railed about Hillary's being questioned about her likability in a debate, about how she'd been written off so prematurely. Merideth was no Hillary loyalist, nor had I had ever known her to have a particular investment in gender politics. Meanwhile Geraldine was sending me lists of links to egregious slurs against Clinton on television and in newspapers. A banished memory came back to me, of an argument with my aunt, a feminist academic who thought I was crazy not to support Hillary. She'd warned me, in a near whisper, that I'd change my tune as soon as I realized how rare an opportunity Clinton presented for women.

I wasn't there yet, but I sure didn't like how much fun the media was having tearing down the girl who'd been called a tight-ass and was now labeled a basket case. A pattern was emerging, not academic or historicized, but live and right in front of me: the double binds, hypocrisies, impossibilities, and improbability of becoming, and being, Hillary Clinton, the first woman ever to get far enough to be taken seriously for the job of president.

The eagerness to oust Clinton from the race was not motivated purely by her gender. I understood that it was interwoven with enthusiasm for Obama, his promise of change. I knew what it was like to object to Hillary's centrism, her history of compromise. I knew that for fifteen years the Clinton team had behaved as if it had no use for the press, a press that had in turn become anxious to chomp the hand that refused to feed it. I knew that the prospect of two decades plus of Bush-Clinton-Bush-Clinton was not just unappealing, but almost un-American. I knew that Mark Penn's strategy was inane and that Clinton had chosen to listen to him.

But what centrist politics and flawed self-presentation should have gotten Hillary was a lost caucus, then a lost primary, and then more lost caucuses and primaries, until at some point she was out of the race and pundits could shake their heads and score her errors. But that was not what was happening in the first week of January. She had lost a single caucus, and instead of simply reporting on it her critics had rolled around in it, celebrated it, made it mean exponentially more than it ever should have. Their ardor for Clinton's abasement had reverberated with an unmistakable vibe, the loosening of a clenched resentment that it had been a chick who had dared be confident about her ability to win the Democratic nomination, who had exercised infuriatingly tight control over the press, who had for more than a year appeared to exert unrelenting dominion over her male competitors.

✶ ✶ ✶

On a subway to Geraldine's apartment to watch the New Hampshire results with friends, I couldn't fathom how I'd come to care so much. My heart was in my throat, my fingers crossed as if at a playoff game, my whole body pretzeled with the intense and irrational desire of someone madly hoping for an impossible upset.

I didn't want Hillary to win the Democratic nomination. I didn't want John Edwards out of the race. I didn't want Barack Obama to suffer a hope-squelching loss. But I knew with primal surety that if I had been a New Hampshire resident on January 8, I would have pulled a lever for the former first lady with a song in my heart and a bird flipped at Chris Matthews, Roy Sekoff, Keith Olbermann and every other guy who'd gotten his rocks off by imagining Hillary's humiliation. That humiliation had been almost assured by a last-minute Gallup poll placing Obama 13 points ahead of Clinton going into New Hampshire.

In baseball anything can happen. The results that began to roll in were not the numbers anyone expected. Women, it seemed, had come to the polls to vote for Hillary Clinton. By the end of the night she would win not only New Hampshire, but 46 percent of its women, compared to 34 percent for Obama.

On MSNBC Matthews recited like a catechism the numbers of every pollster who had forecasted Clinton's loss. Halfway through the night he had his arms crossed defensively across his chest like a shamed schoolboy and was proclaiming that he had been at Saturday night's debate and had thought it "a draw," but that apparently Clinton's performance had been "good enough here for women who wanted to root for her anyway." He said this as if it were obvious that a performance that was "good enough . . . for women" would not have been good enough for any rational political decision maker.

He was not alone in his estimation of female electoral impulses. Flailing for explanations for Clinton's strong showing, pundits soon settled on her purported crying jag. Suddenly the moment that had signaled her uproarious unraveling was being credited with saving her. "I never saw her like that before," said Jack Cafferty on CNN, "Sympathetic. Real." CNN's Gloria Borger informed the audience that "There is a lot of talk tonight about whether Hillary's tearing up made any difference." She noted that a striking percentage of female Hillary voters told exit pollsters that they had decided whom to vote for on that very day.

Tom Brokaw, retired from his NBC anchor spot but sitting in with Matthews for election coverage, was aware of the treatment Clinton had received in the grabby hands of his colleagues and seemed to relish the opportunity to spank them. "The end of the Clinton era—a lot of pundits saying that on this channel and on all the other channels," said Brokaw. "All of that conventional wisdom was turned on its head. This is one of the great triumphs in recent years in American presidential politics, . . . and the rest of us who were saying out loud that this was not going to happen, we've got a lot of explaining to do." Matthews barked back that he had relied on universities that devoted themselves solely to polling. Polling is "a lot less important than letting this process go forward in the way that it should," said Brokaw sternly. Even conservatives were doing some self-flagellating. "The press was dead wrong," said Pat

Buchanan. "We had virtually canonized Obama. . . . The press has been telling us she's gone and the women came out and said no, she's not. What New Hampshire did was stand up and body-slam the national establishment, the press corps, the pollsters, the whole bunch."

And then Rachel Maddow took it one step further. "Do you want to know who they're blaming?" she asked, looking as though she had canary feathers hanging from her mouth. Citing the online news source *Talking Points Memo,* Maddow continued, "They're blaming Chris Matthews. People are citing particularly Chris not only for his own views but as a symbol of what the mainstream media has done to Hillary Clinton." She later added, "People feel that the media is piling on Hillary Clinton. They're coming to her defense with their votes."

At eleven-thirty that night Matthews was finally forced to suck it up. Looking like he was chewing on a lemon, he confessed, "She stood there and took the heat under what looked to be a difficult time . . . I give her a lot of personal credit. I will never underestimate Hillary Clinton again."

The four of us watching at Geraldine's house, not one a Clintonite, cheered like mad.

For the first time in my life my reaction to a political news cycle was mirroring a larger national sentiment, and I was shocked by it. Notably it was also the first time in my life that my reactions as a woman and as a feminist had real-time application on a presidential stage, the first time that women had figured so large both as candidates and as voters. This was what it felt like to be relevant in a presidential contest.

If it surprised me, it was nothing compared to how the Clinton camp felt. A group of them had taken over their hotel's bar in Manchester to drown their sorrows on the afternoon of the primary. Mark Penn was sitting by himself. "No one would go near him at the table," said Elaine Lafferty, "because he was going to get fired." John Coale, a trial lawyer and friend of the Clintons, had brought Lafferty to the bar hoping that she would be able to personally deliver to Hillary her memo on new ways to reach women, strategies that might be useful since, after the predicted loss, the campaign was going to have to change course. Coale stuffed the

memo into Hillary's hands as she passed through on her way to
a radio interview. Returning briefly in the late afternoon, Hillary
pulled Lafferty and Coale aside to say that she loved the ideas and
would like to talk about them further, after she got through the
night ahead.

Bill Clinton, suffering from a bad cold and looking, as Lafferty
described it, "like hell on a biscuit," was the first to offer the sod-
den crowd any hope. "He walked in there at five o'clock and said,
'I think we're going to do better than they say,'" said Lafferty. As
the results began to come in, all hell broke loose. "Mandy Grunwald was screaming. Capricia [Marshall] was having to pick [new]
music. People were screaming at the television," Lafferty said of
the reaction. Lissa Muscatine, a longtime speechwriter for Clinton,
described her night in Washington, D.C.: "I was working on the
non-victory speech, and then it was the 'it's going to be closer than
expected' speech, and then it was the 'wow, this was really, *really*
close' speech, and then suddenly it was the 'Oh! She won! Crap, we
don't have a speech!' speech." Mark Penn would be keeping his job
after all. Except for the demotion of overwhelmed Patti Solis Doyle,
the Clinton campaign was not going to change its course.

As Clinton made her way from the stage at the Southern New
Hampshire University gymnasium after her first victory speech of
the campaign, she leaned in to Ellen Malcolm and grabbed her
hand. "Ellen," she said, "I just became the first woman in history
to win a presidential primary."

✳ ✳ ✳

The Wednesday morning quarterbacking was bleak. Many critics,
it seemed, accepted an interpretation of the surprising results in
which women had cleaved to a weeping Hillary like Golden Girls
to cheesecake.

Judith Warner, blogging at the *New York Times,* wrote, "If
victory came for the reasons we've been led to believe—because
women voters ultimately saw in her, exhausted and near defeat, a
countenance that mirrored their own—then I hate what that victory says about the state of their lives and the nature of their emotions." Returning to a Lewinsky-era refrain about Clinton, Warner

continued, "I hate . . . that [women have] got to see a strong, smart and savvy woman cut down to size before they can embrace her as one of their own."

Obama supporters were dismayed and furious. Melissa Harris-Lacewell wrote on *Slate,* "Clinton cried about being attacked in the debates, but there are no public tears shed for the strain Obama must feel [about an uptick in death threats against him]." Even angrier was Moe Tkacik, a vividly irreverent writer for the women's blog *Jezebel.* Writing to a vocal readership that had shown Hillary leanings, Tkacik exploded: "Dear all you commentwhores who said Hillary's teensy little tear session had swayed your vote to Hillary: Fuck you. . . . Her narrow lead in yesterday's New Hampshire primary is entirely attributable to chicks like you, and you were alllllll chicks. . . . New Hampshire women, after telling pollster after pollster they were ready for change, went inside the booths and had a little cry."

If New Hampshire women had in fact voted for Hillary Clinton because they sympathized with her vulnerability, that was bad. It suggested that although the headline on Steinem's op-ed was patently inaccurate—a woman *had* been a front-runner for more than a year—an inverted version of it was correct: that front-runners were never recognized as women, and that other women jumped to their aid only when they were tied to a railroad track, a locomotive chugging toward them.

I supposed that there were women who recognized in Hillary a wounded, imperiled quality that they responded to as inherently, depressingly female. But I could not shake the feeling that there was something more complex than an appreciation for damp feminine excess or relief at seeing a powerful woman taken down a notch that had made New Hampshire's women rise up for Hillary.

In the days after the primary Harris-Lacewell pointed to a particular dynamic surrounding Obama's candidacy, and her observation felt more resonant than the media line we had been fed about Clinton. Appearing on *Democracy Now,* Harris-Lacewell noted that early in the campaign cycle there had been "a great deal of anxiety about Barack, because he had almost too much white support. . . . It raised some anxieties for African American voters, who were asking, 'Well, if there are all of these people in the media, if there are all of these white voters who are interested in you, does that mean that you're not with us, that you do not share our interests?'" What she was describing was the suspicion that plagued supporters of both Obama and Clinton: if you can win, then you cannot possibly be for real.

Referring to Bob Johnson, the founder of BET and a Clinton supporter who'd made derisive remarks about Obama's youthful drug experimentation, Harris-Lacewell pointed to the fact that support for Obama among black voters had begun, finally, to swell: "When that sort of attack occurs, it actually . . . increases the amount of support among most African Americans," whose reaction she summed up as "Oh, I see. Actually, [the establishment is] not completely for you."

The building volume and visibility of sexism aimed at Clinton post-Iowa, like the increasingly inescapable racism directed at Obama, was a stinging reminder that there was a system in place that had historically excluded anyone who was not white and male, and that those who challenged that system would not only meet with resistance, but would be pitted against each other. In New Hampshire two long-standing misapprehensions about gender had been corrected: the notion that there had never been antagonism to Clinton's candidacy from a reasonable (as opposed to right-wing crazy) male establishment, and that because Clinton had found a way to pass off her power as confident and thus male, she was no longer truly female.

Women who had spent months pretending that Clinton was not a woman suddenly could not help but recognize how she had been treated. Perhaps for some the moment of connection *was* her glistening eyes. But that didn't automatically indicate some lamentably drippy sisterhood. As Harris-Lacewell reported in retrospect, "If you sat at the [restaurant] long enough, you began to hear a ton of hard-working working-class and middle-class white women who said, 'I know what it's like when a young man comes in and takes your spot. You train him, and then he comes in and takes your spot on the job.'" You did the work on the science project; he got the credit. You voiced the idea at the meeting; he said it five minutes later and everyone complimented him. This was not about shared female essence; it was about a shared female experience.

Anita Dunn, who would go on to work as a senior advisor for Obama in the spring, later told the political reporter Anne Kornblut, "I was still neutral during New Hampshire . . . [but] I saw [Obama] walking into these adoring crowds like he was the Messiah. And I saw her out there sweating, with her political career on the line and then choking up because she realized that it was almost over. I would have voted for her."

Some women were voting in response to the humiliation of the media's fetishistic obsession with Clinton's supposed breakdown. "They played that thing over and over and over," said NOW's Kim Gandy. "I think that made women kind of angry. Like, why are they *doing* this to her?" Ellen Malcolm imagined women listening to the media characterization of Clinton's misty moment, and thinking, "*What?* This is the nicest thing I've ever seen Hillary do! I've always wanted to know that she really cared, and she's telling us that she does, and they're just pissing on her because she's crying. And she wasn't even crying!" Jessica Grose from *Jezebel* responded to her colleague Tkacik's rant against weepy women voters in a post that noted that men could be "just as emotional and capricious when choosing candidates as women are," citing her late grandfather, a quiet, mild yellow-dog Democrat who had had a "visceral, irrational dislike of" Hillary Clinton.

Some, like me, reacted to the gloating disrespect from the press. Pam Spaulding of the popular *Pam's House Blend* blog dubbed this phenomenon "the Tweety Effect," in reference to a popular nickname for Chris Matthews. As she defined it, it's "where the misogyny of a talking head in the MSM [mainstream media] so enrages a demographic that they go out and vote in a manner that will put egg on the face of the talking head." Even the liberal blogger Matthew Yglesias conceded, "I don't think pissing off Chris Matthews is a good enough reason to pull the lever for Clinton, but I can certainly understand the impulse."

These points of recognition were about identifying with a certain strain of ill treatment, something feminists are loath to do lest they be accused of capitalizing on victimhood. But feminism was born precisely *because* women faced gendered injustices. To identify and overcome obstacles and resistance was to advance the project of female empowerment. Did the sexism exhibited toward Hillary cast her as embattled and threatened? Yes. But that didn't mean that women responded to it because they themselves loved feeling threatened and embattled or believed that that was their natural pose, or because they loved seeing tough broads brought down. They might have responded because they *hated* that women were treated that way, and because in this instance they had the means to push back: voting for Hillary.

When someone made insinuations about Barack Obama selling drugs or emphasized that his middle name was Hussein, his blackness became accessible not because it was essentially black to sell drugs or have Muslim roots, but because blackness in America has long been an impediment to parity and acceptance, and because manipulated characterizations of blackness have been part of what has been used to enforce that impediment. So too with femininity. To see a woman get taunted for being simultaneously frigid and lachrymose and then get teased for her smarts was not to ascribe to her inherently feminine qualities of frigidity, sentimentality, or unsociability. Rather it was to witness femininity as it has historically been cast, especially when it threatened male power structures: as a laughable, silly, unpleasant, or devalued condition. Women had watched a popular vision of Hillary Clinton, a front-running candidate with whom they may have had a complicated or cool relationship but whose strengths, weaknesses, achievements, and mistakes had never been traditional or one-dimensional, manipulated to fit into retro molds of lightweight (peevish, unpopular, calculating, shrill) feminine illegitimacy. In a cartoon drawn by Pat Oliphant in the days after New Hampshire a blubbing Clinton is shown at a desk, facing Mahmoud Ahmadinejad, Osama bin Laden, Kim Jong-Il and other menacing men murmuring "Aww, she's sensitive—I had no idea"; "Was it something we said?"; and "Buy her flowers." A thought bubble above Hillary's head reads, "You guys are mean!" and in the corner, a miniature Bill remarks, "This is when PMS goes nuclear." In the face of plenty of good reasons to criticize Hillary Clinton, women now realized that for some it still came down to this: the same twisted characterizations used for centuries to bolster the idea that women were unfit to lead.

"We [human beings] like the underdog who is being unfairly attacked," Harris-Lacewell told me. "Part of the reason we come to like Hillary is watching her bear up under pressure, particularly sexist pressure, and we like to watch Barack bear up against the weight of racism." Those who were roused to Clinton's defense were roused not because she was a girl, but because she was being treated like one.

The remarkable thing about what happened in New Hampshire was that standing up for Hillary wasn't really about Hillary at all. "I'm still not voting for Clinton but I've been sickened by the behavior of the national media," commented DBR on *Feministing,* agreeing with a piece I had written for *Salon* to which *Feministing* had linked. Fellow commenter Gretchen wrote, "The night before the NH primaries, I said to my boyfriend, 'I hope Hillary wins.' And he said 'Why? You don't support Hillary.'" The attention women paid to Clinton in those five days was evidence that later media narratives equating support of Barack Obama with a rejection of feminist principles were hogwash. The women's vote in New Hampshire was not a sign of essentialist gynocentric solidarity; it was a show of political and rebellious feminist force more potent than any march on Washington.

But the press's nearly unanimous take emphasized only the impact Clinton's nonexistent tears had on voters' heartstrings. MSNBC's New Hampshire wrap-up included a rehash of how "Clinton's voice quavered." CNN's piece contained a mention of the "almost-tears," a description of how her "eyes welled up this week," and further analysis of whether her "emotions were sincere or faked as part of some strategy to diminish criticism that she is too steely, too cold." The *New York Times* referred to "Mrs. Clinton's unusual display of emotion" as a "galvanizing moment" for many voters, and quoted New Hampshire resident Elaine Marquis, who said, "Women finally saw a woman—perhaps a tough woman, but a woman with a gentle heart."

All three stories failed to include mention of the remarkable fact of which Hillary herself had been immediately aware: that on Tuesday, January 8, 2008, that steely, gentle-hearted woman had become the first in the history of the United States of America to win a presidential primary.

5 THE MOST RESTRICTING FORCES

GLORIA STEINEM'S OP-ED "Women Are Never Front-Runners" began with a description of a fictional female counterpart to Barack Obama, a figure reminiscent of "Judith Shakespeare," Virginia Woolf's imagined sister of William, who had "a gift like her brother's, for the tune of words" but no professional platform from which to express them. In Steinem's formulation "Achola Obama" was a mixed-race lawyer with eight years in the state legislature, a politician whose voice was a unifying force but who could never have been a political supernova like Barack. "Be honest," Steinem wrote. "Do you think this is the biography of someone who could be elected to the United States Senate? After less than one term there, do you believe she could be a viable candidate to head the most powerful nation on earth?"

Contextualizing the electoral fortunes of Hillary Clinton and Barack Obama, Steinem argued that although "the caste systems of sex and race are interdependent and can only be uprooted together," the gender barrier is not taken as seriously as the racial barrier.

She pointed out that "black men were given the vote a half-century before women of any race were allowed to mark a ballot, and generally have ascended to positions of power, from the military to the boardroom, before any women." The pull quote chosen by the *Times* was "Gender is probably the most restricting force in American life."

The response to Steinem's piece from many sectors was wildly positive. Dozens of friends sent me the op-ed, and many called to talk about it. It remained at the top of the newspaper's "most emailed" list for days and was reprinted around the world. Though it seemed unlikely that the piece changed many votes on the day of the New Hampshire primary, it was emblematic of the billowing resistance that Clinton's recent treatment had provoked. "Every once in a while a writer gets to name something that people are feeling that hasn't been named yet," Steinem told me more than a year after the publication of the piece. What she had named was sexism, the thing to which some women were beginning to respond instinctually.

I was surprised by my own reaction to Steinem's piece. It hadn't made me want to vote for Hillary, but it had made me nod my head in agreement that "anything that affects males is seen as more serious than anything that affects 'only' the female half of the human race," and that Obama "is seen as unifying by his race while [Clinton] is seen as divisive by her sex." Steinem observed that because children were still raised by women, some men feel as though "they are regressing to childhood" when faced with a powerful female, and that racist stereotypes of black men as hypermasculine prompt some white men to identify with them as a way of affirming their own masculinity. Yes! These things were true! I couldn't believe that I was having my eyes opened, perhaps even my consciousness raised, by a piece so old-school in its prose, so retro in its tone.

What I did not realize at the time was how many other people found the op-ed old-school and retro in ways that did not make them nod their heads in assent but shake them in fury and frustration.

The piece gave shape and language to an unprecedented moment in American women's history; it was also a grenade, exploding delicate bonds between women of different colors and ages. If "Women Are Never Front-Runners" was received in some feminist quarters with grateful relief, in others it was reviled with a comparable degree of intensity and viewed as a public reopening of deep wounds that had never fully healed.

Second-wave feminism had been riven, and partially unraveled, by divisions over whose interests it was representing. Most visibly emblematized by white middle-class straight women like *The Feminine Mystique* author Betty Friedan, New York Congresswoman Bella Abzug, and *Ms.* founder Steinem, the women's movement of the 1970s was dogged by criticism that it was an ultimately bourgeois project, one that did not take into account the perspectives of women of different colors, classes, and sexual orientations. While in reality the women's movement of the 1970s was powered by a diverse group of white, black, gay, straight, middle- and working-class women, *feminism,* as it was commonly portrayed and popularized, concerned itself most famously and (perhaps) most disruptively with getting women out of the home and into the workforce. This mission did not resonate for millions of women who did not suffer from Friedan's mystical stay-at-home ennui because they did not stay at home. Poor and minority women had always worked, and many were less concerned with sloughing off the repressive bonds of domestic drudgery than with winning economic and social freedoms that might afford them the choice to stay home with their family should they want to. When feminism did catapult some women into universities and professional spheres, women of color were often called upon to pick up the domestic slack, cleaning the houses and caring for the children of those who had reaped feminism's fruits. Through some lenses, privileged (and often racially privileged) women had advanced not by striking new, equitable deals with men, but by consuming those women below them on the power totem pole.

The perceived exclusions of the women's movement were part of what led the poet and activist Audre Lorde to argue that male-female gender distinctions were reductive, and that women themselves experienced such a divergence of identity that feminism failed most of them. The writer Alice Walker, one of Steinem's closest friends, coined the term *womanist* as an alternative for women of color in search of a way to indicate that their feminist perspectives and goals were more expansive than the word had come to suggest.

Competitive tension between female advancement and black advancement extended much further back than the 1970s. While suffragists and abolitionists worked in tandem before and throughout the Civil War—one of the earliest gatherings of the women's movement was the Anti-Slavery Convention of American Women in 1837, attended by both black and white women—alliances ruptured during Reconstruction-era battles over how best to secure rights of citizenship for America's disenfranchised populations. The Fourteenth and Fifteenth Amendments, which granted citizenship, due process, and voting rights to black men but not to women, drove a wedge between formerly cooperative activists. Some, including Frederick Douglass, Elizabeth Blackwell, Lucy Stone and Julia Ward Howe, supported passage of the amendments despite their exclusion of women. Douglass, a longtime advocate of female suffrage who participated in the 1848 Seneca Falls Convention, believed that white women's economic and social privilege put them closer to enfranchisement than black men, and that once black men could vote, black women would enjoy the same indirect empowerment. As he wrote in an 1868 letter to the suffragist Josephine Sophie White Griffing, "Woman has a thousand ways to attach herself to the governing power of the land and already exerts an honorable influence on the course of legislation. She is the victim of abuses, to be sure, but it cannot be pretended . . . that her cause is as urgent as . . . ours." Perhaps the more crucial argument was that, had the amendments included the rights of women, they would not have passed; many activists believed that enfranchising blacks, rather than no one at all, was the more broadly progressive choice. "We rejoice in every extension of suffrage," said Lucy Stone at the 1869 Women's Rights Convention in Chicago.

In staunch opposition were the suffragists Susan B. Anthony and Elizabeth Cady Stanton, who believed that their former allies had sold them out. They were particularly furious that the Fourteenth Amendment allowed the word "male" into the Constitution, surmising that its inclusion would make a future battle for women's rights only more difficult. Stanton's sense of betrayal was particularly rancorous and led her to overt racism. In 1869 she said, "Think of Patrick and Sambo and Hans and Yung Tung, who do not know the difference between a monarchy and a republic, who can not read the Declaration of Independence or Webster's spelling-book, making laws for [prominent suffragists]." Stanton and Anthony formed the women's-only National Woman Suffrage Association in opposition to the Fifteenth Amendment in spring of 1869. In turn Stone and Howe founded the American Woman Suffrage Association, an organization open to women and men who supported passage of the Fifteenth Amendment. More than two decades later the competing groups combined to form the National American Woman Suffrage Association.

Stanton's anxiety about women's progress being delayed by the abandonment of abolitionist friends was prophetic; it would be fifty years before the Nineteenth Amendment gave women the right to vote. Meanwhile blacks were not able to vote freely or safely for years to come. Stopped at the polls by property and residency requirements, literacy tests, and poll taxes, African Americans were beaten and lynched in their century-long struggle to exercise the rights they had been granted in 1870. Ninety-five years after passage of the Fifteenth Amendment, and forty-five years after passage of the Nineteenth, Congress passed the Voting Rights Act.

It was probably predestined that the race between Hillary Clinton and Barack Obama would so agonizingly recall the clashes of allies of the past, between people whose histories of discrimination were linked and, in the case of millions of black women, shared. In 2008 African American men and white women were once again set against each other, in a configuration that provoked a destructive tallying of oppressions, injustices, and suffering and left women of color caught in the middle. It was this explosive conversation that Steinem's op-ed kicked off.

"How can one compare racism to sexism—and if one tries, where do those of us who are disadvantaged both by our race and by our gender fit in?" wrote Jennifer Fang at *Racialicious*. Fang thought, "[Steinem's comparison] redirects our attention away from efforts to break the White male patriarchy that excludes all the Others, but towards in-fighting where we all compete to see . . . who's more oppressed. . . . Is it no wonder, then, that women of colour have long felt alienated by feminists like Steinem?"

"I was deeply, deeply offended," said Melissa Harris-Lacewell. "The part that took me over the edge was the imaginary black woman, Achola." To Harris-Lacewell's mind, Steinem's invented female version of Obama represented "the very worst of what second-wave white feminism does. . . . Instead of engaging with living, breathing women of color, it imagines us in these bodies. 'Imagine this black woman . . . ' But you don't have to imagine a black woman, we exist!" Conjuring one was not only unnecessary, but something that Steinem should have known better than to do. "This is Gloria Steinem, and she's been having these conversations for thirty years," said Harris-Lacewell. "The conversations in which people say 'White feminists: please don't do this.' It's not like Gloria Steinem doesn't personally know women who feel this way, that she hasn't worked with them and written with them and that she doesn't engage with them."

That Steinem might make an argument that women, or even that black women should vote for Hillary was fair enough. "It's not as though race should always trump gender," Harris-Lacewell said, or that blacks or black women vote as a monolith. But, she went on, "[Steinem] chose to make this point *not* by talking about the things that African-American women actually cared about that Hillary Clinton could address better than Barack Obama. . . . No, [instead she implied], 'Oh, you silly black women who are supporting Barack Obama, don't you see he means nothing to you because you are a woman, like me, and like Hillary Clinton, and your relevant issue is your gender, not your race?' I was livid about her use of black women in that way."

Steinem's argument, like so much feminist history before it, had rendered invisible (or imaginary) women of color, blithely presuming them to have the same perspective as the white women whose voices were given a prominent platform, in this case the op-ed page of the *New York Times*.

"[Steinem's piece] left me quite irritable," said Margo Jefferson, a journalist and professor. "But I just thought, 'Well, there goes Gloria.' She's such a good popularizer and always has these good points, but then misses something huge. I chose to take refuge in a certain kind of patronizing of her. It was very predictable. But I was also tired of being too sanctimonious. Yeah, this was an example of what we've been saying for years about feminists being bourgeois and racially exclusive, but I was also trying to check myself, certainly as a black person and also as a woman, because there was aggrieved sanctimony on both ends."

In 2009 Steinem explained to me that she had asked the *New York Times* to select a headline that did not make sex and race seem competitive. They complied, but then used "Gender is the most restricting force in American life" as the pull quote. Steinem said, in retrospect, "That was my fault, because at minimum I should have said 'pervasive,' because I meant that it was the most widespread, not that it was the most severe. They took that sentence and made it the slug on the Internet, and then it was . . . used as a theme for a whole weeklong series on CNN, asking 'Which is more important, sex or race?,' which I've spent my life trying to say are intertwined. They could have taken a sentence in the same piece that said 'The caste systems of sex and race are interdependent and can only be uprooted together.' If they had taken that sentence it would have been more fair. But it was my fault for creating this screwy sentence."

Steinem took the blame for another misleading sentence: "When I said that Negro men had got the vote on paper before women, black or white women." She said that a *New York Times* editor persuaded her that she did not need to delve into the history of black vote suppression because she had addressed it in her 2007 column expressing support for both Clinton and Obama. The editor, said Steinem, assured her that this earlier explanation would cover Steinem in her "Front-Runner" op-ed. "I shouldn't have fallen for that," she said in retrospect. When the fallout came, the *Times* would not let her run clarifications on its website, so she posted an explanation at the Women's Media Center website and withdrew the column from syndication. "Here is the important thing," she said to me later. "If you want to maintain racism, you have to restrict the freedom of the women of the ruling class, of white women, otherwise you don't have the means of reproduction and racial purity. That's how in the South, race and sex have always gone together. White women were restricted and like chattel, and black women were used as workers themselves and forced to produce workers and were everybody's sexual property. . . . It is not possible to be a feminist without being antiracist. It's not possible to be a civil rights person without being a feminist. It's all connected. And that's what made me craziest about this election, and that's what made me craziest about misinterpreting me."

In a *Slate* piece responding to Obama's New Hampshire loss Harris-Lacewell offered what appeared to be a fierce rejoinder to Steinem's piece, puncturing the myth of Barack Obama's postracial slide to victory. Making a point that mirrored Steinem's in some ways, Harris-Lacewell wrote, "What I know for sure is that if black Americans are going to be relevant to American elections, they must rally behind Obama now."

The progressive radio and television host Amy Goodman invited both women on to her show, *Democracy Now*. It was an intense conversation, with Harris-Lacewell hammering home points about the disparities between the ways America apprehends white female oppression and the oppression of African American men and women: "We have got to get clear about the fact that race and gender are not these clear dichotomies in which you're a woman or you're black; I'm sitting here in my black womanhood body, knowing that it is more complicated than that. . . . An anxiety for African American women feminists like myself is that we're often asked to join up with white women's feminism, but only on their own terms, as long as we . . . remain silent about the ways in which our gender, our class, our sexual identity doesn't intersect." Steinem accepted much of what Harris-Lacewell said, bristling only at what sounded like a suggestion that women who sympathized with Clinton and voted for her were acting on racist impulses. Harris-Lacewell responded briskly, "I would not disparage them by claiming they are racist. I would, however, say they're part of the American historical system that responds to white women suffering in very particular ways, and it cannot see African Americans suffering in the same ways."

It was a lucid, energetic exchange about the history of racial and gender politics. It was also painful to watch: two right-minded and quite like-minded women in tormented debate with each other about current and historical injustice. "When I got the phone call from *Democracy Now* I had just gotten back into town [from New Hampshire], and I was exhausted," recalled Harris-Lacewell. "My hair looked awful, I was up against an orange background. It was my least favorite television appearance in about four hundred different ways. But it was also my most favorite television appearance.

I don't think I've ever been angrier on television. I was pissed. And it came out in ways that I think led to very useful analysis." She admitted,"If I made a list of the top people I'd like to go on TV and tell how pissed I am about what they've done to my country, Gloria Steinem wouldn't make the top one hundred. I see myself as being very much on the same side as Gloria Steinem. So it was this weird moment, but one that speaks to the very heart of my political commitments about misrepresentations of African American women."

A YouTube clip of the *Democracy Now* episode circulated; young people saw it. What Harris-Lacewell heard afterward, she said, was that many of them had read Steinem's op-ed and felt uneasy about it but hadn't had the vocabulary, history or context to explain why. "College students and graduate students, other faculty, said, 'What was so useful about it was that you articulated why I have sometimes felt uneasy about feminism in general, or about that op-ed specifically.'"

Asked about whether the fracas reminded her of discord within feminism in the 1970s, Steinem said no, balking even at the inference of second-wave racial exclusivity. Noting that it was infuriating that the women's movement, which she called "more diverse than any other," was accused more often of a lack of diversity than other white, male-dominated social movements, she told me, "I learned feminism from black women. All my lecture partners were black women. They were so far ahead of us. It was true statistically that black women were, from the very first polls in the sixties, more likely to support feminist issues than white women. So this cherished idea that feminists are white middle class? They didn't say Stokely Carmichael was middle class. He was. They didn't say Martin Luther King was middle class. He was. They're always trying to disqualify women with all these adjectives, including trying to divide us from black women. There's certainly racism, God knows, in the women's movement. Of course there is. But in my actual personal experience it was the women of the National Welfare Rights Organization, it was Flo Kennedy, it was Dorothy Hughes, all these women from whom I learned."

Margo Jefferson took a different view. "Flo is a legend, but neither of those women profited at all from feminism and its popularization as much as Gloria did," she said. "And that is certainly because they did not have the background, race, and were not pretty young white women. Do I think Gloria Steinem is a racist? No. But so much of prejudice—gender and racial and class—has to do with the assumptions you're allowed to live with. I have class privilege, and sometimes I'm placed in that position toward people of my own race who have less privilege. Nobody is spared that kind of obtuseness."

Steinem acknowledged, "Yes, I became better known than most women of color I work with," but she pointed to the role of the media rather than the dynamics of the movement itself. Citing several examples in which she refused to participate in magazine stories or pose for pictures that would make her the poster girl for her diverse movement, Steinem recalled being approached by the *New York Times Magazine* for a cover story on pioneer feminists: "I said I couldn't do it unless they included Flo Kennedy, Eleanor Holmes Norton, Dolores Huerta, and others. . . . So they left me out of the cover photo and used Kate Millett, Susan Brownmiller—all white."

Opening up this conversation in 2008 allowed a new generation of women to weigh in. Latoya Peterson, then twenty-four, was writing at the blog *Racialicious,* calling herself a "hip-hop feminist," a term she said reconciled "an often-hostile term, 'feminism,' with a more embracing term, 'hip-hop.'" Peterson told me in 2009, "[Steinem's piece] minimized the balancing act that black women go through, because we're both racialized and gendered . . . and it manifests differently because our sexism is racialized and our racialism is sexualized. Feminists think they can gloss over these things. 'It's not that big a deal because we're still all women.' Well, we're not all women, because you've made it clear that my experience does not matter, [but] you still feel like you know what's best for me. It's that maternalistic streak in feminism that really turns a lot of women of color off. You don't know us, you don't know our culture, you don't know what we've been through, and I'm not going to sit here and be condescended to by a white woman when I could easily go and organize my own people."

One of the ironies of the dissatisfactions stirred by "Women Are Never Front-Runners" and the way the piece resurrected old impressions of a generation's blinkered approach to racial difference was that Steinem, the icon of the women's movement of the 1970s, did not initially want to write the piece at all. She had done so at the behest of a twenty-year-old friend.

As a teenager, Shelby Knox was the subject of an award-winning documentary, *The Education of Shelby Knox,* chronicling her political awakening in conservative Lubbock, Texas. Knox had been raised religious and taken a virginity pledge before launching a doomed battle against the local school board to get sex education taught in high schools. In 2007 Steinem offered Knox room and board in her Manhattan home while she found her footing as an activist and speaker. Upon moving in, Knox papered her bedroom with "Hillary '08" stickers. "I was putting them up by my bed, and I was like, I wonder what Gloria thinks of this, so I asked her," Knox said. Steinem's response was, "I don't think any woman can win—it's too soon." Knox was devastated. "Gloria Steinem cannot be telling me that Hillary Clinton has no chance of winning," she said. "I kept saying, 'But Gloria, don't you want her to win?' And she kept saying, 'I don't know if we want to go through all the ridicule and misogyny or put Hillary through it.'"

Both women were traveling the country, speaking at colleges, and reporting back to each other about the confusion they were hearing from female students disturbed by the animus directed at Clinton but unwilling to believe that the hatred was motivated by her gender since they'd been taught that sexism in America was a thing of the past. Knox in particular was alarmed by the inability of women her age to talk confidently about how they felt about Clinton. She understood why she was more thrown than her mentor. "[Gloria] has had seventy-five years of blatant sexism and talking about it," said Knox. "She told me in 2007 that this was what was going to happen, and that she dreaded it. So, to her, it was just coming true. Whereas my generation had been told we are equal our entire lives. I was hearing young women on campuses internalizing this and thinking they were crazy, that something was wrong [with them] for seeing [sexism]."

The night of the Iowa caucus Steinem returned home to find Knox crying in front of the television. "I was saying, 'This is *sexism,*' raving and ranting," said Knox. "'Yes, Shelby, this is sexism,' Gloria said. 'This is hard. This is what this is.'" Knox recalled that she "got a little pissed at Gloria": "Because I was like, 'Someone

needs to say that this is sexism!' I [was telling her,] 'We're starting
to feel like something's wrong with us, so *you* may know that this
is sexism but you have to say it.'" Steinem responded by suggesting
that Knox herself write a piece. "I said, 'No, Gloria, no one will listen to me. Everyone will listen to you, and if you don't do this then I
will blame you on behalf of my generation forever for what this has
done to us. It makes us think we're crazy. You have to name this,
okay?'" After mulling her own growing anger at the media's misogyny, Steinem drafted her op-ed and showed it to Knox.

Knox, who is white, said that her only quibble was with a sentence about young women denying a gender caste system. To Knox's
mind, Steinem's phrase "Gender is the most restricting force" was
"a throw-away line that explained that white women and women of
color experienced sexism and women of color experienced both racism and sexism but that therefore, statistically, more people would
be affected by sexism. It was not a comparative statement of hardship at all." After some frenzied revisions the piece was published,
and it was Knox who ventured online to check out the responses.
"[Gloria] never looks at any of her things online," Knox explained,
"because the comments often devolve into, 'Oh, that bitch is still
alive?'" In this case, however, the initial comments were positive. "I
ran downstairs and hugged her," said Knox, "and was like, 'Thank
you for doing this for me and for my generation.'"

It was the next day, after Steinem had left for a business trip,
that Knox heard from a former colleague: "[She] was calling Gloria
a racist and a bigot and [said] she had no place talking about black
women's lives and taking on the persona of a black woman. [Knox's
colleague said that she] was there when people were getting lynched
for voting, and how dare [Gloria] leave that out, it must not have
meant anything to her." A startled Knox emailed the piece to a few
of her African American friends to ask what they thought. They
responded, "This is so insensitive and so devaluing and how dare
she write this," remembered Knox. "The most painful ones were,
'This woman used to be my idol and now I hate her.' I was just like,
'Oh my god, this is bad.'"

Knox was particularly devastated because Steinem had often
urged her to reach beyond her own white, college-educated perspective, to research how her cause, sex education, affected women of

different colors and classes. "She was always talking about the interconnectedness of oppressions," said Knox. "She says you can't be feminist without being antiracist. We had these conversations long before this op-ed was ever written." Knox, an emotionally transparent sparkplug, said over and over again how much she adored Steinem. "She gave me a home," she told me. "She is like my grandmother." Knox recalled watching Steinem on *Democracy Now:* "I watched it and I screamed at the TV for Melissa Harris-Lacewell to lay off, because I kept thinking of a dog fight. It's like you've already gotten her in the throat so many times, will you lay off? And Gloria didn't fight back." When Steinem returned home that night, Knox recalled, "she looked seventy-five, which is saying something, for Gloria to look her age. She physically looked devastated. And she said, 'I just can't believe that all of it leads up to this.'" Steinem told me later that after her appearance she thought, "I never should have gone on. I never do debates, and that's what it got turned into. It's crazy and bad for the movement for two women who agree on the issues and will both be for Obama in the general election to look as if we're opposed."

Soon, as Knox remembered it, the narrative became about second-wave women being out of touch. "I kept seeing these comments by young women like, 'They should just die, they should just shut up,'" Knox said. "Gloria was like, 'This crazy idea that you can be a feminist without being antiracist, or that you can be antiracist without being a feminist—Is this what young women are going to think of us?' The entire time I'm going, '*Is* this what young women are going to think of her?' I asked her to do this. I felt incredible guilt."

✳ ✳ ✳

Just as the seal on acknowledging Hillary's gender had broken, so too was Obama's protective postracial layer thinning as people increasingly considered his race and began to interrogate more thoroughly the language of both his opponents and the media. In an interview with Fox News, Clinton, voicing her refrain that Obama's unifying dreams could be made manifest only by someone who knew how to work the system, illustrated her point by stating, "Dr. King's dream began to be realized when President Lyndon Johnson passed the Civil Rights Act of 1964, when he was able to get through Congress something that President Kennedy was hopeful to do . . . but it took a president to get it done." This factually sturdy observation was met with offense by many: Was she minimizing King's role in the civil rights movement, subordinating it to the power of a white man? George Packer argued in the *New Yorker* that Hillary's remarks about Johnson seemed simply to reflect her workmanlike perception that the job of being president was "more about pushing difficult legislation through a fractious Congress than it is about transforming society." But a *New York Times* editorial portrayed the statement as coming "perilously close to injecting racial tension into what should have been . . . an uplifting contest between the first major woman candidate and the first major African-American candidate" as well as to "the distasteful implication that a black man needed the help of a white man to effect change."

What had been a friendly and self-celebratory Democratic field was becoming increasingly charged. Every remark was freighted, every statement of support electrified by anxiety over race and gender.

Jehmu Greene, then thirty-five, had headed up women's outreach at the Democratic National Committee and was the former president of the youth voting group Rock the Vote. She planned to remain neutral in 2008 as she pursued a career as a television pundit on Fox News and CNN. With her background in youth voting, Greene was not surprised by Obama's Iowa win but was shocked by the resulting Hillary-hatred. "Something in me flipped," she said in 2009. "All that shit that started being thrown at her? I took it personally." Greene's plan to stay neutral dissolved; she declared herself a Hillary supporter. "I knew that in coming out for her publicly it would piss people off," said Greene, "but I didn't expect for it to be as personal as it was. The level of animus was definitely surprising. I felt more of the anger came from the fact that I was black, that as a black person I was supposed to put being black before being a woman."

After New Hampshire came the January 26 South Carolina primary. Bill Clinton had been let loose on the state, both because the race was more hotly contested than anyone imagined it would be and because of his history of persuasive power in the South, particularly with African American voters. But as it became evident that Obama was ahead in South Carolina, the former president began to behave erratically.

A year earlier the Clintons had joined Obama and a group of civil rights leaders to walk across the Edmund Pettus Bridge in Selma, Alabama, to commemorate 1965's "Bloody Sunday" march for voting rights. A photograph of the event showed Bill Clinton, holding his wife's hand at one end of the line of marchers, leaning forward, grinning madly at Barack Obama, who was grinning back at him from the other end. I kept a copy of the photo above my desk and captioned it "The Love That Dare Not Speak Its Name." Had it not been for Hillary's presidential ambitions, Obama might well have been Bill Clinton's dream candidate. In many ways Obama was the natural inheritor of Bill's legacy of hope and youth-fueled politicking; he had the elder candidate's way with crowds, his ability to connect. Obama was a young man, as Clinton had been, with a brilliant wife and partner. Bill had been dryly dubbed "our first black president" by Toni Morrison and had worked his whole life alongside and on behalf of African Americans. In another universe Bill might have attached himself to Obama's project and busted a gut to be booster and political papa to the man poised to become the *actual* first black president.

But their union was not meant to be. Hillary's campaign put Bill on the opposite side of the fence from Obama. Instead of being an heir to the Clinton legacy, Obama's mission was to overshadow and discredit it, precisely what the hyperdefensive former president most feared. Obama-loving voters of South Carolina were forcing Bill to reckon with the fact that he was losing his never-fail Bubba charm, either due to old age or because it had been usurped by another compelling politician. After all the consideration about whether Bill would be able to stand up to being upstaged by a woman, what perhaps riled him more was having his legacy toppled by another man. Or at least that's what it seemed like as Bill Clinton talked to reporters in Columbia, South Carolina, on the day of the primary. One asked him about John Kerry, a question he declined to answer, calling it "bait" to get him to say something he shouldn't. Someone else asked why it was taking two Clintons to compete with one Barack Obama. "That's just bait too," he wisely replied. But the reporter had touched a nerve about the limits of Bill's persuasive powers. He got mad. He got a little bit crazy. He said, for absolutely no good reason, "Jesse Jackson won in South Carolina twice, in eighty-four and eighty-eight, and he ran a good campaign. And Senator Obama's run a good campaign."

Bill was, technically, correct. Jesse Jackson had won South Carolina in 1984 and in 1988. But the clear subtext of his words was that Jackson had won South Carolina only because African Americans had voted for him, that Obama was about to do the same, and that because of this, South Carolina didn't really count. Clinton was racializing and thereby devaluing Obama's impending primary success, as surely as anyone had feminized and thereby devalued his wife's victory in New Hampshire.

South Carolina was a landslide for Obama. The morning after his primary victory, George Stephanopoulos asked him to respond to the former president's Jesse Jackson comparison, and Obama killed Bill softly, excusing his remark by noting, "That's his frame of reference . . . that's when he was active and involved and watching what was going to take place in South Carolina." Bill Clinton called Barack Obama black, and Barack Obama called Bill Clinton old. In what should have been the most exhilarating election in modern memory, nobody was having any fun and everyone was pissed off. Bill would go on to accuse the Obama campaign of having played up his comments. He told a Pennsylvania radio station in April, "They played the race card on me," and attempted to reframe the context of his remarks, claiming, "We were talking about South Carolina political history and this was used out of context and twisted for political purposes by the Obama campaign to try to breed resentment elsewhere. . . . Do I regret saying it? No. Do I regret that it was used that way? I certainly do. But you really got to go some to try to portray me as a racist."

Two weeks before Clinton's Jackson remarks an internal Obama campaign memo had leaked; it listed instances of suspect utterances from people associated with the Clinton campaign, from Hillary's King-Johnson comparison to Billy Shaheen's drug insinuations to Andrew Cuomo's egregious assertion that inexperienced politicians would not be able to "shuck and jive" through press conferences.

The memo was evidence that the Obama campaign was indeed tracking, and perhaps looking to capitalize on racially questionable comments coming from their opposition, a strategy that drove lots of Clinton supporters, sick of hearing about the squeaky-clean tactics of the Obama campaign, around several sharp bends. "I don't think I had been as angry about a political tactic as I was at what they did with Bill Clinton," said Jehmu Greene. "Bill Clinton is not a racist. To accuse someone who has done so much for the African American community . . . I'm tearing up when I think about it. The way they turned just the facts into being a racist remark is unforgivable."

A handful of sentences did not wipe out Bill Clinton's history of engagement with African Americans; Jackson himself claimed not to be offended by his friend's diminishment of his historic victories. But the fact that those sentences caused offense to many was something that Bill could not undo, and the harder he tried, the worse off he made it for himself. "There always comes a time when whatever it was that worked for you doesn't work anymore," said Gloria Feldt, former president of Planned Parenthood and a Clinton supporter. "Here was a man who had been called the first black president, and suddenly African Americans were turning on him. He reacted in all the wrong ways. It was very pathetic to see."

Margo Jefferson was surprised by the Jackson remark. "I have had people tell me that it was really not meant to be racially double-edged or to have a signifying subtext," she said. "Some black people have told me that. But I was surprised that he let himself get out of control to that extent." No one likes to think of themselves as a bigot, Jefferson continued, "particularly if they think of their lives as having been progressive lives. Is Bill Clinton a hardcore racist? No. Did he allow himself to make calculated or uncalculated racialist-slash-racist-tinged remarks? Yes. Does that suggest that—hello, we're in America—his racial attitudes are a bit more *complicated* than we think? Yes. That he secretly hates black people? No. That he secretly feels more comfortable when the power is in his hands? Yes, I dare say it does. Sometimes that old-fashioned word of my youth, 'prejudiced,' is very useful. People are filled with prejudices that mutate and expand and disappear. It's all so colored, no pun intended, and inflected."

* * *

The focus on Clinton and Obama became more pointed; they were the clear front-runners, but they were so interested in speaking only to one another that during a debate in South Carolina John Edwards had to remind them that there was a third person on stage. Though both camps would have been loath to admit it, Hillary and Barack had a powerful political chemistry; their every interaction drew the eye. On January 30, a few days before Super Tuesday, which would comprise twenty-four Democratic primaries and caucuses, Edwards dropped out of the race. Despite the fact that his departure left me not knowing who to vote for, I stared in shivering disbelief at the television the next night, as two candidates emerged to debate each other for their party's nomination, neither of them a white guy.

People had lots of critical things to say about identity politics; voting for someone because of who they were and not what they believed was an unsettling proposition for most thinking people. But it also seemed that those who most loudly deplored the corrosive impact of identity politics tended to be those whose identities had been adequately represented in their governing bodies. When the choice between Clinton and Obama became binary, especially given that the policy differences between the two candidates remained minimal, there was practically no way that personal histories, resentments, identifications and rejections could not come to bear; the choice seemed to become unavoidably loaded, emblematic of not only who you agreed with, but of who you were.

In the days before Super Tuesday, 1,000 "Feminists for Peace," including Katha Pollitt, Barbara Ehrenreich and Susan Sarandon, signed a petition supporting Barack Obama. Other feminists, including Steinem, Robin Morgan, Christine Stansell and Blanche Wiesen Cook, shot back with a petition supporting Clinton. Perhaps the most peculiar declaration came from Vagina Monologist Eve Ensler and academic Kimberle Crenshaw, who assailed not Hillary Clinton but her supporters, whom they saw as stark "either/or" feminist bullies who "interrogate, chastise, second-guess and even denounce those who escape their encampment" by voting for Obama.

Margo Jefferson was among the Feminists for Peace. "I was very aware of it as a source of tension with all my friends," she said, "of having to explain my reasoning very carefully every step of the way. One of my biggest struggles was with a childhood black friend who was becoming very pro-Hillary just as I was becoming more pro-Obama. It brought out a lot of old grievances. At one point this friend and I found ourselves arguing over whether Elizabeth Cady Stanton or Frederick Douglass had been the greater betrayer!"

So sharp was the pain of making a choice between Clinton and Obama that superdelegate John Lewis, a Georgia congressman and veteran civil rights leader, said in an interview that his late February change of support from Clinton to Obama, a change his constituents were clamoring for, was more difficult than walking across the Edmund Pettus Bridge in 1965. "All I had to do in Selma in 1965 [was] to put on my trench-coat and my suit, my back-pack and walk and look straight ahead," he told the NBC reporter Andrea Mitchell, who responded, "But Congressman, you got your *head* beaten in. Your face was covered in blood." "This is tougher," he responded. "I'm dealing with friends. People that I love. People that I admire. Part of my extended family." Clinton surrogate Stephanie Tubbs Jones, a congresswoman from Ohio and chair of the House Ethics Committee who would pass away in August of 2008, told the *Washington Post,* "Shame on anyone who . . . put that kind of pressure on John Lewis. I'm not trying to be a martyr. I think Senator Clinton is the best candidate. And the beauty of the United States of America is you have the right to have your opinion, and I have the right to my opinion. . . . If I change my mind, it will be because Senator Clinton said, 'Stephanie, let's make a move.'" But even the narrative of African Americans experiencing pressure was charged and destructive. Danielle Belton wrote on her blog *The Black Snob* that the story line fed another kind of racist fantasy: "'Sweet Jesus! What will happen if these *crazy darkies* don't get their way? *They're attacking their own people for just wanting to practice Democracy. . . . By golly there will be RIOTS IN THE STREETS,*' they shriek, as if our 22 million population . . . will choose this, of all things, to go *Rodney King* over."

"It was the most stressful time in my life," said *Racialicious*'s Latoya Peterson. "Because it's one thing to take hits from the outside; it's another if you're taking hits from your own. All of the old wounds between women of color and white women who are trying to work together in feminism, who don't understand each other, it all bubbled up to the surface and it got very very ugly. . . . It was a complicated history." Peterson said she tried to keep her blogging space as neutral as possible. "Some of my very good commenters left because they felt like the space was hostile to women and to feminism, which is really horrible to hear. It started pitting ally against ally. And it didn't heal. Obama was elected. But that undercurrent of suspicion is still there."

The emotional and historic pulls were felt, in one way or another, by most Americans. But those who got most intensely fetishized, whose loyalties provoked the most curiosity, were black women. There were pressures on them to announce a presidential preference and to extrapolate from that choice which oppressed part of their identity was more essential.

Carol Jenkins, a newscaster and the founding president of the Women's Media Center, found herself being quizzed by CNN host Rick Sanchez about, in her words, "What's worse—being black, or being a woman?" When Jenkins tried to explain that both identities had an impact on her, Sanchez pushed her to choose. In response she wrote a piece called "The Invisible Majority," explaining that "Hillary Clinton's run for the presidency has crystallized our stark unfamiliarity with women. . . . Never has our mainstream media been so insanely obsessive—acting like teenage boys . . . who don't know what to do when a woman enters the room." It was also apparent that a white woman and a black man competing for the biggest job in the world "[didn't] yet translate into possibilities for a woman of color."

In some cases black women themselves presented their political loyalties as statements of comparative identification. *Newsweek*'s Allison Samuels described how her grandmother, "equipped with just a fifth-grade education, sent each of her eight daughters to college (and beyond). . . . I doubt if she knew there was a feminist movement or ever heard the name Gloria Steinem." In her grandmother's lifetime, as well as in her own, Samuels continued, "race, not gender, [was] the defining narrative": "I know that a woman president would change the course of history, too, and many might even argue that gender is far more of an albatross than race. That just hasn't been my experience."

Jehmu Greene's perspective was the inverse. "Sexism is something I've had to deal with my entire career within the Democratic Party," she said. "Speaking specifically from an African American perspective, [black women] are the ones always doing the work [while black men] got all the credit for it, going back to the civil rights movement and to this day. Look at the articulate, inspiring elected officials who are black women, and their trajectory within the party, and compare that to a Barack Obama and it becomes very clear. Carol Moseley Braun, the late, great Stephanie Tubbs Jones, Maxine Waters—we toil away and get the work done and when a microphone is put in front of someone it is usually the black man."

Some women, including superdelegate Donna Brazile, dealt with the constant tugging with humor. Talking with Stephen Colbert, Brazile cracked, "Look, I'm a woman, so I like Hillary. I'm black, I like Obama. But I'm also grumpy, so I like John McCain."

Others were just irritated. Melissa Harris-Lacewell said, "Every time [reporters] would ask me 'Are you going to support him because he's black or her because she's a woman?' I wanted to call them back and say, 'Why don't you call the white guy and ask him, "Are you going to support her because she's white or him because he's a guy?"'"

* * *

In early March, as Clinton was about to get creamed in Mississippi, former vice-presidential candidate Geraldine Ferraro told a California newspaper, "If Obama was a white man, he would not be in this position. And if he was a woman of any color, he would not be in this position. He happens to be very lucky to be who he is. And the country is caught up in the concept."

Ferraro would later state that she was describing a simple electoral fact, that Obama was winning with the help of black votes. But her defensive assertion that had she been named "Gerard" she would not have been tapped by Walter Mondale in 1984 confirmed that she was also suggesting that there was something faddish about the country's sudden eagerness to consider, much less vote for, a black man for president. There *was* an undeniable excitement among some Democratic voters about the fact that Obama was black, and his campaign knew it. To pretend otherwise was disingenuous. The University of Pennsylvania professor of political science Adolph Reed would point out later, "[The] hysterically indignant reaction to Geraldine Ferraro's statement that much of Obama's success stems from the fact that 'the country is caught up in the concept' of a black candidacy [was] no different from the campaign's touting its 'historic' character." But at the same time, in the context of U.S. presidential history, for a white woman to suggest that any black man was "lucky" to be black was a distressing stretch. The implication was that Obama was benefiting from tokenism, that his race was helping him gain a victory he would not have earned had he been female or white.

The Obama campaign justifiably bore down on Ferraro, asking Hillary to repudiate her remarks and remove her from the Clinton campaign finance committee. Hillary said only that she did not agree with Ferraro and noted, "[Both my campaign and Obama's] have had supporters and staff members who've gone over the line, and we've had to rein them in." This was not enough for Obama's campaign manager, David Axelrod, who said in a conference call with reporters, "When you wink and nod at offensive statements, you're really sending a signal to your supporters that anything goes."

Her back against a wall, Ferraro resigned from the Clinton campaign, but then amplified her remarks about Obama, suggesting with increased vigor that he was not only benefiting from his blackness, but that she was being attacked because she was white. Soon Ben Smith at *Politico* found a *Washington Post* story from 1988 in which Ferraro had said, "If Jesse Jackson were not black, he wouldn't be in the race." As more people began calling her racist, Ferraro became more enraged and sounded increasingly . . . racist. "Every time the campaign is upset about something, they call it racist," she said. "I will not be discriminated against because I'm white. If they think they're going to shut up Geraldine Ferraro with that kind of stuff, they don't know me."

In this instance there were few who would defend Ferraro. "Personally, I think Geraldine Ferraro should have apologized," said Steinem in 2009. "I don't think she meant her comments to be taken that way. I have never discussed it with her, so I'm just supposing. But I do believe she should have apologized." Latoya Peterson remembered, "Again, it was, 'Oh I don't think that was racist.' It was just, you know, white. Okay, so it was somebody expressing white resentment? What do you want to call that? You want to call it racism now? You want to call it something prettier today? It's the same thing."

Geraldine Ferraro had grown up in an Italian neighborhood in Queens to become a history-making Democratic politician. Her track was arguably more difficult than that of many liberals born into liberal worlds: she had emerged from an insular and historically xenophobic community, from a culture and a generation with ingrained attitudes about gender, race and religion, to become a liberal congresswoman and a zealous advocate of reproductive freedom. Though much was made of her 1988 line about Jesse Jackson, no one cited a 1984 interview in which Barbara Walters asked her, "The American dream has always been that any young boy can grow up to be president. . . . Are you now the American dream?" Ferraro replied, "If I am, it's not a complete one. Not until you can take not only the gender and remove it or include it in that dream, but also race. When you do that, then the American dream will be complete." Now, in her later years, in the midst of a decade-long fight with cancer, speaking about Hillary Clinton, the only woman in the twenty-four years since her candidacy to compete for executive office, she said things that at best sounded bad—and, truthfully, *were* bad. When she was challenged about them, it was as though her career and her beliefs got obscured, and she fell backward, over a precipice and into old ways of talking about race.

"I got tied in by the Obama campaign on being racist, which I probably will go to my grave with and will never get over," Ferraro told me in a 2009 interview. "And I wasn't, obviously. What I said was not racist. If Hillary had drawn black women the way she drew other women, she would have won. Black women had two choices: race or gender. They went with race. As a mother, if I were a black woman, would I rather have my kids see a black get elected president of the United States? I would, quite frankly. I didn't think there was anything wrong with that. So when this [reporter] said to me, 'What do you think is going on?' I said, 'It's black voters.'" Ferraro was still smarting over what she believed were the Obama campaign's tactics. "They came out against Bill Clinton," she said. "Bill Clinton, who has done more work in this country for African Americans, and people of color throughout the world. To turn around and call him a racist . . . and then me. I was so stunned, because of my record and because of my family's record. . . . I mean, ethnic Italians could be a little tough, but *never* with race. Never with race. So when I heard this stupid-assed comment by [David Axelrod,] who knew me, because I had supported Carl McCall when he ran for governor of New York. I was so active in Freddy Ferrer's campaign when he ran for mayor. And to call me a racist . . . I was like a lunatic."

The controversy over Ferraro opened up a media conversation about racism that extended beyond Clinton's campaign to her supporters. Instead of examining the intolerance of a nation still run by white men, suspicions were trained on the racialized resentments of older white women, increasingly viewed as Clinton's base. As some women expressed growing perturbation both at the sexism they felt Hillary was facing and at the way her triumphs were being ignored while her opponent's victories were being heralded, they found, as Steinem had before them, that it was difficult to express lingering resentments about whose advancements had come first, and at what cost to others, without sounding deeply suspect. The more women pushed to draw attention to Clinton as women's hero, the more comparisons they made between what she was experiencing and what Obama was experiencing, the more awkward the position they found themselves in, both with African Americans who registered their racial resentments and with a generation of young white women dismayed to detect in their elders the traces of racialized exasperation or even intolerance.

"It felt like all the stuff you were afraid might be out there was being made explicit," said *Feministing*'s founder, Jessica Valenti, recalling one incident that shook her. Some Hillary-supporting women were preparing a press conference about media sexism; one of the organizers asked Valenti to participate. Scheduled to speak elsewhere, Valenti recommended another *Feministing* blogger, Jen Moseley. "Jen is black, and had written something about race politics in the election," said Valenti. "The woman got back to me and said, 'We're really not looking for someone who trumps race over gender.' I said, 'I'm not sure what you mean by that,' and she said, 'Well, we want someone who understands that sexism is worse than racism.'" Valenti informed her that *Feministing* probably wasn't the right group for them. "I tried to be diplomatic about it, saying, 'That's just not along our lines of thinking,'" said Valenti. "But she got really upset, and was like, 'Don't you see?' She was clearly hurt and thought I was a big idiot. And I thought she was kind of racist. So it was a tough moment. It was crazy and really sad."

Many older white female Hillary supporters also felt sad that in this historical moment their progressive ambitions to put a woman in the White House were being tarnished, that the sexist stereotypes increasingly applied to them—that they were bitter, angry, desperate—now also included suggestions of racism. When Barack Obama gave his widely lauded spring speech in Philadelphia about race, he cited examples of white racial insensitivity by invoking two specific people, Geraldine Ferraro and his own grandmother, the white woman who had raised him and had confessed to him that she sometimes felt afraid of black men when she passed them on the street. He did not make reference to Bill Clinton, Andrew Cuomo, Bill Shaheen, or Bob Johnson. He did not talk about George Wallace or Strom Thurmond or about George W. Bush, who had left the city of New Orleans to drown. Instead he selected two Americans who stood in for the demographic that was increasingly associated with Hillary support. Critics would accuse him of throwing his grandmother under the bus in this speech, but he was simply playing out a history that, in some senses, had already been written, bringing the painful animus of Elizabeth Cady Stanton and Frederick Douglass back to vivid life.

"Comments that have been made and the issues that have surfaced over the last few weeks reflect the complexities of race in this country that we've never really worked through, a part of our union that we have not yet made perfect," said Obama. "Understanding this reality requires a reminder of how we arrived at this point. As William Faulkner once wrote, 'The past isn't dead and buried. In fact, it isn't even past.'"

*　*　*

In late February a group of women's leaders, journalists and academics, including Gloria Steinem and Carol Jenkins, Beverly Guy-Sheftall and Johnnetta Cole, gathered in New York to discuss the "race-gender split" among feminists. Patricia Williams recounted the meeting in the *Nation*, calling it a kaffeeklatsch at which "old friends broke out the good china for a light breakfast of strong coffee, blueberry muffins and fresh-squeezed orange juice." "We did not want to see a repeat of the ugly history of the nineteenth century," wrote Williams, "when the failure of the women's movement to bring about universal adult suffrage metastasized into racial resentment and rift that weakened feminism throughout much of the twentieth century." How, this group wondered, had this remarkable election been so badly damaged by "media depictions of white women as the sole inheritors of the feminist movement and black men as the sole beneficiaries of the civil rights movement? . . . What happened . . . to the last four decades of discussion about tokenism and multiple identities and the complex intersections of race, gender, sexuality, ethnicity and class?" The group agreed, "Everyone needs to refocus on the big picture. . . . [We wondered] how . . . to reclaim a common purpose, a truly democratic 'we': we women of all races, we blacks of all genders, we Americans of all languages, we immigrants of all classes, we Latinas of all colors."

But the breakfast did not cut it for we feminists who were not yet middle-aged. "I wasn't there, and I don't think anyone under the age of forty was there," said Shelby Knox. "So that was a problem, a problem that I registered at the time." Valenti was even less sanguine about the meeting: "'My friends gathered over china to have orange juice?' I was like, 'Are you fucking kidding me with this?' They declared it over. They declared it resolved. It was like, you don't get to do that! You and four other people don't get to declare this conversation over! That's not how it works, you know?"

For Valenti, the expressed desire to come up with a unifying solution was itself symptomatic of the worldview of another generation. "There is such a powerful desire for this imaginary utopian feminist universe that just isn't ever going to exist," she said. "I think it would be weird if all women connected on some womanly level." She described conferences at which women "want to talk about their vaginal wisdom and their feminine spiritual power." "My mom wants that," Valenti said. "She was like, 'Oh, I want to go to the panel that's about listening to your feminine intuition.' That's part of how they came to feminism, was this idea that being women was truly special and different in a certain way. I get that that's where they're coming from. But it's not where I'm coming from, and I don't think it's where the future is going, especially when you think about issues about people who are transgendered. Your entire movement is built on the idea of womanhood, but a new generation is mucking up what it means to be a woman. Something has got to change."

For many, though, airing the angers of election season, uncovering some forgotten, or repressed, history and forcing people to question where they stood on issues of race and gender was not only necessary, but positive. "It made me very thoughtful about my assumptions," said Margo Jefferson. "You intellectually got a little shaken up, and that was useful. If you didn't get shaken up, then your rages and your bad moods would have just settled back in a more calcified way. Your language and your thinking had to get sharper and more textured. That, I felt, was a potentially very good thing."

Some of the discussions proved instructive, even in climes assumed to be progressive already. Kim Gandy, former NOW president, remembered one conversation within her organization: "The white woman was saying, 'Don't you want your daughters to know that they can do anything?' And the African American woman said, 'What you don't understand is that of course I want my daughter to feel she can do anything, but for me, this would be the first time that I could see someone like me in the White House. Maybe not as president, but in the White House. I could see a family that looks like mine in the White House.' That was a discussion changer. The woman who had been arguing for Hillary sort of stepped back and said, 'Okay.' That was a completely different way of looking at it for her, something she hadn't thought of."

Harris-Lacewell found herself considering how she talked about gender with her daughter. "Sometimes it would get intense and I would grumble, 'I hate Hillary.' And then I would say, 'Oh, wait a minute. I actually don't want you to hate Hillary,'" she said. "I didn't want my daughter to be hating girls. I read to her a book called *Grace for President,* because it was about a little girl of color. It helped me work through what we were doing by not supporting the women candidates. As empowering as it is for me to have Obama in office, he had to beat a girl to get there, and beat a girl again [in] Sarah Palin. So I am keenly aware of them, because our socialization around race and gender is still not there."

Valenti believed that the election offered young women, who perhaps were unaware of the rifts over race that had ensnared their mothers and grandmothers and who perhaps thought their own generation was beyond the tensions, a chance to "lay it all on the table and discuss it." Latoya Peterson agreed that there was relief in the midst of all the tension. "Finally it's all out in the open. All these things that they acted like we were over," she said. "The questions of 'Why are women of color so sensitive?' Well, because racist stuff happens! And then you all make excuses! *That's* what happens. *That's* why we're so paranoid, because you never know who is going to have your back. It was ugly and it was hard and it's sad. [But] I think it will promote progress. Eventually. Everybody's got to get over their hurt feelings first."

Though I thought I understood something of the racially fraught history of the second wave, the election offered many moments of revelation about contemporary tensions. The negative reaction to Steinem's op-ed was one of them. I read and liked the piece; it wasn't for weeks, perhaps months, that I came across the commentary from women who had been angered and hurt by it. Watching the episode of *Democracy Now* made me miserable, realizing how much of this conversation had swept by me. In this instance I was learning about the privileged white perspective on social progress not from a textbook, but by embodying it, gliding approvingly through Steinem's piece without a thought of the voices it ignored. My post facto realization of how flawed the essay was was confusing in itself: I continued to agree with what Steinem said, at the same time that I came to agree with even her harshest critics. It was a lesson in how there were no correct answers.

"The biggest thing when you're trying to be in solidarity with other people who are different from you," said Peterson, "the first thing you have to acknowledge is that there is so much that you don't know and that you will never know. A lot of people don't do that. They feel like because they've read something, because they've talked to a few people, they can say 'Oh, I understand the black experience. Oh, I get it.' You don't get it. You all miss all the nuances because it doesn't happen to you."

This was the lesson that Shelby Knox took away: "I learned that you can never speak *for*. You can speak *about*, but you can never speak *for*, and even if you have a forty-year history with interracial cooperation and you think you understand a black woman's experience, you're denying people's lived experience by speaking for them. It's hard for me even now to say that [Steinem] made a mistake. If she made any mistake it was probably embodying a black women at the beginning of the piece. . . . I realized that in order to not repeat the mistakes of the women before us, of some in the second wave and definitely the first wave, silencing the voices of women of color . . . we have to step aside and invite people to speak for themselves."

Steinem herself would later write about her unwilling debate with Harris-Lacewell, "Though at moments, I felt as if forty years of effort to link issues were going down the drain, even this human contact may have been better than none; I think we ended up on microscopically better terms than we began." She cheered herself up, she wrote, by conjuring the memory of her friend and lecture partner, the late Florynce Kennedy. "Flo would have found a purpose even in conflict," wrote Steinem. "I could hear her voice giving one of her wise lessons: 'The purpose of ass-kicking is not that your ass gets kicked at the right time or for the right reasons. It's that it keeps your ass *sensitive*.' . . . Suddenly, the hard things of the recent past had a purpose, and they weren't so hard anymore."

Valenti recalled seeing Steinem speak at a conference after the primaries: "I think the election must have made a real impression on her. All she was talking about was race. I was like, *damn*. She was *great*. Before that, I had never heard any mainstream feminists own up to the fact that the second wave was—not necessarily explicitly racist, but that it was a white, upper-middle-class straight woman's movement. Or that that's who got the most attention. The only people I heard talking about that were younger feminists or academic feminists. When I saw Gloria talking about all this stuff, I felt so heartened, not for her, but for me. Because she's fucking Gloria Steinem. She can say whatever she wants, right? But she's obviously still learning. That's a pretty great thing, especially in a movement that seems to be overwhelmingly stagnant on a lot of things. It was good for me to see someone who was obviously affected by this experience and has changed her tune a little bit. Like I can do the same thing."

6 ALL ABOUT THEIR MOTHERS

DECIDING WHO TO vote for in the primary might have been easier if it hadn't been for my mother. Unsentimental, her politics listing left of Hillary's, my mom seemed barely interested in Hillary Clinton. I laughed when my friend Merideth brusquely chided me for my Edwards support by asking, "Are you going to call your mother and ask her permission to vote against Hillary?" It had never crossed my mind that my mother would care a whit if I voted for Hillary, let alone that she might vote for her herself. So I was floored when, the day after Iowa, I picked up the phone to hear her say, "I'm very sad." When I asked why, she replied, "Whether or not it's Hillary, any woman who is aggressive enough to make a go of it is going to be too aggressive to be likable."

The sentiment rattled around in my head for the weeks between Iowa and Super Tuesday, when I would cast my vote in New York. My mother's discouragement, which I think surprised her as much as it did me, was a reminder of how Clinton was lugging around questions about the future and remembrances of the past as she hauled herself from state to state. It was also my window on what was about to become a media fixation: the generation gap between women when it came to Hillary Clinton.

I had been resisting the idea that Clinton's presidential bid was a once-in-a-lifetime opportunity for women. I was confident that there would be many more female presidential candidates coming down the pike. But many older women clearly found this sort of optimism infuriating. They saw my generation's lack of enthusiasm for Clinton as naïve complacency. Sure, I knew that it was well past time for a female president, but I assumed that there would be loads more satisfactory models to choose from in the future. My mother created a flicker of worry that this was perhaps a careless bet. Her sadness, along with the torrent of ill-disguised resentment unleashed at Clinton since Iowa, shook some of the breeziness out of me, made me feel flashes of guilt for not having stood up for Hillary from the start.

But you don't vote for a candidate out of guilt. And you don't vote because your mother calls you. As primary day approached I didn't know what to do with these percolating qualms or, for that matter, with my political impulses. I had never had trouble articulating what I believed, but for the first time in my life I did not know what I believed. I did not know who to vote for.

I was not alone. *Feministing*'s founder Jessica Valenti told me two years after Super Tuesday, "Up to the day, I considered not voting at all. I didn't even know that I could do it. It was horrible. Horrible." Valenti, whose site did not endorse either candidate, finally voted for Obama. "But it was rough," she said. "I was not happy afterwards."

Valenti's experience was so like my own, and so different from Geraldine Ferraro's, who told me in 2009, "I didn't cry when I voted for myself [in 1984], but I went into that booth and I looked at [Hillary's] name . . . I'm beginning to well up now thinking about it. It felt like Susan B. Anthony was standing beside me saying, 'Pull that lever.' Which sounds so stupid. But I felt the struggle [for women's rights], and it just smashed me."

I would have given anything to feel that conviction, but I simply didn't. It was humiliating to be undecided in the weeks, days, hours before the first primary in my memory in which my vote would make one iota of difference. John Edwards's disappearance from the race had shown me that supporting him, while in general accordance with my political beliefs, had also provided a cop-out. Had I been able to vote for Edwards I would not have had to get my hands dirty by choosing between two similar candidates whose differences increasingly seemed to swirl around their race and gender. I would not have had to admit, or even consider, the role my gender and my feminist politics might have in my decision making. Now I had to face Hillary Clinton. Alas, she was my destiny.

I felt the pull of Obamamania, had considered how thrilling it would be to see the country come alive with excitement for a young person, a man beholden to few in Washington, who had lived around the world and took a reasoned approach to foreign policy. When I ran my own (useless, inevitable) calculus of oppression, I concluded that in the United States, race (especially when combined with class) remained a more formidable barrier to political and economic parity than gender. That meant that on some level, Clinton stood in for all those pushy white broads, the ones who were coming to steal college admissions letters and seats in Congress from the white men to whom they had historically belonged, while Obama could more comfortably be regarded as an exceptional black man, not the harbinger of a larger threat to established power. If Hillary's success was less exceptional—and there were certainly fewer African Americans of either gender in federal elected office than there were women—did she deserve my vote as much as Barack did?

But here was the part that I had been trying to ignore: Hillary Clinton was a woman, and so was I. I knew that my president didn't have to look like me, any more than she had to be a person I wanted to have a drink with, but I couldn't pretend that it didn't mean something to me, something more important than I'd realized, that we had never had one who looked like me before. Oddly, this realization didn't galvanize me as much as it gave me pause. However much I protested that I would never vote for someone just because she was a woman, I was realizing that a vote for Hillary would be an emotional decision as well as an intellectual and political one. And if that were true, then I would be conforming to every dismissive assumption about why and how women vote, fulfilling a feminized and thus devalued expectation of Democratic womanhood.

The morning of Super Tuesday I was reporting on primary voters at the ticker-tape parade for the Giants, who had just won the
Super Bowl, when I came upon Brian Murray from Long Island, a
young fan who had his fists in the air, frozen as if they'd been there
since the last dramatic moment of the big game. I asked him if he
was planning to vote. "No way," he said, lowering his arms. "But I
wouldn't vote for Hillary Clinton, if that's what you were going to
ask." I hadn't been going to ask. Brian and I blinked quizzically at
each other for a moment. "I bet you voted for her, right?" he said.
I didn't respond. I did not want to be the girl that everyone, from
Obama-supporting progressives to a politically apathetic Giants
fan, assumed I was, the one who chose the woman in part because
she was a woman.

In fact, a few hours earlier, with a few final clicks of the levers
and the pull of the big metal bar, I had emerged from the booth a
shaky but now official Hillary Clinton supporter. I actually assumed
my new identity would be short-lived. As the East Coast polls began
to close on Super Tuesday it seemed likely that this would be the
night that had been forecast since the Iowa caucus, the night that
the senator from Illinois would halt Clinton's drive to the White
House. When I walked into the grand ballroom of the Manhattan
Center Studios that night to report on Clinton's Election Night celebration, the mood was practically funereal.

But when the first results showing Clinton leading in Massachusetts and New Jersey began to appear on the screen, the listless party
began to swell and sway. The crowd, liberally studded with young
people and with black and brown faces, cheered and yelped the news
that Clinton had won Massachusetts, the state that liberal legend
Ted Kennedy and 2004 candidate John Kerry had tried to secure for
Obama by making surprise endorsements. "We know how badly
Senator Kennedy and Senator Kerry wanted that state," Jonathan
Mantz, Clinton's finance director, told me over the din. "The fact
that we're winning it is very gratifying." It was gratifying in precisely
the same way Clinton's New Hampshire win had been: after all the
months of being treated as the establishment candidate, Hillary was
being revealed as an outsider, providing thrills by escaping the fate
to which the real establishment—guys who ran the media, guys who
ran the Senate—was trying to consign her.

Clinton's Super Tuesday address was closer to lyrical than any she'd given to that point, full of rhythmic invocations of those Americans "on the day shift, on the night shift, on the late shift with the crying baby . . . all those who aren't in the headlines but who have always written America's story." There was also an increasingly progressive aura about her as she talked up the rebuilding of the American infrastructure and revamping of the GI Bill of Rights.

Clinton was learning, a little late, about establishing herself as part of a narrative of social progress. Early exit polling showed that once again it was women voters who were enabling her respectable showing, and she tipped her hat to them by mentioning her own mother, "who was born before women could vote and is watching her daughter on this stage tonight."

✶ ✶ ✶

> *I cannot wait, 'til 2008*
> *Baby, you're the best candidate*
> *Up in the Oval Office*
> *You'll get your head of state*
> *I can't leave you alone*
> *'Cause I've got a crush on Obama*

So went the hook of a brain-eating ditty that lit up the Internet in 2007. The viral *Obama Girl* video starred a pneumatic twenty-six-year-old model, Amber Lee Ettinger, who swung her hip-hugger Obama panties to the beat and presented America with its first vision of what youthful female support of Barack Obama looked like. Though the clip was meant to be comedic, the vision of Ettinger boogying in her bikini, inviting Obama to "Barack [her] tonight," came terribly close to how the media would portray one half of a generational divide among Democratic women: Obama Girls were the postfeminist sylphs who had fallen for Barack and cared not a bit for the earnest politics of their forebears, angry, punishing harpies who did not dance in their underwear but shook their pruny fists as young women rejected not just Hillary, but them, and the women's liberation they had given their lives for.

These characterizations reflected the wishful thinking of a

media hungry for any tale that might involve both a catfight and the implosion of feminism. But a white male press could not fairly be blamed for imposing a self-serving template on this tale of generational strife. Responsibility fell squarely at the feet of the ladies themselves, women on both sides of the generational chasm, who were airing their shrill differences and infusing them with a desperate gravity, as if they had been spoiling for a fight for years. In fact, they had been, and their conflicts had very little to do with Hillary Clinton, but swirled instead around the future and what remained of the women's movement.

From many angles the old-versus-young setup was grossly exaggerated. The briefest scan of any Clinton rally turned up teenage girls cheering for Hillary with a force that threatened to pop their heads off their bodies, high school guys offering restrained applause, demure twentysomething couples listening attentively. Even Obama Girl Amber Ettinger confessed that she was "very impressed with Hillary Clinton. . . . I watched the recent debates and I liked a lot of her answers." There were plenty of middle-aged women—including the well-known writers and pundits Barbara Ehrenreich, Katha Pollitt, Eve Ensler and Arianna Huffington—flocking to the Obama campaign. But the nuanced story was not as much fun to tell as the one in which the young women of America were thoughtlessly brushing off not only Hillary Clinton but with her their commitment to female political empowerment.

It was also true that throughout the primary season young people, including young women, turned out in unprecedented numbers to vote for Barack Obama, while Hillary's most reliable base consisted of white women over forty. The reasons for this dynamic began with the fact that the Clinton campaign was not good at addressing young people and the Obama campaign was great at it. If John and Elizabeth Edwards had been prescient in hiring bloggers as a way into the netroots, then Obama's use of technology, from blogs to Facebook to text messaging, was masterful. Obama did not assume that young voters were consuming the same culture or watching the same news that their parents were. He went to where they lived, where they socialized, to their phones and to their college campuses.

Jehmu Greene, who as president of Rock the Vote until 2005 was a specialist in youth voting, said, "He was doing all the right things that for the past ten years of my career we had been trying to convince candidates to do." Under-thirty voters had been regarded as unreliable, not worth the resources it took to reach them, ever since George McGovern's 1972 presidential hopes were undone when the young idealists who had made him the Democratic nominee failed to show up for him on Election Day. Most candidates, in Greene's words, assigned youth outreach to "some ghettoized cubicle" at campaign headquarters.

Barack Obama knew he could not rely on already registered Democrats, who appeared more likely to vote for Clinton, and so he took a chance on wooing new voters. Realizing that the Internet had reinvented the possibilities of political participation and provided candidates with a way of speaking directly into the ears of the young, his team made young people an integral part of its grassroots approach.

Greene said in retrospect that if Clinton's team "had targeted young women and incorporated them into their organizing efforts the way the Obama campaign did, she would have had way more support." The Clinton campaign instead took the traditional skeptical view of young voters, communicating with them tepidly and ineptly. Greene told me in 2009 of how the campaign had reacted when she'd called to offer her help after Clinton's Iowa loss. The thirty-five-year-old most recent president of Rock the Vote, an African American woman who had been in charge of women's outreach for the DNC from 1998 to 2000 and a former associate of Terry McAuliffe, Greene was precisely the kind of person Clinton's team should have been all over. The campaign could not seem to figure out what to do with her. "I ended up having to reach out to them I don't know how many times to say 'I want to *help*!'" Greene recalled. "'You have a *problem* with young people! This is my *expertise*!' It took a while for them to come around." Though Greene first contacted the Clinton campaign the day after the Iowa caucus in January, they did not officially announce her endorsement of Hillary or deploy her as a surrogate until mid-February, more than six weeks and many contests later.

Clinton often tipped her hat to the pre-Nineteenth-Amendment nonagenarians attending her rallies in wheelchairs. Only after her much derided Iowa concession speech, at which she was shown on television surrounded by a crowd of disconsolate dinosaurs, had her campaign cottoned to the fact that she had a little generational problem.

In the weeks before Super Tuesday Clinton engaged her deeply private twenty-seven-year-old daughter to speak at campuses. Chelsea was perhaps the sturdiest of all Hillary's personal credentials, and so effective a stand-in for her mom that, as the *New York Times* reported, at an hour-long February appearance at the University of Wisconsin–Eau Claire she nimbly held forth on "Medicare Part D, the distinction between the chronically and occasionally uninsured, health care premium caps, Pell grant allowance maximums, income contingency repayment programs for financial aid, sugar-based ethanol and carbon sequestration . . . Romanian reproductive policy and the design of the internal combustion engine." Oh, the Tracy Flick genes were strong, and Chelsea was a whiz.

But she could not compete with Obama, who had been beguiling undergrads for more than a year with limpid lines like "I've become a vehicle for your hopes and your dreams, but I can only carry it so far. . . . It's going to be you who carry it forward." He meant it, and he was proved right. The Obama campaign was so grassroots that kids themselves were self-starting campaign initiatives, making their own buttons and pamphlets. Clinton still shipped in the machinery from out of town.

In March, the young feminist Shelby Knox was dismayed when she arrived in her hometown of Lubbock as a Clinton volunteer and found no Clintonites in sight. Meanwhile, she said, "there were Obama supporters from the college on every street and Obama signs everywhere." A speaker at colleges around the country, Knox knew that there was an eager youthful following for Clinton, but when she walked into campaign headquarters "it was literally all older white women from out of town." The women explained that their unfamiliarity with Lubbock meant they weren't sure which thoroughfares to populate. Knox marshaled the feminist alliance from Texas Tech University, asking them, "Regardless of your political beliefs, can you please help me?" With her hastily recruited collegiate volunteers she canvassed Lubbock, holding signs for Hillary. Hillary wound up winning Lubbock, but as Knox learned, "Hillary campaigns around the country were being run by older white women, which was so unfortunate."

Younger women were there for the asking; it's just that nobody, besides Barack Obama, was asking. Worse, Hillary's older supporters were choosing to *tell* young women, in no uncertain terms, exactly what they thought of their electoral loyalties.

That the Clinton campaign was failing to seek out or address women under thirty did not seem to figure into the estimations of older Clinton supporters, who quickly worked themselves into high dudgeon over the perfidy of the next generation.

Steinem was gingerly dismissive with the sentence in "Women Are Never Front-Runners" that Knox had first objected to: "What worries me is that some women, perhaps especially younger ones, hope to deny or escape the sexual caste system; thus Iowa women over 50 and 60, who disproportionately supported Senator Clinton, proved once again that women are the one group that grows more radical with age."

Evoking an only slightly more cerebral version of the writhing Obama Girl, Steinem's characterization was doubly perplexing to young people who could not sense anything radical at all in Hillary Clinton. She was not selling herself as a history-making barrier buster or as an inheritor of a bold social project. Even as she absorbed more of John Edwards's populist message and economic policy ideas, she was still being cast as the conservative, allowing Obama to wear the progressive mantle as he coasted on his uncast war vote and allowed the young liberals he was so assiduously courting to project their every progressive fantasy onto his comparatively blank slate.

Steinem's discouraging take was polite compared to the can of censorious second-wave whup-ass that her Women's Media Center colleague Robin Morgan was about to open on young women. Morgan, then sixty-seven, had been a member of New York Radical Women and Women's International Terrorist Conspiracy from Hell (or W.I.T.C.H.). Sometimes credited with coining the phrase "The personal is political," Morgan in 1970 composed the blistering, movement-defining manifesto "Goodbye to All That," a venomous adieu to what she viewed as the sexism of left-wing male politics. On the day before the Super Tuesday primaries she published "Goodbye to All That #2" on the WMC website. This time she was not gunning for the liberal male establishment; she was gunning for everyone, *everyone* who was not supporting Hillary Clinton, taking particular aim at her jejune counterparts.

The piece had all of the retro flair of Steinem's op-ed with little of the insight. "Good-bye to a misrepresented generational divide," Morgan wrote, before ensuring that that divide was about to get a lot starker. "Goodbye to some young women eager to win male approval by showing they're not feminists (at least not the kind who actually threaten the status quo), who can't identify with a woman candidate because she is unafraid of eeueweeeu yucky power, who fear their boyfriends might look at them funny if they say something good about her." To those benighted young women, Morgan delivered from on high a famous statement by Harriet Tubman: "I could have saved thousands—if only I'd been able to convince them they were slaves."

Morgan would go on to tell the *New Yorker*'s Ariel Levy that the publication of the piece elicited more than eight hundred emails a day, and that only one in fifty were negative. That seemed a low estimate, given how many young women failed to warm to Morgan's characterizations of them as boyfriend-pleasing, power-averse dopes who didn't recognize their own servitude and used the word *yucky*.

"This is all incredibly offensive to me—not because of who I support in the presidential primary, but because of who I am, a younger *feminist* woman," wrote Ann Friedman at *Feministing*. "This crap is merely annoying when it comes from the mainstream media. It's *really* disappointing and hurtful when it comes from within the women's movement."

Jessica Valenti said in 2009, "[Censure from Morgan and her compatriots] was hardest because all of your fears about what older feminists thought about you were made extremely explicit. They just think I'm a mommy-hating idiot who's voting for Obama because my boyfriend is." Because *Feministing* did not support a candidate, Valenti said the site was inundated with hate mail from older women. "Ideologically there was a rift, because theirs was the idea that you have to support Hillary because she's a woman and if you don't that's not feminist."

This was the heart of the complaints about young women: they did not realize to what degree their gender was an impediment to parity, and had not considered that having a female leader would create a trickle-down effect that would empower all women. "Younger people don't get how the impact of having a woman in that particular office will have an impact throughout the world," said Geraldine Ferraro in 2009.

Michelle Goldberg, a young feminist and fervent Obama supporter, hit back at her elders and indulged in some generational characterizations of her own in a piece in London's *Guardian*. Calling Morgan's essay "a hysterical screed accusing female Obama supporters of being, essentially, blinkered bimbos," she bemoaned the fact that "otherwise admirable, even heroic women seem to identify with Clinton so profoundly that they interpret rejection of her as a personal rebuke," and in their responses were "lashing out in all kinds of counterproductive ways, doing far more damage to feminism than a Clinton loss ever could."

The hard truth, Goldberg asserted, was that the majority of young Democratic women were supporting Obama. "Maligning and disparaging them is no way to recruit them into a movement," she wrote. "[And] the more leaders of the movement insist on conflating their noble struggle for social justice with the fate of an uninspiring and nepotistic candidate, the less relevant [second-wave feminism] will be. Many progressives . . . see Clinton as cynical and narcissistic, pandering to interest-group sectarianism even as she compromises on important principles. It would be a hideous shame if they came to see feminism the same way."

But Clinton diehards continued to conflate support for their candidate with feminism itself, and to vilify anyone who opposed her. In February fifty-seven-year-old Marcia Pappas, the president of NOW's New York chapter, fired off a press release in which she called Massachusetts Senator Ted Kennedy's endorsement of Obama "the ultimate betrayal" of women and an "abandonment." Many feminist bloggers, and even other chapters of NOW, promptly repudiated Pappas's comments; *Feministing*'s Ann Friedman called the release "unhinged." The *New York Times* used the fracas as a peg for a column by Susan Dominus about escalating generational conflict between feminists, embodied by Pappas and Jessica Valenti.

The title of the *Times* piece was "Feminists Find Unity Is Elusive," a headline that could have run at any time in the past fifty
years, or even the past hundred and fifty. The myth of a feminist
monolith—some accredited synod that takes away your disposable
razor and issues you a gift card for two free abortions—had been
used against women's rights activists for years, by critics from Phyllis Schlafly to Rush Limbaugh to Katie Roiphe, antifeminists eager
to paint themselves as gallant heretics, charging the forbidding
fortress of the women's movement. In truth feminism was, at its
cohesive best, a loose banner hoisted by women of different colors,
classes, sexual identities, professional ambitions and religious affili-
ations, who sometimes managed to put their tussling aside to work
for a shared goal; at its cannibalistic worst, it was a self-destructive
mash-up of competing priorities and identities.

The story of the roiling, ever-evolving debate within feminist circles was as old as feminism: the National Woman Suffrage Association versus the American Woman Suffrage Association, womanism
versus feminism, Betty Friedan versus The Lavender Menace, Betty
Friedan versus Gloria Steinem, Catharine MacKinnon versus Ellen
Willis. But for some in the media, hope sprang eternal that this
would be the moment that the loose-knit coalition might unravel for
good. The generational resentments made public during the primaries had been simmering for a long time. The election simply turned
up the flame and made those resentments public.

For years Valenti and her cohort had been chafing against the
older women who represented and ran institutional feminism,
organizations like NOW, NARAL, Planned Parenthood, the Feminist Majority. According to many young women who began their
careers banging on the doors of these umbrella organizations, institutional feminism treated them with the kind of disrespect against
which women of the 1970s had bucked and strained. The young
women did not feel listened to; they felt judged for their short skirts,
as if their elders could not look past their piercings to their brains.

"The main reason I founded *Feministing*," Valenti told me in
2009, "was because I was working for a women's organization, and
there was all of this lip service being paid to how important younger
women were to the movement, but no one really wanted to hear
what we had to say. They wanted us for photo-ops, and on their

young feminist advisory boards that had no real power. When push came to shove, they were not interested in our opinions."

Valenti started *Feministing* not long before the April 2004 March for Women's Lives, a massive event that offered ample evidence that older feminists coveted young blood but didn't know what to do with it once they got it. I covered that march for *Salon*, and the feeling there was that a decades-old carapace of backlash had cracked. Tens of thousands of young women showed up, their faces open and expectant. I watched women in their twenties swarm a golf cart carrying an aged Betty Friedan, and saw one nearly pass out from excitement upon meeting Gloria Steinem. "Oh my god! I love you!" she gasped. The gamine crowd went nuts when Hillary Clinton made a surprise appearance. Here they were, aligning themselves with their elders, anxious to throw their fists in the air and be a part of the largest gathering of women since 1992, the year Hillary arrived in Washington and the unprecedented election of four women to the Senate made it the Year of the Woman.

Organizers had crowed happily as they gazed upon the sea of young faces, but could offer the juvenescent crowd only well-intentioned but sad displays of paleofeminism. *Cagney & Lacey*'s Tyne Daly and Sharon Gless, Wonder Woman Lynda Carter, *One Day at a Time*'s Bonnie Franklin and *Moonlighting*'s Cybill Shepherd ensured that there was full representation of television's prime-time line-up from early 1980s. Ashley Judd, the Indigo Girls and *Saturday Night Live*'s Ana Gasteyer nudged the median age of entertainment acts toward forty, but what was there for anyone in their twenties? Heaping piles of condescension.

Whoopi Goldberg brought a hanger on stage with her, saying in an almost accusatory voice, "You understand me, women under thirty? This is what we used!" It was an attempt at communication, but it came out sounding like she was scolding a generation for its privilege, when that privilege was actually a right, a right that women had fought for and won, ensuring that the next generation might take it for granted. On the Metro the night before the march I'd overheard a young man in low-slung jeans ask what a coat hanger stood for. "That's how women used to get abortions," his young female companion replied. "Haven't you ever seen *Dirty Dancing*?" This was the world that the activists who organized the march had made, one in which comprehension of the atrocities of illegal abortion came via sixteen-year-old movies.

The women who had banished those hangers from the contemporary consciousness were not sure that forgetting they had existed was such a good idea. In part their distress was human: a keening desire for recognition, for appreciation and for credit due a generation that, as the columnist Gail Collins would suggest in a 2009 book, had changed *everything* for women.

Aging must have brought its own frazzled anxiety, creeping fears of irrelevance and invisibility, of not wanting to go softly anywhere, for the lives they lived had been loud. From this came the agitation and annoyance with young women: Would they treat so carelessly the freedoms their predecessors fought so hard for? Would they forget them? Would they undo them? The young ones, after all, were lucky, spoiled, their paths cleared by those who whacked through thickets of resistance. Older women sometimes sounded angry that young women's lives were easier than theirs had been, that they could afford to have more fun with their feminism, with their power, with their opportunities. Now those whippersnappers were going to push their worn-out progenitors aside just at the moment they might have taken their triumphant presidential bow.

This made some fanatical about Hillary in ways they would not otherwise have been. NOW's Kim Gandy, a strong Hillary supporter, remembered the surprise she felt watching some fervently liberal women who had sat out previous elections because the Democratic candidate was imperfect on issues like same-sex marriage or the war. When it came to Hillary, though, they were forgiving. "The hard-liners became apologists!" Gandy recalled. "They gave Hillary a pass. The historical commitment to seeing a woman president overrode everything." Gandy tried to reason with some of them, to remind them, "If you think she's going to make the ERA the number one priority as president, you're crazy." But for those who had given their hearts to Hillary there was no reasoning. "They wrote all their hopes and dreams on her, in the same way that other feminists who didn't support her wrote their fears on her."

This wasn't just about politics or policy. It was about mortality. "Older women felt this was their last chance to see a female president," Steinem pointed out in 2009, "and younger women knew they would have another chance." The sense that time was running out strengthened the older generation's identification with Hillary, a woman they thought was being pushed off-stage too soon. As Leslie Bennetts wrote, "Not only is Clinton well beyond the age when our culture deems women to have lost most of their value, but so are all too many of her supporters—and there are few things this country is less interested in than aging women." Robin Morgan's screed asked even more directly, "How dare *anyone* unilaterally decide when to turn the page on history, papering over real inequities and suffering constituencies in the promise of a feel-good campaign? . . . We are the women who changed the reality of the United States. And though we never went away, brace yourselves: *we're back*!"

They wanted so badly to be back, to lay claim to the most public, emblematic, political victory, and instead they were being reduced to carping mommies, the role they had worked so hard to break out of. In February Letty Cottin Pogrebin, one of the founders of *Ms.* magazine and a devout Clinton supporter, appeared on PBS with her adult Obama-supporting daughter, Abigail. "When a woman finally deserves to be where she is, somebody comes in and undercuts her," Cottin Pogrebin explained, while Abigail made the (dubious) claim that she had never experienced sexism growing up, in part *because* she was raised in a feminist environment. Cottin Pogrebin echoed Marcia Pappas's bathetic language when telling host Maria Hinojosa that Abigail's "abandoning Hillary" was a very serious thing, adding that younger women choosing Obama "hurts." Abigail ended the interview by wailing "Mommy!" in an effort to get Letty to stop kvetching at her about Hillary. It was all faintly embarrassing.

Perhaps because many of these conversations were taking place at kitchen tables, between actual mothers and daughters, women on both sides of the divide gave in to the impulse to lay out their differences about Hillary on the mother-daughter framework. Conversations were shot through with echoes of mothers who yearned for gratitude, or just the assurance that their children would be able to take care of themselves once they were gone. For many of the senior combatants there was a fear that younger women, so flip about the feminism that had landed them in law school and board meetings, would allow a roll-back that would condemn their own daughters to car pools and vacuuming.

Writing in *Slate,* the firebrand Linda Hirshman pondered the possibility that young women were supporting Obama as a way of flipping off their mothers, citing the respected young author Courtney Martin, who had confessed one of the reasons she was not supporting Clinton: "Because she reminds me of being scolded by my mother." Hirshman also cited a piece of mine, in which I wrote that the pressure from elder feminists was like being told that I had "some kind of ovarian, fallopian responsibility" to vote for Hillary. "I suppose I must offer the obligatory reassurance that neither all women nor even all feminists need to march in lockstep to the polls to vote for Hillary Clinton," Hirshman wrote. "But I want to amplify that with the additional caution that *just because your mother did it does not make it wrong.*"

Hirshman had a beef with the next generation that would extend beyond the election. In 2009 she launched an attack on *Jezebel*, a blog aimed at young women, noting that although "from a certain perspective, the *Jezebel* writers look a lot like the natural heirs of feminism," their propensity to revel in their sexual emancipation by flaunting erotic triumphs and misfortunes, all in the name of good fun and an aversion to victimhood, contributed to an erosion of feminist principles. "Feminism was never only a liberation movement," Hirshman wrote. "It was a claim that liberation would open up a better life to women, a life of meaningful work and satisfying sexual relationships (among other things)."

Hirshman told me in 2010 that she had been initially thrilled to discover the feminist energies of the web, and believed young logged-on women to be rigorous political thinkers. "But then I started reading the blogs day in and day out," she said, "and [I saw] an absence and indeed a rejection of political thinking." Hirshman didn't object to the sexual focus of young feminist bloggers: "There was a tremendous amount of writing about our sex lives in the 1970s. But it was about how we wanted to have orgasms. How we wanted to try out our sexual partners before we committed to them for a lifetime. These are selfish things and the beginning of all politics." What she saw on the blogosphere was a self-interest of a different sort—personal revelation without much thought about the collective good of women. "It was the utter absence of the fundamental rules of social-movement politics: that you act collectively, identify your interest, and put it first."

The feminist journalist Debra Dickerson took a slightly less cerebral approach to her criticism of youthful activism, writing after the election, "Today's feminists need to blog less and work more."

Gripes about the feminist blogosphere were, from many perspectives, dead-on. The Internet featured an extreme openness about sex—good sex, bad sex, straight sex, gay sex, sex work and sex toys—indicating that feminism's inheritors believed that the personal was worth posting. Feminist bloggers treated their revelations with a crassness and nonchalance that sometimes seemed at odds with their serious-minded critiques about body image and objectification. Bloggers had a way of having it both ways, of firing off biting posts about the ill treatment or sexualized diminution of a female politician or actor at the same time that they published provocative photos of themselves or described sex acts—sometimes disempowering ones—in graphic detail. The self-exposure and self-celebration had all the hallmarks of a narcissistic Internet; it betrayed both an intellectual inconsistency and an eagerness to abandon the appearance of political self-seriousness. It was a transparent effort to contradict rusty but still damaging stereotypes of feminists as sexless succubi. And it made many second-wavers crazy. *Feministing*'s logo was the image of a mud-flap girl. Didn't these women know how hard their predecessors had worked to escape the mud-flap girl? But young women were eager to tip some of feminism's sacred cows.

As Ariel Levy reported, when the former child star Robin Morgan became involved in the women's movement and appeared on Johnny Carson's show in 1969 to talk about feminism, she marched off-stage when Carson tried to show clips of her pubescent television appearances, so vehemently did she object to the frivolous diminishment of her work. When Levy herself appeared on *The Colbert Report* to flog her book, *Female Chauvinist Pigs,* which picked apart many of the contradictions of purported sexual empowerment, she just laughed as Colbert hobbled toward her in high heels. When Valenti later appeared on the same show to promote her manifesto, *Full Frontal Feminism,* she gamely joked, "Nothing says feminism like a naked woman's body."

There were structural realities that shaped the tone and attitude of the feminist blogosphere. For many of the young women who ran independent blogs, women who lacked the boost of the feminist establishment to catapult them into (slightly) more remunerative spotlights as activists or writers, feminist criticism was something they produced on the side while working other jobs. Frequent posts and instant commentary written for little or no money often meant a decrease in intellectual heft. For those writers lucky enough to be paid for their work, their sometimes hourly enunciations had little in common with the deliberate, reported, long-form journalism and scholarship of the 1970s. An Internet maw demanded to be fed; posts had to go up, quick and often dirty.

But the Internet gave feminism something older women could not: an expansive new life and more abundant points of entry. When she first sought to get into feminist organizing, Valenti said, "you had to work for certain organizations, or have certain inroads with Gloria Steinem or Robin Morgan or Jane Fonda. The thing with the blogosphere was you could just build up your own audience and all of a sudden your voice was important."

Channeling their energy online, young feminists pushed the movement forward, making it more accessible to millions of women, reclaiming it for future generations who communed differently from those who had staged marches and sit-ins and consciousness raising in earlier decades. Models of activism that had once worked no longer pertained; women of the 1960s and 1970s did not have email, text messaging or the Internet, in effect a massive clubhouse in which to congregate, communicate and organize. This new wave of young people did not long for figureheads and spokespeople and megaphones—though if there was a young icon, Valenti was it. Gone were the days in which everyone read any one text or watched any one movie. Now everyone could produce their own texts and engage in multiple conversations without having to be geographically present or even visible. Online feminism afforded the option of pursuing activism in private. Young women, especially very young women, could explore feminist ideas without committing to a public brand, attending a meeting, wearing a T-shirt; they could read a feminist website at the same time that they played Beyoncé and shopped at gap.com. Perhaps it made feminism a less radical and less radicalizing choice, but it also made it far more available.

In turn, young women came aboard sooner. And because they did not have to go out of their way to seek a feminist community, many young people were coming upon online feminism by chance, not in reaction to instances of injustice or misogyny. What was often hard for older women to remember was that the young women creating a new feminist realm had not had the same experiences they had, both in broad poetic post-second-wave terms and also purely in terms of age. At the beginning of the twenty-first century women were surely still passed over for promotions, talked down to in meetings, sexually harassed, abused, asked to carry undue domestic burdens, paid less, objectified, disrespected and inadequately represented in government. But the younger a woman was, in any era, the fewer of these gendered data points she encountered, precisely *because* she was young and hadn't yet been exposed to them.

Debra Dickerson said it herself, even as she excoriated young feminists at *Mother Jones*: "Honey, you haven't seen sexism yet." Bingo. As Leslie Bennetts said in 2008, "We used to have a saying in the women's movement: 'It takes life to make a feminist.'" Much of what women learned about how their gender impacted their status—economically, socially, politically, professionally—came with time, with babies, with promotions and raises and marriages, with challenges that most young women had not encountered. That didn't mean that ten years later they would have voted for Hillary Clinton (though women over thirty did vote for her at higher rates than did their younger counterparts). It just meant that yelling at them about what they had not yet lived through was not going to do anyone any good.

☆ ☆ ☆

There was another serious, structural issue at stake in the disagreement between mothers and daughters: the youthful attempt to repair racial rifts within the feminist movement, an approach that academics and young women called "intersectionality." A new generation of feminists, acutely aware of what they perceived as the myopia of their predecessors when it came to racial, class and sexual variety among women, extended their gender activism to incorporate work around race, ethnicity, poverty, disability and sexual identity. Intersectionality meant not only stretching the feminist conversation to include new voices; it meant de-emphasizing gender as the single locus of oppression. Many young women saw this shift as unambiguously progressive, catalyzed by the diversity of the Internet and as an achievement of which they could be proud.

"If the blogosphere hadn't happened, we would still be in the same place we were in fifteen years ago," Valenti told me in 2009. "The only reason that intersectionality is talked about more often in mainstream feminist conversation is because mainstream feminists and national organizations were forced to take the issues on by blogs; they couldn't ignore it once so many people were talking about it." Online, conflicts about racial and economic and physical privilege continued to flare, but at least everyone was talking about it. The slow, imperfect move toward inclusion was the thing that earlier generations had failed to do effectively. That young women were aiming to correct it was seen in some quarters as a rebuke to traditional feminist organizations; crowing about the value of intersectional feminism sounded like an insinuation that young outsiders were more capable of improving the movement than the women who had created it, women who did not necessarily see the changes as improvements.

Until 2008 this conversation had been largely academic; it took place on blogs and in women's studies departments. But the election was bringing the differences of opinion into stark practical—and often personal—relief.

Latifa Lyles had worked at NOW since her early twenties, had been elected national membership vice president at twenty-nine and was an exception to a vision of the country's feminist organizations as forbidding to young women and women of color. During her tenure at NOW she had felt supported; she had been mentored and respected and believed that traditional feminist structures were inclusive. Until the election. "Despite how wonderful the election was in so many ways, it was a low point for me in the feminist community," Lyles told me in 2009. "The conversations that ensued—is sexism worse than racism, is racism worse than sexism, the sense [from older white women] that it was their time, the [voiced resent-ments about how] 'We had to wait for black men to get the vote!' Suddenly NOW felt like an organization and a culture that I did not know. I thought we had evolved into a better place."

Lyles began to see eye-to-eye with her outlying blogging sisters about the practical effects of intersectionality, of broadening and diversifying the conversation. "We had a progressive organization, but we didn't even have the language or the sensitivity to have these conversations!" she said. "You have to have diversity in your social justice work. Not just because it looks and feels good, but because [without an attention to issues besides gender] we harm ourselves and it's a detriment to our progress."

But older critics, the ones who saw their gender as the most cen-tral inhibitor of political parity, the ones who were weighing sex-ism against other oppressions and pointing out that women often came last in line, worried that the breadth of intersectional pri-orities thinned the interest in women, vilified older white women and left feminists too unfocused to move forward. "A movement that uses intersectionality as a lens but banishes white, bourgeois corporate older women might be a vehicle to glue what remains of feminism together, but it will struggle to achieve social change for women," argued Linda Hirshman in the *Washington Post*. She thought, "[The Clinton campaign] revealed what many in the move-ment know—that if feminism is a social-justice-for-everyone (with the possible exception of middle-class white women) movement, then gender is just one commitment among many. And when the other causes call, the movement will dissolve."

Hirshman regarded intersectionality as a step back into familiar patterns in which women put themselves last. "Everything is always a contest of one good against another," she told me in 2010. "You put your good against a competing good. Everyone since Hobbes has known these rules of social-movement politics. But you can't have politics if you don't take care of yourself. If you care for your-self first, *then* you make alliances with other people." The feminist movement, Hirshman argued, "had to be good girls and look after everybody but themselves. So when time came and people said 'It's more important to put a black person in the White House than a woman,' they said, 'Of course, you should go first.'"

Gloria Feldt recalled that at the 2004 march on Washington young, black and Latina feminist organizations insisted that the demonstration focus not just on reproductive rights, but on the kinds of social, economic and sexual challenges faced by poor women and women of color. "If we were going to build a coalition that would bring the women of color groups in, [they] made it quite clear that they needed the issues to be broader," she said. "So it became the March for Women's Lives. And then nobody knew what it meant. It diffuses everything."

Had that march taken place just four years later it might have looked very different. In 2004 the nascent *Feministing* had a minuscule readership. By 2008 Valenti had published two books and had more than half a million readers a month. In 2008 the march might have been covered by other blogs, such as *Racialicious, Salon*'s women's blog *Broadsheet, Slate*'s women's blog the *XX Factor,* or *Gawker* offshoot *Jezebel,* none of which existed in 2004. Celebrities might have included a generation of self-identified young feminists, such as Emma Watson, Andy Samberg, Adrian Grenier, Nellie McKay, Amy Poehler, Kate Winslet, America Ferrera, Lady Gaga, and Eliza Dushku, though a celebrity presence would likely not have been the galvanizing force. Conversation—and inevitable disagreement—about the impact of the march, the quality of the speakers, and the voices that were included and excluded might have been hashed out by young feminist journalists like Ann Friedman, Dana Goldstein, Ariel Levy, Amanda Fortini, Sheelah Kolhatkar, and Kira Cochrane, writing for the *American Prospect,* the *New Yorker, New York* magazine, *Portfolio,* and the *Guardian.* Maybe it was the early grab at Internet real estate by women like Valenti, maybe it was a backlash to backlash, maybe it was a swelling of the female media ranks related to Hillary Clinton's presidential run, but by 2008 feminism was not only far hipper than it had been in decades, but young people were taking control of the message. If the March for Women's Lives was a stilted mixer in which teenagers and mothers and grandmothers gaped awkwardly at each other, a matter of a few years would have seen emboldened youngsters turning up the music and owning the party.

But we didn't have a March for Women's Lives in 2008. We had a presidential election, and that was the event onto which the messiness of era, age and difference spilled.

★ ★ ★

The yawning generational divides of 2008's election season were not exclusive to feminism. Time—and success—do funny things to social movements. Urgency gets lost; resentments build.

In July 2008 a live microphone caught Jesse Jackson, the revered civil rights leader, the man who was with Martin Luther King Jr. when he was assassinated in 1968, whose runs for the presidency in 1984 and 1988 helped make Barack Obama's candidacy possible, saying that he'd like to "cut [Obama's] nuts off" because he was "talking down to black people." Obama ran a race-light campaign, very different in tone from Jackson's earlier forays. Obama had not relied on Jackson for advice (though tellingly Jesse Jackson Jr. was one of his biggest backers), nor had he made much reference to the legacy of Jackson or his contemporaries. This fostered the perception of a lack of gratitude. To some Barack Obama's refusal to make his racial identity his priority was maddening, as was his distance from the history of black leadership. Obama carried none of the DNA of the civil rights movement; his political career had not originated at the pulpit; he did not rely on the counsel of leaders like Jackson or Reverend Al Sharpton.

In an entry on the *Huffington Post*, Brooklyn's Democratic congressional candidate Kevin Powell attributed Jackson's comments to a black generation gap, to the fact that while civil rights battles had made it possible for young African Americans to succeed in business and politics in ways that would have been unimaginable forty years earlier, their successes were often met with "a heavy resentment from the established black gatekeepers." Feeling frustrated and powerless, "some old school leaders have taken to chastising younger ones every opportunity they get," Powell wrote. Voicing sentiments that could have come from any number of young feminists, Powell continued, "The days of marching and protesting are over. The days of voting for someone just because they are black are over. . . . The multicultural legion of young Americans who've flocked to Obama's campaign suggest that we want leadership that builds bridges, not that is stuck in the rhetoric and realities of the past. . . . Yes, I must represent the concerns of blacks and Latinos in East New York. But I cannot ignore the Hasidic Jews in Williamsburg or the young white professionals in Fort Greene. They are all my people."

There were similar sensibility shifts within the gay rights movement, with some young people eager to move beyond the Stonewall-era, then AIDS-era history of their predecessors. In a 2009 *New York* magazine story Mark Harris described how online "there's no topic, from politics to locker-room etiquette . . . that cannot quickly devolve into 'What are you, 17?'—'What are you, some Stonewall-era relic?' sniping." Harris might as well have been channeling Robin Morgan in his description of what middle-aged gay men said about their youthful counterparts: "They reek of entitlement. They haven't had to work for anything and therefore aren't interested in anything that takes work. They're profoundly ungrateful for the political and social gains we spent our own youth striving to obtain for them. . . . They think old-fashioned *What do we want! When do we want it!* activism is icky and noisy. They toss around terms like 'post-gay' without caring how hard we fought just to get all the way to 'gay.'" Harris also reported on how youngsters perceive his plague-era compatriots: "We're horrible scolds. We gas on about AIDS the way our parents or grandparents couldn't stop talking about World War II. We act like we invented political action, and think the only way to accomplish something is by expressions of fury. We say we want change, but really what we want is to get off on our own victimhood. We're made uncomfortable, or even jealous, by their easygoing confidence. We're grim, prim, strident, self-ghettoizing, doctrinaire bores who think that if you're not gloomy, you're not worth taking seriously."

It all sounded so familiar, movement to movement.

A June 2009 Pew Research Center survey determined that the United States was experiencing the widest generation gap since the 1960s, when so many of the movements that were thrown into the spotlight by the 2008 elections had first coalesced. The Pew survey found that almost 80 percent of people polled believed that there was a major difference between what young people thought and what older people thought, the largest spread since 1969, when 74 percent of Americans polled saw major differences of opinion between older and younger generations.

Those young radicals from 1969 were now the elders, but it was their modern-day juvenile counterparts, the ones they bitched about being less radical, about being complacent, who were making manifest social progress that they could only have dreamed of forty years earlier. Products of this generational chasm included our first black president, a man whom eighteen- to twenty-nine-year-olds voted for by a two-to-one margin, and a widening acceptance of homosexuality and gay partnership, especially among young people. It also included the calm, if perhaps overly rosy assumption that women were so capable of winning the presidency that it was not incumbent on other women to support the first one to take a serious crack at it.

Anyone who lived through the 1960s should have known that the younger generation wins. The best anyone could hope for was that there would be some acknowledgment, some meaningful exchange before young women picked up their satchels and moved into the future.

And as difficult as it may have been, this election gave them exactly that. For all the kvetching and the carping, what didn't get reported was that many young women were not only listening to senior voices, but were expressing gratitude and acknowledging that their eyes had been opened to the challenges Clinton was facing, whether or not they were voting for her.

Some, like *Shakesville*'s Melissa McEwan, the blogger who had worked for John Edwards and initially dismissed Clinton as part of a corrupt political dynasty, described to me in 2009 her building "awareness of the ten metric fucktons of shit Hillary had to put up with to get where she was. . . . I just started admiring the hell out of her." Others admired her too, even without deciding to support her. Courtney Martin laid it out on *AlterNet*, explaining, "I . . . am an Obama voter, but was and will continue to be an avid Clinton supporter. I hate the sexist coverage that she endured . . . but that doesn't change my vote. My feminism is not just about gender equality in government, but also about racial justice, global security, community ethics, etc., and I resent being made to feel as if there is a 'right' way to vote if I am a feminist." In a *Nation* article excoriating those who assailed feminist Obama voters, Valenti wrote, "Let's focus on tangible goals: fostering youth leadership, working from the margins in and using intersectionality as our lens—instead of just a talking point. Let's use this moment, when our politics and emotions are raw, to push for a better, more forward-looking feminism."

The points that second-wavers seemed to think were falling on tender, deaf ears were actually being considered seriously. As twenty-five-year-old Jessica Grose wrote at *Jezebel,* "Hearing Abigail Pogrebin say that she has never encountered sexism makes me wonder if we do take the women's rights movement of the 60s and 70s for granted. . . . Have we stopped fighting a battle we didn't win?" And twenty-four-year-old Obama supporter Rebecca Wiegand told me in 2008, "[Going into the election] I felt very post-feminist. I felt like, I'm a woman and I'd love to have a woman president, but I also have many other issues I care about and the Iraq war is a big one, and I'm not going to make my decision just because I'm a woman." Over the course of the campaign, Wiegand said, "there has been a lot of anger toward Hillary that's felt really intense and misogynistic. . . . And it's made me realize we are still dealing with the gender issue. I don't think we know what to make of a woman in power, or make of Hillary. I don't think the world is as postfeminist as I was feeling that it was."

In some cases the sentiments of dissenting young women were practically love letters from a purportedly ungrateful generation. Responding to Linda Hirshman's piece about her mother issues, Courtney Martin wrote in the *American Prospect,* "I have gained an immeasurable amount from the wise, older women who have challenged my views on this election and other issues within a context of complexity. These women have made me a better thinker, a better writer, a better feminist, and a better human. And because of them, I will not cower, but I promise to be grateful. I will not forget, but I must also move on. I will not be a dutiful daughter, but I promise to be an impassioned, authentic, and brave inheritor."

What many of these young women were telegraphing was their willingness to see, to really see, through the prism of Clinton's campaign and their elders' reaction to it, that sexism was not a thing of the past. Whether it made them pull a lever for Hillary Clinton was practically immaterial—if not to Clinton's presidential prospects, then to the future of feminist engagement.

At least some older women heard this and shouted back. "I learn as much from them as they do from me," Steinem said about younger women. When I asked her if she thought the overzealous sex positivity and profanity of Internet feminism were weakening the movement, she replied, "As a person who walked around with a button that said 'Cunt Power' on it while I was wearing a miniskirt, I don't know that that's the case."

It was true, Steinem acknowledged, that many of her contemporaries "were not appreciated enough for the hard work and the sacrifice and so on. But you cannot now exact that price from your daughters. Even Susan B. Anthony said, 'Our job is not to make young women grateful. It's to make them ungrateful.'"

7   BOYS ON THE BUS

IN EARLY SPRING, in response to my *Salon* coverage of the election, I started receiving email messages from men who wanted to talk to me about Barack Obama. "Seriously . . . he's the bomb," wrote one friend from college. "To walk above the bitter bickering . . . to shoot straight, to continue to inspire, AND to continually remind us that we are responsible for our own democracy and future. . . . We need him." Another acquaintance expressed how much he admired "that Barack and Michelle Obama seem to have a very healthy thing going on with their family," and invited me for a drink by suggesting, "Yes We Can have a glass of wine."

This swollen-hearted adoration for the presidential candidate was startling coming from a usually ironic cohort. If my correspondents' bliss made me chafe slightly in those weeks after I cast my vote for Hillary, I believed it was because theirs was an enchantment from which I was now barred.

Then I began to get emails from a guy I'd been to dinner with six months earlier. "Hey, I don't mean to be confrontational," began his first missive, which went on to detail his hatred of the Clintons' political history, his dismay at how Hillary was conducting her campaign, and his fury at her front-running presumption. None of his antipathy had anything do with Hillary's gender, he assured me. In one of his notes he confessed, "Personally, I feel like vomiting every time I hear her hectoring voice."

My friend Geraldine, by the spring a strong Obama supporter, told me about a drink she'd had with a man who was ardent in his love for Barack and who made a series of legitimate complaints about Clinton before telling her that whenever he heard the New York senator's voice he was overcome by an urge to punch her in the face. Geraldine's date sounded chivalrous compared to one of my lifelong friends, a man with whom I had shared approximately one million beers and two million cigarettes as teens sorting through our nascent political beliefs. He said that when *he* heard Clinton speak he wanted to punch her in her uterus.

A pattern was emerging in the liberal, privileged, predominantly white climes in which I worked and lived: young men were starry-eyed about Obama and puffed with outsized antipathy toward Clinton. Swearing up and down that it wasn't because of her sex, they'd reel off dozens of reasons for not wanting to vote for her. But I was made uncomfortable by the persistent note of aggression that marked their reactions to Clinton, and puzzled by the increasingly cult-like devotion to Obama, a man whose policy positions were not so different, after all, from those of his opponent. Hating Hillary had for decades been the provenance of Republican blowhards, but now men on the left were spewing vitriol about her voice, her looks, her presumption—and without realizing it were radicalizing me in my support for Clinton more than the candidate herself ever could have. And it wasn't just me. I was hearing similar dismay not only from fellow Clinton voters, but from female Obama supporters put off by the Hillary-despising virus that had infected their progressive male compatriots.

On the morning of the Louisiana primary my friend Becca O'Brien, then a policy advisor in New Orleans, received five separate calls from male friends around the country. They were just campaigning on behalf of their candidate, Becca understood. "[But] the presumption was that I was undecided because I was a young woman and they could talk some sense into me. . . . With straight

white male progressive friends, I feel something that makes me viscerally angry and afraid—the viciousness of the rebuttals to the
suggestion that [Obama's and Clinton's] policies are roughly equal
or that Clinton's have some benefits, the outright dismissal of any
support of her . . . The whole 'Hillary Clinton is a monster' theme
is so virulent."

After hearing from Becca I put out feelers, asking friends and
colleagues to pass along the message that I was curious to hear from
young women who were experiencing disturbing pressure from their
Obama-supporting male friends. Within twenty-four hours I had
an overflowing inbox; my voicemail was full; I had women practically climbing through my windows to tell me of their perplexities
and aggravations. Those who contacted me were almost exclusively
well-educated professionals, mostly white and very liberal, and they
were complaining about their male counterparts. They described
outright sexism as well as less well-defined suspicions that these men
were uncomfortable with powerful women. The women who were
supposedly rejecting feminism and diving deep into the embrace
of the "Yes We Can" dude down the block were instead calling
me out of earshot of their Obama-loving boyfriends, some expressing gendered discontent for the first time in their lives; more than
one young woman voiced her own surprise, midlitany, at "sounding so feminist." Most contrary to the popular narrative of the election—that young women voting for Obama had no investment in
Clinton—was that the majority of women who contacted me were
Obama supporters, or at least Obama appreciators.

Dana Lossia, a twenty-nine-year-old labor lawyer in Brooklyn,
called Obama "the most inspiring, amazing person, a different kind
of politician." She was no fan of Hillary's and hated how she'd run
her campaign, but she wrote, "I've been really bothered by what I
perceive as sexism [among some male Obama supporters] and have
spent hours defending [Clinton]. . . . It's the intensity of their irrita-
tion with her that disturbs me more than their devotion to Obama."

Thirty-one-year-old Maggie Merrill was an urban studies graduate student at the University of New Orleans whose anxieties were
sown early, when a young family friend began talking as if every
right-minded person would support Obama over Clinton. "I got the
sense that this idealistic, highly educated, progressive man, regard-

less of the fact that he'd been raised by liberal women, was uncomfortable with the idea of a woman being in power," Merrill told me. She spoke with alarm about the Obamamania in Louisiana: "These young men get glassy eyes and start spitting out vague things about how Barack Obama is going to save humanity. Really, have you seen their eyes? It's this faraway look. It's scary."

Yes I had! In February, March, and April 2008 I saw that look on scads of scruffy volunteers lining the streets of Brooklyn and Manhattan, spreading the word. In grouchier moods I considered speaking with them about preaching, choirs, and possible relocation to suburban Ohio. In more sanguine moments I appreciated their ardor but wondered if the thing they thought Barack Obama might be saving humanity from was a threatening woman in the world's most powerful job.

Jessica Valenti, who spoke at fifteen colleges during the election cycle, told me in 2009 that in her travels she encountered "a lot of women who were voting for Hillary, and a lot who were voting for Obama. And *all* of them felt like their progressive male friends were sexist." Shelby Knox was also touring colleges, where undergraduate women told her things like "My boyfriend is so supportive of Obama and I guess I agree with him, but something about how much he hates Hillary feels mean." Some students, Knox recalled, told her about a banner at a fraternity that read "Bros before hos." "The girls told me, 'They say it's not sexism,' and when I ask them why they're calling her a ho they list all these things—her vote on the war, that he's more progressive, that she's a Clinton and she only got there because of her husband. But even if it's not explicitly misogynistic, it's just there."

Molly Cohen, a senior at Brown, fought with her boyfriend after he began telling her "about how, objectively, Hillary Clinton was a bitch," Cohen told me in 2009. She said other male classmates insisted that she watch the popular Will.i.am video, in which celebrities strummed guitar and sang along to an Obama speech. "It felt like they thought I needed to be converted or something," said Cohen. Anytime she said anything positive about Clinton her male friends attacked: "[They behaved] as if I didn't understand that I was siding with the bitch." At the same time they insisted that their distaste for Clinton had nothing to do with the fact that she was a woman. "These were liberal guys," Cohen said. "They were the guys fighting for Palestinian rights. And then it came to a woman and it was like, 'She's a bitch.' Wait, what about the sensitivity you just showed to all the people of the world?" Cohen wound up voting for Clinton. Why? "Mostly because I was so frustrated by the male Obama supporters."

Letters to left-leaning publications and blogs bubbled with enmity toward Clinton. As Katha Pollitt wrote, "Vats of sexist nastiness splattered across the Comments section of hundreds of blogs and websites. It's as if every obscene phone caller and every exhibitionist in America decided to become an amateur political pundit." Latoya Peterson, already dismayed by the racially inflected language of the feminist community toward Obama, was also troubled by the sexism coming from progressives. "Conservatives you expect it from," she said. "But when you look at liberal men, like black male pundits—I understand they [were] infuriated by this whole election cycle, but it is never cool to call somebody a cunt. It is never cool to tell somebody to shut up." Peterson stopped reading *Jackand-JillPolitics,* the blog cofounded by the comedian and *Onion* editor Baratunde Thurston, even though she agreed with much of what he wrote about Clinton's race baiting, because the atmosphere on the blog and in its comments section was "beyond sexist for Hillary." Peterson's blog, *Racialicious,* was often critical of Hillary. "But I never allowed anybody to call [Hillary] a cunt," she said. "I never allowed anybody to call her 'Shillary,' 'Shrillary.' . . . I can't allow gleeful misogyny to continue unabated."

The trouble was that because everyone was liberal and officially down with female empowerment, the many women who couldn't cite actual uses of the words *bitch* or *cunt* found themselves troubled by their inability to specify the sexism they sensed. "I don't think anyone in my peer group . . . would be comfortable saying, 'I'm not ready for a woman president,'" said Alex Seggerman, a twenty-four-year-old art history Ph.D. student. Seggerman was an Obama voter but noticed people making remarks like "She's had plastic surgery" or "Her attitude is off-putting," which she heard as "expressions of some deeper issues with the fact that she is a woman." "People can always come up with reasons they don't like the candidate they're not supporting," said Dana Lossia, the

Obama-supporting labor lawyer. "But no one disliked Joe Biden or Chris Dodd as much as they dislike Hillary." She'd never heard her friends say anything explicit: "[They never say] anything where I could say, 'That's a sexist comment.' It's just that I can't understand why they hate her so much."

It was a contemporary iteration of Betty Friedan's problem that had no name, a maddening cycle of vague hunches and self-righteous denials that left many of us feeling as though we were going insane. Even Valenti was disoriented by it; she was particularly hamstrung because, as she pointed out, she made her living identifying sexism. "You'd think I'd be able to find an example," she said, adding, "Because it's not [always] explicit sexism, it makes it impossible to argue with people, because if you say something, then you're the wackadoo feminist."

Those who did attempt to articulate their apprehensions about how Clinton was being discussed provoked defensive eruptions. The journalist Jessica Wakeman, an Obama voter, wrote that her commitment to pointing out the sexist treatment Clinton was receiving from the media was considered "really not cool" by her mostly male friends. Becca O'Brien, the New Orleans political advisor, told me that, after examining polling data indicating that white men were disproportionately breaking for Obama, she had posted the chat headline "National Gender Bias Puts Obama Ahead of Clinton." It prompted a phone call from a furious male friend and an argument that escalated, O'Brien said, to "a new territory of outrage. . . . [He told] me that it showed fundamental flaws in my judgment and ability to read polling data."

At least, as Gloria Steinem told me drily in 2009, the guys on the left were trying to deny any sexism. "It's a big step forward that they feel they have to hide it," she said. "In the old days, they did not."

✳ ✳ ✳

The reluctance to extend enlightened democratic thought to women's priorities, like so much else in 2008, stretched back hundreds of years, to Abigail Adams, who wrote to her husband in 1776, "Whilst you are proclaiming peace and good-will to men, emancipating all nations, you insist upon retaining an absolute power over wives." It recalled that terrible fissure between abolitionists and suffragists, and the words of Sojourner Truth, who observed at the meeting of the American Equal Rights Association in 1867, "There is a great stir about colored men getting their rights, but not a word about the colored women; and if colored men get their rights, and not colored women theirs, you see the colored men will be masters over the women, and it will be just as bad as it was before."

More immediately it evoked the 1960s, when women in antiwar, student, and civil rights movements realized that the freedoms and respect they were fighting for were not being applied to their own status within those groups in which they labored. The men gave the speeches, led the rallies, and wrote the manifestos, while women were called on for secretarial and sexual purposes. The 1966 annual meeting of Students for a Democratic Society was disrupted when women attempting to address gender inequity were pelted with tomatoes. The next year, when the vocal feminists Jo Freeman and Shulamith Firestone were among a group of women who rushed the stage to speak at the National Conference on New Politics, a male conference goer urged, "Cool down, little girl. We have more important things to talk about than women's problems." At a large antiwar rally organized to counter Richard Nixon's January 1969 inauguration, the SDS activist Marilyn Salzman Webb took to the stage and began, "We as women are oppressed." She plowed forward as rowdy lefties in the crowd heckled, "Take it off!" "Fuck her!" "Rape her in the back alley!"

The principles that guided the civil rights movement helped shape the feminism of many women, black and white. But in that movement too there was rampant sexism. Stokely Carmichael's infamous comment that "the only position for women in the SNCC is prone" may or may not have been meant seriously, but it nonetheless illustrated exactly what alarmed many women on the left in the 1960s and 1970s: in the civil rights and the later Black Power movement women were again the pamphleteers, typists, coffee brewers, and sexual outlets, while their radical brothers became the revolutionary heroes, a situation that, in conjunction with the racial exclusions of the feminist movement, helped give birth to womanism as well as predominantly female and black-run organizations like the

National Welfare Rights Organization, the National Black Feminist Organization, and the Combahee River Collective.

Robin Morgan's original "Goodbye to All That," published in the leftist paper *Rat,* excoriated "the male-dominated peace movement" and bid farewell "to the dream that being in the leadership collective will get you anything but gonorrhea." The groundbreaking rock critic and feminist Ellen Willis wrote in 1969, "A genuine alliance with male radicals will not be possible until sexism sickens them as much as racism. This will not be accomplished through persuasion, conciliation, or love, but through independence and solidarity. Radical men will stop oppressing us and make our fight their own when they can't get us to join them on any other terms."

Almost forty years after Willis's prediction, the generation of liberal thinkers that was reviving progressive activism online was finding contemporary gender resentments troublingly reminiscent of the 1960s and 1970s. In 2005 Markos Moulitsas, founder of the lefty blogging powerhouse *Daily Kos,* ran an advertisement on his site for the reality show *The Real Gilligan's Island*; the ad depicted scantily clad Gingers and Mary Anns throwing pies at each other. When some readers registered their opinion that the spot was degrading to women and therefore not appropriate for a progressive website, Moulitsas responded, "I find such humorless, knee-jerk reactions, to be tedious at best, sanctimonious and arrogant at worst." Claiming that he would not let "the sanctimonious women's studies set" control the content of his site, he continued, "Feel free to claim that I'm somehow abandoning 'progressive principles' by running the ad. . . . Feel free to storm off in a huff. . . . Me, I'll focus on the important shit." Moulitsas later withdrew his reference to "women's studies" but let the rest of his commentary stand. Here was a vivid expression of a modern online youth movement's attitude toward women, embodied by one of its most recognizable figureheads; it was a progressivism in which those who balked at the objectification of women were sanctimonious, humorless, and tedious, in which women's concerns about their representation did not count as "the important shit."

Former NOW vice president Latifa Lyles told me in 2009 about attending the 2007 Yearly Kos Convention. She was awed by the obvious importance accorded the gathering: every Democratic presidential candidate save Joe Biden was in attendance. The netroots movement had become so powerful that politicians understood they had to woo the blogosphere, a remarkable development. Lyles was impressed by the influence of a youthful, left-wing media that had not existed just a few years before. But she said, "It was mostly white men, even in this young group. It wasn't that [women] were not welcome. . . . It just felt weird. Here were all these people my age! This great power was being wielded by this incredibly power-ful youth group. And there were so few women represented. It felt like a missed opportunity."

Static between the online left and its female denizens was par-ticularly fierce because the blogosphere was born during the period during which the Democratic Party strategy for securing majori-ties in the House and Senate hinged in part on running anti-abor-tion Democrats. The idea was that if women could just stifle their impulse to prioritize reproductive rights, Democrats could stack Congress with lawmakers who would pass broadly progressive legislation that would benefit millions of Americans—*including women,* proponents of this strategy always hastened to add. Party loyalty would bar antichoice Dems from standing in the way of judi-cial appointments, women were assured, so no actual reproductive rights would be risked.

This scenario was not much fun for those who felt keenly that hard-won, always imperiled reproductive rights were central to women's freedom, equality, and ability to participate fully in the democracy. The choices were either playing nice as those rights got traded away, or raising a stink and getting cast as self-inter-ested enemies of the greater liberal good. The scheme was possi-ble only because it was assumed that Democratic women—thanks, ironically, to their social progressivism and commitment to issues of choice—would not leave the party; we had nowhere else to go. When NARAL, a group built around the fight for reproductive free-dom, chose to withhold support from the antichoice Democrat Jim Langevin in the 2006 Rhode Island Senate race and endorse pro-choice Republican Lincoln Chafee they earned the ire of the liberal blogosphere. "NARAL, and many people here, whined and cried about Langevin," wrote Moulitsas on *Daily Kos,* "the way they whined and cried about Harry Reid, because of those Democrats' personal opposition to abortion. Didn't we know, they demanded, that choice was a core principle of the Democratic Party? . . . The hell it is. . . . Single issue groups have hijacked [the Democratic Party] for their pet causes." This was how women with an investment in reproductive rights were cast by this new young left: as single-issue whiners too stupid and self-obsessed to understand the priorities of their own party. As Steinem told me in 2009, "Freedom of speech is also a single issue. Reproductive freedom is no less pervasive in its own impact than freedom of speech. A single issue is any issue not one's own, that's my theory."

In 2009 the impact of deemphasizing reproductive freedom in order to build a Democratic majority would be made manifest in the struggle to pass health care reform. Some of us had bought the line that if we just held our noses and voted for the antichoice Democrats, women and men of every stripe would benefit from the legislation they would pass. We were rewarded with purportedly "progressive" legislation that included proposals from both the House and the Senate for the sharpest curtailment of abortion rights since the Hyde Amendment, thanks to Democrats like Bart Stupak and Ben Nelson. The health care wrangling prompted some Democratic women to put their foot down at last. As Kate Harding wrote in *Salon* in 2010, "The party will not get a dime of my money as long as it could help a candidate who doesn't trust grown women to make their own medical decisions." Pamela Merritt, also known as the blogger Shark-Fu at *Angry Black Bitch*, told *Salon* at the end of 2009, "The woman of the year is the re-awakened feminist— the women who pulled together in coalition to protest Stupak and defeat Nelson, the women who are now organized to demand reproductive justice in a way that has never happened before." Women in the Senate threatened to vote down health care legislation if it included anti-abortion measures.

"I feel like individual women who were outraged [about Stupak] were a lot more engaged than they would have been prior to the 2008 election," said Women's Media Center head Jehmu Greene in 2009. Harding agreed, to some extent: "I think anti-Clinton bullshit woke some women up, though not enough." Even Moulitsas seemed to have thought further about the place of reproductive freedom in his party's politics. During the Stupak conflagration he urged readers to stop donating money to the Democratic Congressional Campaign Committee, in part because it was supporting Democrats who wanted to "get in the way of a patient and her doctor . . . on a LEGAL procedure." Instead, Moulitsas wrote, "give to those elected officials who best reflect your values."

☆ ☆ ☆

In the spring of 2008 a conveniently nongendered campaign narrative was getting cemented: Obama was the progressive candidate, Clinton practically a Republican. This assuredness was slightly confounding. Yes, Clinton was hawkish as she continued to chew her way through primary states, but she had the better health care plan and was talking more about economic policies that benefited the working class. It may have been true, as her critics snorted, that Clinton's dive toward populism was an example of pandering to her increasingly secure blue-collar base. I failed to see how that differed from Obama's playing to his privileged, educated base. Both candidates appeared to be consummate politicians. But my friends continued to swear that Obama was different and to issue cutting renunciations of Clinton's supposedly more centrist centrism. In April Markos Moulitsas agreed with a commenter who wrote, "It's bizarre, but I don't really consider [Clinton] a Dem anymore."

That didn't make sense to Mia Bruch, a thirty-three-year-old writer who would have voted for Obama but was foiled by a voting-roll snafu. Even though she was supporting him, the liberal Bruch felt a "great distance" from her partisan peers. "You already see this idealistic longing projected on Obama," she said. "People talk about him as a secular messiah who will bring us political salvation. There's no sense of what is plausible." Bruch pointed to health care: "Hillary's policy is the more politically progressive one, but this has somehow been ignored, and Obama was projected upon as the progressive redeemer."

The image recalled George Packer's observation in New Hampshire that Obama shed a forgiving light on the country itself. "At times," Packer wrote, describing a rally, "Obama almost seems to be trying to escape history, presenting himself as the conduit through which people's yearnings for national transformation can be realized." National transformation, yes, and also personal trans-formation. As the Obama-love threatened to break the bonds of reason in some of my peers, I was reminded of a woman I'd met on Super Tuesday standing outside the legendary Manhattan grocery store Zabar's holding an Obama sign. Sixty-two years old, white, a teacher of English as a second language, Kathy Kline gestured to the young people standing around her. Beaming, she grabbed my arm. "One of the great things about Obama's influence is that not *once* have I felt like an old white woman," she said to me.

After eight years of the Bush administration I understood the longing to once again feel pride and inspiration. More than that, I understood the value of electrifying the electorate. The possibil-ity of engaging generations and populations that had historically felt shut out of the political process was one of the only arguments that shook my strengthening Clinton support. But I wasn't sure that it was automatically more liberal than the mandated health care plan Hillary was proposing. It was fair and perhaps smart to prefer unifying inspiration over policy mechanics, but it was neither fair nor smart to pretend that the latter did not exist or didn't count. Obama's 2004 red states–blue states speech had been moving, but it was also a gracious invocation of centrism. His lyrical language made flesh would have looked a lot like Hillary's voting record. Kim Gandy, who was surprised by the often blind devotion to Hillary from some of her NOW constituents, was equally taken aback by others' idealization of Obama. "They're both moderates [but] they turned her into a warmonger and him into a peacenik," she said.

The *Sacramento Bee* published an article in January about a field organizer for Obama who instructed fellow volunteers to stay away from policy questions when talking to voters, instead focus-ing on "one of the campaign's key strategies: telling potential vot-ers personal stories of political conversion." Campaigners were told "to hone their own stories of how they came to Obama." Kathleen Geier, writing for *Talking Points Memo* on the same day she cast her vote for Obama, nonetheless reported being put off by the slav-ish devotion of her compatriots: "How can we truly bring about real political change if the movement the Obama people are build-ing is devoid of ideological content? . . . Such a movement becomes a cult of personality rather than [an] engine for social justice and

political transformation." Responding to the *Sacramento Bee* article, Geier observed that the language of "coming to Obama" was
"the language of evangelical Christianity. . . . But he's not Jesus!"

In late March Tom Hayden, Bill Fletcher, Jr., Danny Glover and
Barbara Ehrenreich wrote in the *Nation*, "All American progressives should unite for Barack Obama. . . . We take very seriously
the argument that Americans should elect a first woman President,
and we abhor the surfacing of sexism in this supposedly post-feminist era. But none of us would vote for Condoleezza Rice as either
the first woman or the first African-American president." As surely
as Gloria Steinem had substituted an imaginary Achola for Barack,
these avatars of political enlightenment were simply sliding in one
woman, one whose politics were in stark opposition to Clinton's, to
stand in for another woman they didn't like. Just as underhanded
was their calling forth a younger, more radical Clinton—a woman
who could never have maneuvered her way to the presidency with
her politics intact—as enemy to her older self: "We believe that the
Hillary Clinton of 1968 would be an Obama volunteer today, just
as she once marched in the snows of New Hampshire for Eugene
McCarthy against the Democratic establishment."

In Democratic circles Obama loyalty, like white masculinity
itself, had become normative. If you were a liberal and you were
not for him, that deviation was always—in the spirit of the Condoleezza Rice comparison—linked to politically empty harebrained
femininity. As Amanda Fortini wrote in *New York* magazine, "A
woman I interviewed described the atmosphere of Obama-Fascism
in her office: '[My male colleagues] feel only idiots would vote for
Hillary. There's this kind of total assumption that of course any
thinking person is voting for Obama.'"

Ashley Johnson, a senior at Princeton, was an undecided voter
leaning toward Obama. She told me, "If I did end up voting for
Hillary, people are making me feel like I am making a superficial
decision based on her gender." But, she continued, aside from the
fact that a vote for Hillary Clinton was not exclusively attributable
to some dank, pheromone-driven sisterhood, she had a real question about why, if the candidates were politically comparable, it
would be so bad to be pleased to vote for a woman. "If I did end up
voting for Hillary," said Johnson, "would part of me be very proud

that I was voting for the first female candidate? Yes." Like Johnson, I wondered when it had become so half-witted to want the cycle of white male presidential power to be broken by a woman.

Though his supporters often made clear that they were not voting for Obama *because* he was black, his race had been a factor in his decision to run for president. Jodi Kantor reported in the *New York Times Magazine* that when the Obamas first discussed the campaign with David Axelrod in 2006 Michelle had asked her husband, "What do you think you could accomplish that the other candidates couldn't?" Although, in Kantor's words, "an Obama agenda would not look very different from that of Hillary Clinton or John Edwards," Barack's response was, "When I take that oath of office, there will be kids all over this country who don't really think that all paths are open to them, who will believe they can be anything they want to be. . . . And I think the world will look at America a little differently." This was true. This was crucial. To acknowledge that an Obama presidency would represent the beginning of an overdue correction in long-standing underrepresentation, that it would change the scope of possibility for the millions of American children who were not white, to admit that these ideas informed a vote for him—none of that invalidated a simultaneous appreciation for his policy ideas or his leadership style.

☆ ☆ ☆

If progressives were failing to give women's history its due, it was hardly to be expected that the mainstream media would do any better on this score. Chris Matthews announced in February that one of Obama's speeches sent a "thrill going up [his] leg," while open disregard for Clinton and her supporters among even left-leaning commentators became ever more common as she defied their prognostications by continuing her primary march and winning big contests. The more Clinton upended the expectations of the boys on the bus, the more those boys reverted to Moose lodge–style japery toward her and her sex. It was no surprise to hear the conservative strategist Bill Kristol, appearing on *Fox News Sunday,* observe that "the only people [supporting Clinton] are the Democratic establishment and white women" and suggest that while Democrats would be crazy to follow their establishment, "white women are a problem. . . . We all live with that." It was more jarring to hear the NPR correspondent Juan Williams, brought in as Kristol's nominally liberal stooge, chuckle heartily at the joke. When the former *Boston Globe* columnist Mike Barnicle appeared on MSNBC's *Morning Joe* and joked that Clinton reacted to Obama "with just the look, the look toward him, looking like *everyone's* first wife standing outside of probate court," Joe Scarborough, Willie Geist, and guest host David Shuster laughed and laughed.

Newsweek's Jonathan Alter had kicked off pleas for Clinton to leave the race in February with a column headlined "Hillary Should Get Out Now," suggesting that quitting her campaign before the March 4 Ohio and Texas primaries would be the "graceful" choice, since he predicted high odds of Clinton "looking bad" in the two big state contests. Clinton won Ohio and Texas and was now profiting from a new self-image: the resilient fighter who would not back down, even when media men were pushing her to give up. What those media men could not grasp was that their belittling, butt-slapping approach to her was actually fueling her robust new persona. The more states Clinton won, the more loudly they mocked her and called for her to quit, the more they looked like heavies.

On MSNBC's *Tim Russert* in April, Russert asked Andrew Sullivan and Christopher Hitchens to comment on remarks Clinton had made about how she was not going to be "bullied out [of the race] by a bunch of guys." Their responses—about Clinton's "self-pity and self-righteousness," about how Sullivan could not be a misogynist because he'd admired Margaret Thatcher, about how Thatcher was a real feminist "in the sense that we're post gender"—were like a *Saturday Night Live* sketch in which boorish midcentury patriarchs, soaked in martinis and cigar smoke, reassured themselves that women's lib was really a passing trifle. Hitchens took particular delight in his role as caveman provocateur, saying of Clinton's "welling up and sobbing," "if she knew how it made her look . . . alternately soppy and bitchy, she'd stop it." They were trying desperately to ruffle feathers; it was unclear whether they knew that by doing so they were only strengthening Clinton's position. At the end of the segment Russert thanked both men "for writing and thinking and talking with intelligence."

In a postprimary article Michelle Goldberg, the Obama supporter who had expressed such anger at older feminists who disparaged the next generation, would concede that the media reaction to Clinton had been repugnant enough to catalyze female support. She acknowledged that it was difficult to watch "professional media types sing smitten fanboy hymns to Obama and, at the same time, spend hours dissecting Clinton's laugh and cleavage."

None of this meant that young women were swaying in time to the words of Robin Morgan; it merely demonstrated that the reactions to Clinton, especially from the left, were making as much or more of an impact on women who had thought, in part thanks to the liberal company they kept, that sexism was a thing of the past. Even more than the exhortations of second-wave feminists, the attitudes of Democratic men were eye-opening. As Fortini wrote in *New York* magazine, "The past few months have been like an extended consciousness-raising session, to use a retro phrase that would have once made most of us cringe. . . . This is, admittedly, depressing: *How can we be confronting the same issues, all these years later?* But it's also exciting. It feels as if a window has been opened in a stuffy, long-sealed room."

☆ ☆ ☆

As the candidates set up camp in Pennsylvania before the late-April primary, the politics of gender, race, and class were proving ever more complicated. Pennsylvania had a huge working-class population and was chock-full of seniors, two of Clinton's strongest demographics. In April the University of Pennsylvania scholar Adolph Reed wrote a piece for the *Progressive* titled "Obama No," in which he accused the Illinois senator of being "a vacuous opportunist, a good performer with an ear for how to make white liberals like him," and described the "disturbingly ritualistic and superficial" enthusiasm of young Obama supporters. I didn't share Reed's harsh perspective on Obama's candidacy, though I certainly agreed with him about Obamamania, and about something else he observed: "Increasingly, Obama supporters have been disposed to cry foul and charge racism at nearly any criticism of him, in steadily more extravagant rhetoric." As Obama supporters were ever more certainly avowing the progressive superiority of their candidate, they had fixed on another explanation (besides birdbrained female solidarity) for why people were still voting for Clinton: racism. Assumptions about the age, class, and whiteness of Clinton's base made it easy enough to assert that perhaps those who were supporting the woman were doing so in part because of an unwillingness to vote for a black person.

I hoped that Pennsylvania was a state that might challenge the ugly idea that Clinton's late-primary surges were fueled largely by racial intolerance. In eastern Pennsylvania Clinton support was multiracial, led by Philadelphia's then very popular African American mayor, Michael Nutter. Nutter wasn't just backing Clinton. Like Reed, he was openly disdainful of Obama. "This is not the Martin Luther King oratorical contest," he told *Bloomberg News* in late March. "It's a contest for president of the United States." But the Pennsylvania primary wound up challenging what was fast becoming my own idealization of Clinton and her supporters.

In April political reporters were running stories describing how exhausted the electorate was by the ongoing primary battle; Democratic pundits were agonizing over the money being spent by two Democrats working to expose each other's weaknesses. But on the weekend before the primary an improbably merry Hillary Clinton was shouting "Isn't this exciting?" to a crowded high school gymnasium in Bethlehem, Pennsylvania. "We love you!" came a young female voice from somewhere in the bleachers at the precise moment that paramedics wheeled in an empty stretcher. For one discombobulating second I wondered if the rally might have produced an Obama-esque scenario in which a twitterpated youngster collapsed in Beatlemaniac ecstasy for her candidate. The stretcher was actually for a middle-aged guy who'd had a brief diabetic episode, but the fact that the possibility had even crossed my mind was testament to the buzzing enthusiasm that characterized many of Hillary's spring events. This renewed exhilaration contradicted the fretful story line about how everyone was sick of the election and how John McCain was growing stronger while Democrats grew weary.

Clinton's packed Bethlehem gathering, on the heels of a rally drawing thirty-five thousand for Obama in Philadelphia, suggested that many people were actually thrilled that the choice was ongoing.

The mechanics of the primary system typically meant that presidential races were tied up after a few early contests. That was great for candidates who wanted to rest up and amass money before the general election, and for political parties eager to avoid the appearance of internal strife. But quick nomination battles were less salubrious for voters who lived outside of Iowa, New Hampshire, or perhaps, in a lucky year, the Super Tuesday states. Those people rarely had a chance to watch their votes make an impact on their party's nomination. This lengthy season was allowing voters to evaluate and engage with the candidates, arguably increasing their investment in those candidates for the general election. Perhaps more vitally it was forcing the candidates to engage with voters—to listen to them, visit with them, hold their babies, and hear their stories, and while they were at it lay down campaign apparati that would come in useful in the fall—all around the country, not just in the few states with early primaries.

The stretched race was transforming the candidates. Obama, something of a delicate flower going into the primaries, quick to pout and easily injured, was toughening up. And Clinton, who had approached her early campaign with the muscular determination of a Clydesdale, seemed to have recovered a bit of the freewheeling what-the-hell attitude that had served her well in New Hampshire. In early April she finally demoted Mark Penn; the well-liked pollster and strategist Geoff Garin was now at the helm alongside Howard Wolfson and Hillaryland stalwart Maggie Williams, who had taken Solis Doyle's job in February. Clinton was flashing snap and smile on the stump, plainly enjoying her role as plucky underdog. Losing the burden of inevitability had loosened her up and given her something to fight for: a nomination most people understood to be *just* beyond her grasp, that could in turn translate into a message about how she was fighting for people. She was making whooping campaign promises to big blue-collar crowds who cheered her on. She had also gotten better at appealing to women; she wasn't selling herself explicitly as a feminist champion, but her role as hard-working populist long shot offered female voters another way to embrace her as a symbolic heroine.

Roles had flipped somewhat, especially with working-class voters: now Clinton was the candidate with emotional appeal and

Obama was cast as the thinker. "She wasn't a cerebral 'have hope' candidate," said EMILY's List Ellen Malcolm. "She was conveying: 'I get it. I know what health care reform means to you. I know why you're scared about the college education system for your kids. I know that you want investment in jobs.' The Obama message of change in many ways was a very cerebral message that resonated with people wanting a different kind of politics. . . . But when it came down to brass tacks about who was going to make a difference, Hillary being scrappy and showing her expertise [made people believe] that she's the one who's going to fight for me."

"By the time we hit Pennsylvania, she was in charge of her own campaign," Ann Lewis told me in 2010. "We went out with less money [than Obama] and did a woman-centered campaign." Lewis said she was prouder of her work with women in Pennsylvania than anywhere else; rather than concentrating exclusively on the western parts of the state, Lewis and her team focused on the suburban counties surrounding Philadelphia that were tougher to take from Obama, playing up the campaign's "The Hillary I Know" approach, in which friends and associates testified to Clinton's humanity. It had been a fixture of the campaign since the start, but was put into full effect in Pennsylvania, bolstered now by a candidate who was increasingly comfortable showing off that humanity.

Much would be made of Clinton's negative campaigning in Pennsylvania, but I wasn't watching her television ads. I was listening to her address crowds, a warmer and more talented speaker than she'd been at the start. She was talking about ending tax cuts for those making over $250,000 a year, bringing back manufacturing jobs, going after student loan companies, forgiving school debt for those who went into nursing, teaching, and law enforcement. I wasn't just defensive about Clinton anymore; I was more excited than I could have imagined about her candidacy, her insistence on staying in the race, the fact that people all over the country were seeing a woman and a black man compete to be president.

On the night before the primary I heard Chelsea Clinton tell eight thousand people packed into the University of Pennsylvania's Palestra basketball arena that her mother would be a better president than her father because "she's not only more progressive but more prepared than he was." Someone in a presidential campaign was crowing about being "more progressive"! My brother and I took my mother to that rally, and we watched her watch Hillary speak; she was so pleased to be seeing this woman run for president, so pleased that she'd be able to vote for her the next morning. I wished I could be less sentimental about how watching women's history refracted through my mother's eyes made me feel, but I couldn't. It made me so happy.

If my euphoria in April was comparable to the level of Obama fanaticism I deplored, it came with the knowledge that there was no good way for it to end. Obama-lovers could pray without equivocation for their candidate to fly straight on till morning. I could cross my fingers all I wanted about Clinton's upward trajectory, could celebrate her turn to the left. But I knew, on some level, that even if she found a way to pull it off she would be hated for it. I also knew that there was very little chance of a win that would be accepted as legitimate. There was already too much rumbling from the Clinton camp and Clinton supporters about the ethically bankrupt idea of counting votes from unofficial primaries in Michigan and Florida. Meddling with superdelegate counts and illegitimate primaries was no way to win an election.

I also could not shake a memory of waiting to listen to Clinton in Bethlehem. While most of the crowd had assured me that they loved Hillary but would be thrilled to vote for Obama if he became the nominee, a woman named LeeAnne followed up on her husband's assertion that "Obama has some decent things to say" by noting, "I don't even know what his name is. Bahama Mama? Osama?" As LeeAnne spoke the crowd around her shifted uncomfortably. One man said firmly, "His name is Barack Obama." LeeAnne looked abashed. "Fine. I'll learn it," she said. "I just love Hillary. I love everything about her. And I heard that what's-his-name doesn't salute the American flag." At this about half a dozen people in line corrected her misapprehensions about Obama's patriotism. "That's just not the case, and you shouldn't believe gossip about him being a Muslim, either," said a woman wearing two Hillary buttons. "Even if he were Muslim, that's no reason not to vote for him," said a man named Charles Johns, who said he was an Obama supporter but was there to hear Hillary anyway.

After that, even in those weeks that I was feeling my most unrestrained appreciation for Hillary, I caught myself looking at some impassioned Hillary supporters with suspicion. On primary morning a thirtysomething white woman drove into the parking lot of the polling station where I was reporting, yelling out her car window, "I wanna vote for Hillary! I'm a Republican, but I want to vote for Hillary!" Instead of considering that this woman's zeal demonstrated that a hunger for female political leadership stretched beyond the Democratic Party, I stiffened. Maybe she was racist. Later that day, in a working-class Catholic neighborhood north of Philadelphia, Hillary voters told me that they would not vote for Obama because "there was something about him" they didn't trust.

Some of what I saw in Pennsylvania forced me to acknowledge that imputations of racism among Clinton supporters were as warranted as my own attribution of misogynistic impulses to some Obama voters. The very defenses I offered up about Clintonites—we were progressives who wanted the same things Obama supporters did, why should our commitments to social justice be called into question?—were precisely in tune with the "I can't be sexist, I'm a liberal" line coming from my uterus-punching Democratic compatriots.

The crucial question was how much Clinton and Obama themselves were stirring up, or capitalizing on, the prejudices of their supporters. Some of the charges thrown at Clinton strained the limits of credulity. In May she would defend her choice to stay in the race by noting, "My husband did not wrap up the nomination in 1992 until he won the California primary somewhere in the middle of June, right? We all remember Bobby Kennedy was assassinated in June in California." The reference was read by some as suggesting that perhaps Obama would be killed before the convention, an interpretation that I found implausible and unfair. But others were angry and bewildered simply at the fact that Clinton would unnecessarily summon the memory of Kennedy's tragic murder in the context of a fraught and historic political contest. "This is completely inappropriate in light of the fact that hate groups and white supremacists are . . . increasing the threat rhetoric," wrote Pam Spaulding at *Pam's House Blend*. "Why stoke the crazies even more with this kind of (presumably) careless remark?"

It was undeniable that some of the most egregious comments about Obama's race had come not just from Clinton supporters, but

from her friends and associates, including Bob Kerrey, Billy Shaheen and Andrew Cuomo. Clinton had not walked out of the room
when Bob Johnson made comparisons between Obama and Sid-
ney Poitier, and she had not harshly repudiated Geraldine Ferraro.
Maybe she'd been reluctant to publicly excoriate an ill woman in
whose footsteps toward executive office she alone had so far followed. But the fact remained that her gentle admonishment did not
telegraph distance from or disgust with Ferraro's remarks. More-
over the desire to profit from American racism and xenophobia had
been written into the Clinton campaign's DNA, evidenced by Mark
Penn's March 2007 memo, in which he wrote that he could not
"imagine America electing a president during a time of war who is
not at his center fundamentally American in his thinking and in his
values." In May Clinton would comment to *USA Today* that her
opponent's support among "hard-working Americans, white Americans," was weakening. One of my favorite bloggers, Shark-Fu from
Angry Black Bitch, wrote in response, "I've lost respect for this
woman, her candidacy and the entire Clinton legacy. . . . I lift this
vodka cran in a toast to the most amazing free fall from inspiring
politician to complete gaping asshole of my lifetime. You've come a
long way baby will forever have new meaning."

There were questions, though, about why Clinton was drawing
so much flack for her missteps while Obama's gaffes drew so little.
Paul Krugman wrote in the *New York Times* about "the inability
of many alleged progressives to see that the news media created the
narrative of Hillary Clinton as race-baiter in much the same way
that . . . they created the narrative of Al Gore as congenital liar—by
assembling a montage of quotes taken out of context and willfully
misinterpreted." It may or may not have been true that some Clinton comments were taken out of context or misinterpreted. What
was certainly true was that Pecksniffian sanctimony over the purity
of Barack Obama's campaign glossed right over many of that campaign's own imperfections.

"The unctuousness, the holier-than-thou-ness of some of these
people really annoyed me," said Gloria Feldt in 2009. "As if Barack
Obama has always been totally pure. What are they smoking? The
man came out of Chicago politics, for god's sake." It helped that
Obama was a much better apologizer than Hillary was. When a

memo from his campaign referred to Hillary as the Democrat from "Punjab" (a reference to her many Indian donors), Obama promptly apologized. When his advisor Samantha Power, the Pulitzer Prize–winning genocide expert, gave an interview to the *Scotsman* and said of Hillary, "She is a monster, too—that is off the record. . . . You just look at her and think, 'Ergh,'" the Obama campaign issued a statement decrying her comments and Powers resigned immediately. But apologia and self-correction flatter a man more than they do a woman. As the linguistics professor and writer Deborah Tannen pointed out in a 1996 essay, when it was reported in 1995 that Hillary had expressed remorse about the impact of her health care plan on her husband's administration, she was criticized by a political scientist who said, "To apologize for substantive things you've done raises the white flag," and by a woman in Florida's state cabinet who snipped, "I've seen women who overapologize, but . . . I believe you negotiate through strength."

Obama supporters legitimately attacked Hillary's infamous "3 a.m." ad, depicting vulnerable children in their beds, for its fear-mongering negativity. But a January Obama campaign mailer employed those same alarmist tactics against Clinton's health care plan. The brochure showed a white couple sitting at a kitchen table, sorting through bills. "Hillary's health care plan forces everyone to buy insurance, even if you can't afford it," read the text. A few critics did notice; Ezra Klein pointed out that Obama had practically reanimated "Harry and Louise" from the deadly anti–health care ads of 1993, and Paul Krugman wrote, "I know that Obama supporters want to hear no evil, but this is really, really bad." On MSNBC's *Morning Joe* in March Zbigniew Brzezinski, an Obama supporter and former national security advisor to Jimmy Carter, compared Clinton's record of international diplomatic travel to the number of countries visited by his travel agent, and asked, "[If John Kennedy in 1960] had been running not against Nixon but against Mamie Eisenhower, would someone say that Mamie Eisenhower is better prepared to be president than John Kennedy?" Still, it was Hillary who was publicly branded as the negative campaigner with the rogue surrogates.

In February Obama gave a speech at Tulane in which he said of Clinton's campaign attacks, "You challenge the status quo and suddenly the claws come out," a characterization he might not have made about a man. Not long after that Obama told a reporter, "I understand that Senator Clinton, periodically when she's feeling down, launches attacks as a way of trying to boost her appeal." This evocation of a woman "periodically . . . feeling down" piqued the interest of some female television reporters, including Norah O'Donnell, who said, "It's getting a little personal," and Andrea Mitchell, who concurred and added, "Frankly, you know how deeply we interpreted every comment to look for some sort of racial motivation. . . . When you start describing a female candidate as being 'down' and 'striking back' . . . that's a little edgy, don't you think?"

One of the more ineffable complaints about Obama was that his team was a little too masculine, a little too fratty for comfort. Like Clinton's, Obama's campaign was designed by men; but unlike Clinton's, it was also largely staffed by men. With the crucial exceptions of Valerie Jarrett and later Anita Dunn, his closest advisors and strategists were men, and the vibe of the campaign, as described by both reporters covering it and those who did business with it, was clubby, sports-obsessed, and testosterone-fueled. Conversation within the ranks was dotted with "buddy" and "man"—dude talk, the kind of back-slapping repartee in which men, including some of the men in the media, could participate, but to which women found no easy entrance. There would be a spate of stories in September 2008 about how women working for Obama in the Senate made an average of 83 cents for every dollar made by men working in the same office. The numbers were misleading, but the explanation for the wage discrepancy was not particularly comforting: the average female salary was lower than the average male salary not because women were being paid less for the same jobs, but because they were not in the highest-level and best-remunerated positions. Of Obama's five highest paid staffers, only one was female, and only seven of his top twenty.

In May Peggy Agar, a reporter for a Detroit ABC affiliate station, approached Obama during his visit to the Chrysler LLC plant, asking, "Senator, how are you going to help the American autoworkers?" Obama waved Agar off, saying, "Hold on one second, sweetie." The clip gained YouTube traction, and within hours Obama left a

message for Agar apologizing for failing to answer her question and
for referring to her as "sweetie." He called his use of the word "a bad
habit." His apology was timely and polite, but he was right: he had a
"sweetie" habit. He had addressed a female factory worker in Allen-
town, Pennsylvania, by the same diminutive, and ABC soon found
footage of him telling one female supporter, "Sweetie, if I start with
a picture I will never get out of here," and another, "Sweetie, if I
start doing autographs, I won't be able to get [out]."

The remark generated the opposite of outrage from the media: on
Good Morning America a practically purring Diane Sawyer asked,
"Don't you think it's going too far to care about that stuff?" Actually, no, it was not going too far to care about that stuff. To care
about it did not mean that people should have changed their votes
or their minds about Obama or his candidacy. But caring about
that stuff was the only way to understand how language can convey diminishment, whether that diminishment is based on gender,
race, age, or power. "Sweetie"—redolent of sugar and spice and all
the rest of that stuff little girls are supposed to be made of—was an
endearment. It was a warm word. Many women, myself included,
enjoyed being called "sweetie" by people they cared about. That did
not mean that we would have enjoyed being addressed that way by a
presidential candidate, especially in response to a question about the
future of American autoworkers, and especially when the word was
part of a larger professional brush-off. Was it the most sexist thing
a man could say to a woman? Certainly not. But whereas racially
inflected remarks from Clinton had been pored over and parsed, the
media seemed eager to sidestep the fact that Obama's reliance on
the "sweetie" diminutive reflected some basic patriarchal attitudes.
Much of the defensive maneuvering happened around the question
of whether his elocution was premeditated or malevolent. Surely it
was neither. As Whoopi Goldberg said on *The View,* the senator
likely "meant . . . no disrespect." But good intentions don't render
anyone incapable of disrespect or condescension, any more than a
good record on race rendered Bill Clinton incapable of disrespect
and condescension. Words are often both spontaneous *and* sexist.

The merry masculinity of Obama and his team was shrugged
off as no big deal, but it was persistent enough to continue to draw
attention after the primaries and into his administration. When, in

December of 2008, photos surfaced of Obama's wunderkind speech-writer Jon Favreau groping the breast of a cardboard cutout of Hillary, he apologized but was not publicly reprimanded or dismissed by his boss; he was hired to work in the White House. Less than a year into Obama's presidency the *New York Times* ran a front-page story about the president's habit of playing golf and basketball with high- and midlevel male staff members. The sports-heavy, lady-light vibe of an Obama White House made critics uncomfortable. While the choice of how and with whom to blow off steam might seem an awfully benign thing to get bent out of shape over, this was precisely the kind of pastime that throughout history had ensured the unceasing replication of patriarchal power structures. The ones who play ball, golf, cards, who smoke cigars and drink bourbon while speaking informally of power and policy are the ones who have the boss's ear, who understand him best and can manipulate him most successfully.

Barack Obama, the man with a silver tongue but a tin ear for lots of things having to do with women, should have known this but apparently didn't. He called the controversy about his all-boys basketball games "bunk," and in the words of reporter Mark Leibovich, he defended himself against the notion that the time spent with male advisors sent any kind of message in part by "point[ing] out that he is surrounded by strong females at home." This was an argument that not only echoed one made by George W. Bush's female adherents, who had equated respecting women with being henpecked by them, but also stank of long-entrenched sexism. Of course Obama was surrounded by women at home: that is one of the oldest gendered circumstances known to humankind; women at home are where they have always been. The question Leibovich and many of Obama's critics were getting at was where the women were *at work*.

My soreness over "sweetie" had less to do with the remark itself than with the determination to not acknowledge that it might reflect a societal approach to gender and power that was fundamental to why we had never had a strong female presidential contender before, just as comments about Obama's name signified the obstacles that long had come between African Americans and the presidency. But giving voice to these ruminations would only further flesh out an image of me as a finger-wagging L. L. Bean shopper affixing a Hillary '08 sticker to my Camry. Reciprocally, when I encountered odes to Obama's greatness, visions of dorm rooms humid with bong water and bedecked with Shepard Fairey posters floated into my head. We Democrats had become George Bush's soldiers, divided into "for us or against us" camps; nothing blurred our focus on our chosen candidates. I found myself fighting with Merideth, the friend who had first railed to me about how deplorably Clinton was being treated early in the race. Now Merideth spoke angrily about Clinton's answer to Steve Kroft's question on *60 Minutes,* about whether Obama was a Muslim. I had heard Clinton's immediate response, "Of course not," as definitive. Merideth had heard her later answer to Kroft's repetitions of the question, "No, there is nothing to base that on as far as I know," as equivocal.

I disagreed with the press's notion that the prolonged race was damaging the candidates, but I certainly noticed the toll it was taking on my affections for my fellow Democrats. American liberalism, unconsciously unfriendly to powerful women. American feminism, unconsciously unfriendly to African Americans. What was fascinating was the nearly identical rhythm of the unfriendliness in both camps: the vague doubts, something that the speaker could not quite articulate that made him or her distrust Obama or despise Clinton. There was the valid sense from Clinton supporters that people didn't sling racial epithets as easily as they called women bitches, that nobody joked about watermelons and fried chicken with the get-a-sense-of-humor brio attached to PMS and castration jokes. And the equally valid sense from Obama supporters that racism toward Obama was deeper, more insidious than what could be put on a bumper sticker, that Hillary's privileged racial and economic caste meant she could probably handle the period jokes. As Obama's former pastor Jeremiah Wright summed up, "Hillary ain't never been called a nigger." Both sides saw themselves in competition; they rarely realized how much they echoed each other. Baratunde Thurston, the blogger whom Latoya Peterson stopped reading during the primaries, wrote about his retrospective revelation that much of what offended him about how Obama was discussed closely resembled what offended female Hillary supporters. "I had an epiphany," he wrote, "*that which I most dislike about the darker sides of her and her campaign is just what some people see in me....* I spent hours and days even, researching all the race-baiting and ugliness going on in the media and among Clinton folks, but I never bothered to try to find out what was driving some of Hillary's staunchest supporters."

During the race, despite some agitation from within her camp and much clamoring from her supporters, Clinton did not give what was referred to within the campaign as "the women's speech," in which she would address with depth and nuance her place in history and women's relationship to power and public life. Clinton held back because she and her advisors understood the risks. Ann Lewis told me in 2010, "I just thought she was going to get beat up again. No way was Chris Matthews going to say he's going to get a thrill up his leg. They would just have said, 'Every time she's in trouble, she plays the gender card.' It was painful because so many of our friends and supporters hoped that she would do it. They wanted her to speak up for them as only she could. But it wouldn't have been in her best interest." Then there was the fact that Obama had given his speech on race in response to controversy over the sermons of Jeremiah Wright. "We didn't have a natural hook," Clinton advisor Lissa Muscatine told me in 2009. "We didn't want to do it in response to the race speech. The struggle was how to do it in a way that was compelling and substantive but also not regarded as 'Oh, he did the race speech, now she's going to do a woman speech.'"

But during Clinton's victory speech in Philadelphia on April 22 she offered an almost Obama-style articulation of how this often painful process was moving the nation forward. She noted that her victory party was taking place in the city where the country's founders had set down a vision for democracy's future, a vision in which "neither Senator Obama nor I were fully included." Citing abolitionists, suffragists, unionists, and all those who had ever marched and protested—the predecessors of those who were now campaigning and fighting and yelling at each other—Clinton said, "because of them, I grew up taking for granted that women could vote. Because of them, my daughter grew up taking for granted that children of all colors could attend school together." And now, Clinton continued, children will grow up "taking for granted that a woman or an African American can be the president of the United

States of America." She seemed to see the other side. This hell, she was saying, was worth it.

* * *

True to form, the media did not react to Clinton's Pennsylvania win by sending her flowers. Instead her victory seemed to elicit an unprecedented wave of aggression. The calls for her to drop out became pointed, propelled now by serious alarm: her insistence on competing and winning against Obama was making him look bad. In *Time* Joe Klein criticized her insubstantial attack tactics against Obama, claiming that they had damaged her reputation, but that "that was nothing compared with the damage done to Obama, who entered the primary as a fresh breeze and left it stale, battered and embittered . . . no longer the darling of his party." In addition to the questions about his pastor and insinuations about his relationship with former Weatherman Bill Ayers, it was during the Pennsylvania primary race that Obama had been quoted at a fund-raiser saying that those Americans who clung to their guns and their religion were bitter. It was, by rational measures, an ultimately compassionate observation about those who had been economically devastated by Reaganism and then by two Bush administrations, but it had not gone over well with blue-collar folks, especially because on the campaign trail, as Klein noted, Obama "seemed to look on the ceremonies of working-class life—bowling, hunting, churchgoing and the fervent consumption of greasy food—as his anthropologist mother might have, with a mixture of cool detachment and utter bemusement." Obama's difficulty connecting with working-class America was beginning to cause Democrats concern about the general election. And they were blaming Hillary for it.

It was true that the Clinton camp had thrown some stones. But since when was it owed to any candidate that he or she escape the dents and dings of political competition? Just as voters and commentators had considered the impact on Hillary's electability of her abysmal strategic team, her personal and political baggage and her early trouble connecting with voters, it was now fair to evaluate how Obama performed as his opponent got stronger, as he accumulated baggage of his own, as he lost the glint of tender newness.

But pundits were sure it was incumbent on Hillary to drop out. When they fantasized about her exit in January it was because she had lost Iowa. When Jonathan Alter suggested she drop out in February it was because she was likely to be humiliated in upcoming big contests. Now that it was Obama who was losing and being humiliated, the prescription, oddly, remained the same: Hillary had to go. It was a media barrage that Melissa McEwan dubbed "Take Your Boobs and Go Home."

A *New York Times* op-ed castigating Clinton for running negative ads about Obama in Pennsylvania suggested, "It is getting to be time for the superdelegates to . . . settle a bloody race that cannot be won at the ballot box." Maureen Dowd nudged Hillary to take a cue from an old Dr. Seuss poem that the children's author had in 1974 applied to Richard Nixon. Dowd's verse went, in part, "The time is now. Just go. . . . I don't care how. You can go by foot. You can go by cow. Hillary R. Clinton, will you please go now!" On *Countdown*, *Newsweek*'s Howard Fineman suggested that it was time for "some adults somewhere in the Democratic Party to step in and stop this thing." Keith Olbermann agreed, saying, "Right . . . somebody who can take her in a room and only he comes out," a comment that led the *Huffington Post* columnist Rachel Sklar to headline an item "Olbermann's Idea for Beating Hillary: Literally Beating Hillary." Olbermann later apologized for his remark, calling it "a metaphor."

More arresting was an appearance by Ken Rudin on *CNN Sunday Morning* in late April, in which the NPR political editor said, "Let's be honest here, Hillary Clinton is Glenn Close in *Fatal Attraction*. She's going to keep coming back, and they're not going to stop her." In evoking Close's character Rudin was summoning a bunny-boiling virago whose bullet-riddled demise in a bathtub represented one of the most graphic cinematic punishments of aggressive femininity available to the American imagination. So outrageous was Rudin's comparison that it prompted *Sunday Morning* cohost Betty Nguyen to suggest, in response to Rudin's admission that he'd been partying all night at the White House Correspondents Dinner, "Maybe that explains the Glenn Close analogy." Rudin later apologized, claiming he wished he hadn't made the "facile and dumb comparison." But he had created a meme. Two weeks later Tennessee Con-

gressman Steve Cohen, an Obama supporter whom Nancy Pelosi
once called "the conscience of the freshman class," was asked about
Clinton's presence in the race and replied, "Glenn Close should have
just stayed in the tub." It was as if the id of every guy who had built
up resentments toward powerful women had staged a coup against
the superego, making it open season not just on Clinton, but on
all noncompliant women. Penn Jillette heartily joked on MSNBC's
Morning Joe in May, "Obama did great in February, and that's
because that was Black History Month. And now Hillary's doing
much better because it's White Bitch Month, right?"

Only a few people were calling foul. At *Media Matters* Eric
Boehlert wrote, "Looking back through modern U.S. campaigns,
there's simply no media model for so many members of the press to
try to drive a competitive candidate from the field while the primary
season is still unfolding. . . . Strong second place candidates such
as Ronald Reagan (1976), Ted Kennedy, Gary Hart, Jesse Jackson, and Jerry Brown, all of whom campaigned through the entire
primary season, and most of whom took their fights all the way
to their party's nominating conventions, were never tagged by the
press and told to go home."

The media was not presenting the fight between Clinton and
Obama as a norm for close presidential races. Instead we were being
told that in continuing to compete with him, in not letting him just
win, Clinton was behaving like a headstrong child or a demented
movie villain. Here were echoes of the strategies that in recent years
had bedeviled reproductive rights activists faced with one antichoice
Democrat after another. Couldn't they see that in prosecuting their
own self-interested aims they were imperiling the greater good?
That if they would just stand down, Democrats would win, which
would be good for everyone, *including women,* but that if they continued to make their self-serving stand we would wind up under
Republican control and everyone would suffer, because of *them*? As
with the siren song about antichoice Democrats, this argument was
painful for those of us on the other side of it. *Of course* we wanted
a Democratic president and a Democratic majority. *We were liberals,* or Democrats, or radicals, or progressives, or whatever we
called ourselves, who were invested in reproductive rights or in the
Clinton campaign precisely because we cared about liberal politics,

because we believed fervently in making the country a better place for more people. It felt almost sadistic, the maneuverings of those who would trade on our rights or dismiss our candidate early and then accuse us of undermining a progressive agenda.

☆ ☆ ☆

My birthday, May 6, was the day Clinton lost North Carolina and won Indiana by a margin so slender that it was clear that this was, truly, the end. At a restaurant with three longtime girlfriends, conversation was strained; two of us were for Clinton, the other two for Obama. We would each start to talk and then cut ourselves off, not wanting to argue when we were supposed to be celebrating. Partway through the meal I checked my phone and saw the night's results. The reality of Clinton's fate began to settle heavy in my belly.

As we walked home after dinner, Geraldine, the friend with whom I'd started down this road four months earlier, tried to talk me out of my funk, explaining how much better I would feel once I made the inevitable switch of allegiance to Obama, how good it felt to support him, how much easier it was than backing Hillary. All I heard was a pod person, someone talking to me from the other side of the invasion of the body snatchers: Just give in; it's so much easier this way. I nodded, understanding that soon I would be a pod person too, that my frustrations would subside. I just wasn't ready to go there yet.

On the day of the last Democratic primaries, in Montana and South Dakota, Hillary Clinton was running for the Democratic nomination pretty much in name only. When my colleague Caitlin Shamberg, a video producer at *Salon,* and I tried to check in for her New York speech that evening—usually an arduous process of negotiating with officious campaign staffers—her press people practically threw our credentials at us. They were not laminated or hung on lanyards as per usual; they were simply pieces of paper on twine. I thought of Monty Python's dead parrot sketch: Hillary '08 had shuffled off its mortal coil, rung down the curtain, and joined the bleeding choir invisible. It was an ex-campaign.

When Hillary finally arrived at the lectern she gave her preconcession speech. She thanked South Dakota, which she had won. She congratulated her "friend" Obama, who she said "inspired so many Americans to care about politics and empowered so many more to get involved, and our party and our democracy [are] stronger and more vibrant as a result." She spoke of "mothers and fathers lifting their little girls and their little boys onto their shoulders and whispering, 'See, you can be anything you want to be.'" The crowd shouted, "Denver! Denver!" and she did not rebuke them. She said that the next day was her mother's birthday. She said she was going to take a day or two, confer with advisors. She suggested that her supporters visit HillaryClinton.com, a plea for help in paying down her monster campaign debt. There was a friendliness and a camaraderie about her speech, a weary but warm sense that those in the room had been through a lot together. Clinton was commencing the delicate process of turning her enormous ship around. As we walked out of the building, Caitlin, an Obama supporter from the beginning, said to me, "That speech made me like her more than I ever have before. It almost makes me wish she *would* take it to Denver. She's way more fun than I ever thought she'd be." I went home and went to bed, feeling flat and resigned, already pulling away from the campaign, distancing myself from the avidity I'd somehow generated for Hillary and her presidential project.

When I logged on to my computer the next morning there were three hundred emails from Obama-supporting readers, friends, and colleagues, all expressing barely cogent rage at Hillary. She had not conceded! She had not given Obama his night, his moment in the sun! She had held her speech in a building without cell phone service to keep reporters from learning that she had lost the primaries! She was plotting to use the superdelegate system to steal the nomination! She was going to destroy the party and the country in her preening bid for monomaniacal power!

This would be the last moment of the primary during which I felt as though I inhabited a different planet than everyone else in my party, that I had heard a different speech, seen a different person, been in a different room than everyone else. But I can't say that I was unhappy that they had heard what they did. If they thought Hillary was telling them to fuck off, that was okay with me. For just one last day, before I joined their ranks, I wanted them to fuck off too.

8 THINGS TO DO IN DENVER IF YOU'RE FEMALE

Four days after Hillary Clinton's un-concession I dragged myself out of bed at the crack of dawn on a Saturday to travel to D.C. to watch her throw in the towel for real. I dressed in jeans and a ratty T-shirt, a sign of how much I didn't care about this event. But somewhere along the northeast corridor, as I began a draft of what would be my coverage of the speech, I wondered if maybe when I got to Union Station I shouldn't buy a nicer shirt. My sartorial reconsideration was not singular; when the train pulled in, several grouchy New York reporters hit Tiecoon and Express, searching for garments that conveyed something closer to respect than what they'd pulled on that morning. I can't say that my hastily purchased black button-down shirt (its material suitable for protecting human life during reentry into the Earth's atmosphere) will ever see daylight again, but it still hangs in my closet, and I think of Hillary whenever I catch sight of it there.

Clinton had spent days trying to figure out what she was going to say. Her advisors were split between those who believed she needed to emphasize her endorsement of Obama and those who felt she must, at last, truly address the women who had supported her. Speech-writer Sarah Hurwitz was caught in between. "I think [Hillary] was thinking it through herself," said Ann Lewis. "What she wanted to accomplish, what she wanted people to remember about her." Lissa Muscatine was arguing on the side of the ladies. "This was obviously a speech that was going to be parsed over and over again and psychoanalyzed by the press. . . . It was going to be a historic moment," she told me in 2009. "To me, the most important thing was that it be genuine, both in conceding to and endorsing Obama, and in conveying to the eighteen million people who supported her, especially women, that the end of her campaign didn't mean she was abandoning them. I felt you could do both in one speech." Muscatine continued, "I felt strongly—vehemently, actually—that she had to speak directly to women and let them know that she was not simply going to recede into the woodwork and become acqui-escent about these issues because she lost the race." Muscatine was concerned that this had not been reflected in early drafts of the speech and wrote Clinton a long memo about it. "These people had come out for her in droves, especially in the last months of the campaign. Their hearts and emotions were tied up in the campaign, and her loss was shattering for many of them. They were counting on her. I really felt she had a duty and obligation to speak to those women even as she was endorsing Obama." There were big argu-ments within the campaign. Clinton's strategist Geoff Garin pushed strongly for keeping the emphasis on Obama; her aide Jim Kennedy contributed a sentence about 18 million cracks in a glass ceiling. At some point Hillary wrested control of her own speech, staying up all night to rewrite it and find the balance between Barack Obama and her campaign's place in women's history. The morning of her speech, hours before she was to give her address, some advisors were still pressing her to cut the parts about gender.

The National Building Museum was air-conditioned, but it couldn't keep the scalding heat from seeping in. The throng inside the large room glistened, their faces slick with perspiration and, even before Clinton began speaking, some tears.

When she took the podium Clinton issued a lengthy round of thank-yous before turning to her final task as presidential contender, rallying her supporters to her opponent's cause. She was, as she had always been, a good girl. She praised Obama, yelled "Yes, we can!" with a convincing show of enthusiasm, and did her damnedest to start a slightly lame and wordy chant: "We must help elect Barack Obama our president!"

But then she took a moment, the moment many of her supporters had been longing for since she entered the race, to unfurl some feminist plumage. "I know there still are barriers and biases out there, often unconscious," she finally said, and the room roared in relief and affirmation. "You can be so proud that, from now on, it will be *un*remarkable for a woman to win primary state victories, *un*remarkable to have a woman in a close race to be our nominee, *un*remarkable to think that a woman can be the president of the United States." She paused. People screamed. "And that is truly remarkable."

Clinton was making sure no one forgot that it was she who had made a footprint on history and then stamped up and down until her size 8½s made the mark indelible. "To those who are disappointed that we couldn't go all the way, especially the young people who put so much into this campaign," Clinton said, "it would break my heart if, in falling short of my goal, I in any way discouraged any of you from pursuing yours." I looked at the crowd of kids, the ones who had been sitting on their parents' shoulders all over the country for so many months, watching Clinton and Obama campaign. "As we gather here today," Clinton said, "the fiftieth woman to leave this Earth is orbiting overhead. If we can blast fifty women into space, we will someday launch a woman into the White House." Her crescendo was the line to which she will be forever tethered, a sentence far superior to any about not baking cookies: "Although we weren't able to shatter that highest, hardest glass ceiling this time, thanks to you it's got about eighteen million cracks in it."

Wary throughout the campaign of turning herself into too much of a symbol, Clinton had given the speech of her life, perhaps to her own surprise. Muscatine, who had worked with her since her days as first lady, explained that Hillary's particular brand of feminism had always been more focused on the nitty-gritty of policy issues than on soaring feminist rhetoric. "She was always about things like pay equity, breast cancer coverage, health insurance, or even going around the world talking about women and microfinance," said

Muscatine. "Her championing the cause was not emotional in the way you and I might feel about feminism. We might be motivated by an accumulation of all these little stupid obstacles thrown at us because we're girls, or women. . . . It's not that she's emotionally detached, exactly, but she doesn't come at these issues with a huge amount of emotion that other people try to project on her." Instead, Muscatine said, Clinton has always been focused on the practicalities of progress, what kinds of concrete improvements she could make. In their days at the White House they used to argue about it: "I used to tell her, 'You are not using the symbolic power of your position.' She would say, 'That's not going to effect systemic change, or make a lasting impact.' My argument was, sometimes you effect the change through the symbolic act."

In her concession speech Clinton gave in and made the symbolic gesture, and it was a corker, though as some of her advisors had predicted, the media wanted to hear only one thing: her enthusiasm for Obama. At MSNBC Rachel Maddow was moderating a panel discussion about the speech. Months later she told me that she heard the speech and knew the story was Clinton's embrace of her piece of American history, but all her colleagues wanted to talk about was the not-breaking news that Clinton had endorsed Obama. "The stuff about millions of cracks in the glass ceiling no longer being remarkable I thought was huge," Maddow said. "But look back . . . [and] see how much the commentary focused on [that part of the speech]. None of it. It was all 'She endorsed him!'" As a moderator rather than a commentator, Maddow had a mandate to direct conversation, not offer her own opinion, but she gave it a shot nonetheless. "I said something like 'Obviously what we saw here was an incredible statement about women . . . am I right?'" she recalled. "Everyone just replied, 'I think her endorsement of Obama was blah blah blah.' Even as a person who helped to decide what the point of discussion was in the mainstream media, I was alone."

I looked around at the people waving their flags, hoisting their kids, and cheering for her. My phone began to vibrate with calls from my mother, my cousin, my girlfriends, all watching from their homes. As Clinton stepped off the stage I saw a text from Geraldine. "I am completely losing it," she wrote. It was then that I lost it too. Sprinting from the press area, where Clinton's reporting squad were saying their good-byes after months on the road together, I found space behind a pillar. Next to me was Matt Drudge, who seemed not to realize or care that I was stupidly sobbing. I was so tired. Tired of caring so much about a woman I hadn't meant to care about at all. Tired of arguing with my friends. Tired of being angry at people I'd never been angry with before. Tired of being identified with Hillary even when I didn't like her. Tired of resisting the fact that maybe I did like her quite a lot.

Shelby Knox watched the speech alone at Gloria Steinem's house. Steinem had traveled to Washington for the address with batches of buttons she and Knox had made together; they read, "Hillary Supports Obama and So Do I!" She had discouraged Knox from attending the speech. "She knew I was going to lose it," said Knox in retrospect. Knox admitted that she had indeed cried through the whole concession and was still disconsolate when Steinem returned home.

When I asked Steinem in 2009 what she felt at Clinton's concession she answered without pause, "Relief." "I hate conflict," she said. "If I'd been [Hillary] I would have quit after Iowa. I know I'm in the wrong business." This jibed with the sentiment she voiced to Knox. "I asked her if it was as horrible in person as it was on TV," Knox recalled, "and she said, 'No, it was like a party.'" Knox was angered by Steinem's nonchalance, remembering that she said, "Think about it, Shelby: we don't have to talk about this anymore. We don't have to do this anymore." Knox tearfully pointed out that now we would also not have a woman president. "Gloria said, 'But Shelby, we will have a woman president. And you'll see it.'"

It was the young women who were supposed to have been optimistic and breezy about the future, the old ones who were meant to feel pessimistic, but here was Steinem, buoyant and dry-eyed in the face of a youthful lachrymosity. "Why are you crying?" Knox remembered Steinem asking her over and over again.

When Knox told me this story I remembered my own blubbing at the end of the concession speech. I remembered the message from Geraldine: "I am completely losing it." I also remembered a passage from a profile of Steinem that Nora Ephron wrote in 1972, at the Democratic convention in Miami. After watching the National Women's Political Caucus get sold out by the Democrats, including George McGovern, Ephron found Steinem in a hotel lobby and began to walk with her to her next meeting. Ephron described their conversation, "'It's just so difficult,' [Steinem] says, crying now. I begin babbling—all the pressures on you, no private life, no sleep, no wonder you're upset. 'It's not that,' says Gloria. 'It's just that they won't take us seriously.' She wipes at her cheeks with her hand, and begins crying again. 'And I'm just tired of being screwed, and being screwed by my friends. . . . They won't take us seriously.' . . . She is still crying, and I try to offer some reassuring words, something, but everything I say is wrong; I have never cried over anything remotely political in my life, and I honestly have no idea of what to say."

The intervening decades had provided Steinem with lots more experience in bucking up and carrying on. But Knox, her skin unthickened by age and repeated disappointment, and I, who like Ephron would not previously have imagined myself crying over anything political, and Geraldine, who had not even voted for Hillary— we were all momentarily gutted by the loss. There was certainly something to be said for the dignity and forbearance that came with experience, but I suspected that it had been Steinem's youthful intensity and sensibility, her impulse to cry over something political, that had helped affirm her dedication to staying in her business, despite her avowed discomfort with conflict.

There was something else at the heart of Knox's angst. "I couldn't say what I wanted to say," she recalled, until Steinem's repeated assurance that she would see a female president in her lifetime finally made her blurt out, "But *you* won't. And I wanted *you* to see it." Reminded of her looming mortality by a twenty-year-old, Steinem looked slightly taken aback, Knox recalled. "Then she hugged me and said, 'I might, you know. It could happen in the next twenty-five years. But I also got to see Hillary run, and I got to see young women like you get angry about it and know that it was going to happen. I will get to see Sasha and Malia move into the White House. I got to see all of this happen."

★ ★ ★

As Clinton's threatening shadow began at last to recede, tributes started to stream in from feminist pundits who had backed Obama and were now comfortable extending some tepid "You go, girl" plaudits. Then there were those who were sticking to their anti-Clinton guns, reminding us that Hillary's loss was no one's fault but her own, that she may have been a woman, but she was no icon. Maybe if she hadn't voted for the war, maybe if she hadn't been married to Bill, maybe if she'd been more of a true feminist, maybe if she'd been more like them—then, maybe, these people could have gotten excited about her as a presidential candidate.

My gut reaction, as I recovered from my unexpected bout of emotion, was that though we all might wish that our groundbreaking leaders come in prettier packages, we get what we get. We got Hillary Clinton. In no small part we got her thanks to the reasons so many couldn't abide her: her ambition, her ruthlessness, her marriage, her centrism, her hawkishness. I couldn't think of many women of sterling liberal character who would have succeeded where she failed to satisfy all feminists while also winning Ohio.

It was all well and good that little girls might grow up knowing that women could run for president and break voting records; Clinton and Obama had each received more primary votes than any other presidential candidate in history. I was perhaps more gratified that those little girls would know they were not responsible for embodying the highest expectations for their gender's civility and decorum because one hellaciously difficult woman had been there before them and knocked everybody around pretty hard.

As each primary approached I was sure that Clinton was toast; again and again I got a thrill from watching the talking heads collapse into paroxysms of annoyance at this woman who would not quit. After one particularly wild election night, perhaps it was Ohio, I received an email from my cousin, a Clinton skeptic who had come to appreciate the senator's dazzling ability to drive her critics around the bend. "I hope she never stops running," my cousin wrote. "Even after he's elected." It had nothing to do with Obama. We were young women, drunk on the fun of watching an older woman refuse to concede to anyone's expectations. At the party after the Pennsylvania primary I bumped into a *New York Times* journalist who said, with great theatrical weariness about the fact that this primary had not clinched it, "Well, see you in Guam." But a smile played across her lips. This was funny. Actually, it was hilarious.

There was some hand-wringing about where the next female

contender would come from, but I did not feel particular alarm. Who knew the name Bill Clinton before 1992? Who knew the name Barack Obama before 2004? Who, ten years earlier, could have imagined that beleaguered First Lady Hillary Rodham Clinton would come so close to getting her own intern in the Oval Office? People came out of nowhere and surprised us. What turned out to be my dedication to—and, after all these years, my identification with—Hillary Clinton had surprised me.

To have voted for Hillary, to have deviated from my peers, had sometimes made me feel as though I wore a big red H on my chest, but learning to acknowledge and embrace my affinity for this woman proved to be not only an extraordinary political experience, but one that reshaped my appreciation for a certain kind of powerful woman.

But now it was over. Hillary had to let go.

Some of her supporters, however, did not.

✳ ✳ ✳

In the bitterest days of the race there had been speculation that Hillary's flock would not go gently into the Obama campaign. It had seemed a silly prediction, born of the bad tempers and competitive antipathies of the primary. In the heat of things, Michelle Obama herself had said that she would have to carefully consider whether or not to support Clinton if she won the contest. Overblown prognostications about ornery Clintonites spoke to the vilification of Clinton's imagined coven and the eagerness to lay blame at their feet. They were going to ruin everything.

Five days after Clinton's concession I got my first inkling that the myth of the unforgiving Hillary die-hard had some basis in fact. I was in Washington, speaking on a panel at the annual convention of EMILY's List. My fellow panelist Katrina vanden Heuvel, editor of the *Nation,* was receiving a surprisingly chilly reception from the audience, largely, it seemed, because her magazine had endorsed Barack Obama for president. When she mentioned DNC chairman Howard Dean in her speech, the crowd booed. Was this, vanden Heuvel asked, about Dean's decision not to count votes from Michigan and Florida? Nope, they replied. It was about his behavior toward Clinton and her supporters.

It was true that Dean had not spoken up against sexism or about the historic nature of Clinton's campaign as soon as he might have. It was widely assumed, though never confirmed, that privately both he and House Speaker Nancy Pelosi were rooting for Obama, and that one or both of them exerted pressure on Hillary to get out of the race. "They were silent when it came to sexism," said Jehmu Greene, who had worked as the head of women's outreach at the DNC until 2000. "Nancy Pelosi should have spoken up; Howard Dean should have spoken up; Harry Reid should have spoken up."

After Clinton's defeat, Dean, who apparently did not watch a lot of television, claimed that he had not been aware of the misogyny directed at Clinton until a friend sat him down, around the time of Clinton's concession, and showed him back-to-back clips of some of the ugliness. Once he'd gotten a taste, several sources confirmed, he had been genuinely horrified. Within days of Clinton's concession he told the *New York Times,* "The wounds of sexism need to be the subject of a national discussion. . . . Many of the most prominent people on TV behaved like middle schoolers." But it was a strategic error: Clinton supporters only heard way too little, conveniently way too late. Dean would bring up the issue repeatedly in the months after Hillary's concession, asserting in a November panel discussion that sexism was the most "underwritten" story of the election. I made repeated attempts to contact Dean to speak about that underwritten story for this book, to no avail.

Dean's post-Hillary tip of the hat to misogyny was part of a larger trend among Democrats: a sudden, partywide enthusiasm for talking about gender. On some level this was terrific. But for those Hillary defenders who for months had been compiling and disseminating carefully catalogued lists of every talking head who ever called Clinton a castrating, cankled cauldron-stirrer, it was rather deflating to hear the people they'd been desperate to reach suddenly tumble to the idea that sexism was the most underreported story of the year.

Most of the women who were angry about Clinton's fate, the women at EMILY's List and beyond, were angry for some perfectly

legitimate, and amply precedented, reasons. A period of recalci-
trance was to be expected after protracted political battle. In 2004
it had taken Howard Deaniacs months to return to the Kerry fold.
But their reluctance had not been monitored with the same lip-
licking zeal, in part because the Dean-Kerry rivalry had not been
plumped by the personal sting of identity politics. The length and
ferocity of the Clinton-Obama competition had given supporters
time to truly sink their teeth in and invest unreservedly.

Many of Clinton's staunchest supporters were women who had
dedicated their lives to Democratic politics, had just had their hearts
broken and now felt isolated and taken for granted by their own
party, a party that was doing little to meet them halfway. Major
Democrats were reacting to Clintonite bellyaching by broadcasting
their assurance that once feathers were smoothed Clinton women
would come back and vote like the good Democrats they were. In a
profile of Keith Olbermann in the *New Yorker* MSNBC executive
Phil Griffin described how Olbermann appeared to Clinton voters:
"He turns out to be a jerk and difficult and brutal. And that is how
the Hillary viewers see him. It's true. But I do think they're going
to come back. There's nowhere else to go." The presumption that
Democratic women's loyalty would ultimately not waver was historically sound, but it was precisely the attitude that most infuriated
Hillary supporters in the aftermath of her campaign. Their party
and their media, both kept alive in large part by female dollars
and votes, had not treated them with respect, and then shrugged
their shoulders at their anger, because they understood women to
be strapped by their reproductive organs to the DNC.

Yes, there were suddenly lots of panel discussions, web forums,
and newspaper stories devoted to the subject of sexism in the primaries. But the tendency to focus on two reductive questions—*Did
Hillary face sexism?* and worse, *Did her campaign fail because of
sexism?*—did not allow for much nuance or thoughtfulness. Of
course she had not failed because of sexism. She had failed for a host
of reasons that, sure, probably included sexism. Everything about
Clinton's campaign was marked in some way by her gender, but the
suggestion that sexism was exclusively or even largely to blame for
her defeat was not only implausible, it was the kind of overwrought
conclusion that did no favors to those who propagated it. There had

been instances in which sexism had *helped* Clinton garner the outraged support she needed to remain in contention. But few in the media wanted to hear answers this complex. Few were interested in talking about sexism unless it could be made into a simplified game of aggrieved blame laying. And so it was those who were willing to simplistically and grievously lay blame—and even more, who were willing to jump up and down and point fingers—who attracted the media spotlight.

Thus were born the PUMAs, a small, loose collective of rabble-rousers who helped to fill the news void between primary season and the political conventions. With cameras and microphones trained on them after months of feeling dismissed, ignored or simply talked over, a tiny but vocal number of Clinton supporters—and as far as I could discern, some Republicans posing as Hillary Democrats—became the summer's media darlings by fulfilling every fantasy of affronted femininity, promising to make a scene at the convention in Denver and vote for McCain in November. They were the perfect foil for anxious Obama supporters who needed someone to blame everything on and found themselves short a Hillary.

PUMA stood for Party Unity My Ass. Those who rallied under its banner had a temperament distinctly different from that of the politically dedicated women I'd met at EMILY's List. The PUMA expressions of loyalty seemed tailor-made to corroborate every hoary, bigoted cliché about Hillary's defenders being irrational harpies. They damaged everyone who had ever supported her.

✳ ✳ ✳

Meanwhile, despite a stagey "Unity" tour designed to show Clinton and Obama as a cheery team, Obama's campaign appeared not to be attuned to the more understated and rational distress of Clinton's following. In high-level meetings with Clinton donors, Obama advisors made precious little attempt to address her supporters' reservations or to entice them by asking what their concerns and priorities were. Instead, many donors reported, the sell was stupidly cold: *Sorry she's out, now please give us your money.* It made handing over the dough more difficult than it might otherwise have been.

Ann Lewis told me in 2010 of a phone conversation she'd had

with an individual donor. This was when she and other Clinton campaigners were "being good soldiers" over the summer, "talking to 'Women for Hillary' groups, getting them to get out and support Obama." "I used a line I had been using a little too easily, which was, 'Look, if Hillary can do what she's doing, which is so hard, then surely we can do this,'" Lewis recalled. "The woman said to me, 'Yeah, but she's a better person than I am.'"

Naturally some Clinton supporters harbored the hope that Obama would ask her to be his running mate, felt that it would be not only a courteous but a brilliant move that would deliver him her 18 million voters and unite the fractured party into an unstoppable whole. Obama supporters were understandably less thrilled by this idea. At a Unity breakfast at the New York Hilton in July I watched Clinton give one of her fulsome postdefeat speeches, with Obama befuddled next to her; he looked unsure of what to make of his once formidable opponent, now grinning widely beside him. In the ladies room after the speech members of a group called Women for Obama grumbled about Clinton's cat-that-ate-the-canary appearance. "You'd never know she lost," they said. "She makes him so uncomfortable," said another. "He better not choose her as a running mate," said a third. The whole ladies room line nodded in vigorous agreement.

Rumors swirled that Obama might pick another woman for the ticket, a choice that would suggest he understood the importance of having female executive leadership. Names began to float; Kansas Governor Kathleen Sebelius seemed the most serious possibility. The vocal PUMAs were not just unimpressed by this; they were steamed. Some remained so besotted by the idea of *their* woman as *the* history maker that they would not be satisfied unless Clinton or someone from her direct bloodline was the first female to breach the Oval Office. Even some of the more reasonable Hillary loyalists were dismayed by the more systemic problem that this imagined plan laid bare: the paucity of women in government left a pitiful few to choose from, and the names being bandied about seemed pallid substitutes for the steam engine Clinton had become.

Obama was in a bind. His smartest choice would have been to pick someone immediately, chilling the hopes of Hillary's monofocused flock. Instead he made a tone-deaf move: at just the moment he was supposed to be making nice with Camp Clinton, he appointed her estranged ex-campaign manager, Patti Solis Doyle, to his campaign's team as chief of staff for his yet unnamed vice president. To those who had paid attention to the power dynamics within the Clinton campaign, hiring the scorned Solis Doyle seemed a sure signal that her former boss was not even being considered as a vice-presidential pick. One of Clinton's top donors called it the "biggest fuck-you I have ever seen in politics."

Most discouraging about the Solis Doyle appointment was the degree to which it confirmed that neither Obama nor his advisors were hearing the reasons many women felt alienated from their campaign. Many sources within the Obama campaign reported that the organization was blindsided and mystified by the backlash over the appointment. This was the strategic problem with having a frat-house campaign, a dynamic related to the one that Latifa Lyles had described about the lack of diversity at NOW: beyond a failure of political correctness, the preponderance of men in the Obama camp meant that there was no one around to understand or explain that, intentions aside, hiring Solis Doyle was a nasty rebuke to those who had given their hearts and their pocketbooks to the Clinton campaign. So bereft was the Obama campaign of women that, John Heilemann and Mark Halperin would go on to report, it was Solis Doyle herself, once aboard, who would clue in the Obama team that picking another woman might not go over swimmingly with Clinton's supporters. Obama's announcement that he would be running alongside Joe Biden came late on the Friday night before the convention, getting things started with a flash of disappointment for Hillary's delegates who had perhaps held out some hope.

Clinton had not released her delegates, and in Denver many of them were hoping to make a symbolic gesture by voting for her on the first ballot. This made sense to me. They wanted their place in history, no different from Shirley Chisholm's or Ted Kennedy's delegates before them. They weren't threatening a takeover. Those I spoke to said they would vote for Obama on the second ballot. But their motives were made to seem nefarious thanks to the exploitive coverage of the small band of disruptive PUMAs.

"This is where you see the civil war!" said Chris Matthews from an outdoor stage in the sweltering Denver heat, while behind him two small but boisterous groups chanted "Obama! Obama!" and "Hillary! Hillary!" at each other. Matthews looked beside himself with happiness as he declared, "We're at ground zero!" He was in fact about six blocks away from the Pepsi Center, the crowd behind him probably no more than a hundred strong, and at least one of them was dressed as a toilet for reasons that appeared to have nothing to do with Clinton or Obama. Media mirages were made from miniature tableaux of political discord played out in front of a couple of well-placed television cameras. The PUMAs were making Chris Matthews's night. They held aloft Clinton signs and hand-markered cards reading "Stop Delegate Intimidation!" and "South Jersey PUMA." A small group holding "McCain" signs started a melodic chorus of "Clintons for McCain, sweetie, Clintons for McCain, sweetie," in reference to Obama's bad habit. Next to them a man in an Obama hat shouted, "You're all irrelevant! Jesus!"

The press, and especially MSNBC, thought the Hillary wraiths were relevant; in fact they seemed to think they were the most important story to be told about the convention, without regard for the fact that every national political convention in modern history had become a locus for agitators. The reporters did not take into account that during the convention antiwar protests drew thousands of people, compared to the dozens who made noise about Hillary. They did not take into account that on Monday of the convention Code Pink, the antiwar protest group, had hijacked a presentation by Nancy Pelosi, screaming "Liar! Liar!" "You said you'd impeach Bush!" "You lied to my face!" I had witnessed this demonstration, and it was far more disruptive and newsworthy than the people dressed as commodes milling around Chris Matthews's stage. No, Matthews and his colleagues were taking the grounded gripes with the way Clinton had been treated, the longer-standing concerns of liberal women about their place in their party, the simple desire of Clinton delegates to cast their symbolic votes, and representing it all via this small and overheated gathering. The media was putting a kabuki mask of unhinged wrathfulness over the saner impulses of most Hillary supporters.

In Denver Marie Wilson, head of the White House Project, told me, "There is such a fear of women coming into power that when they protest, they are given more weight. Just the fact of women saying they support their candidate and want to make their voices heard sounds more scary than it would be if it were guys. That's just part of backlash." Wilson saw the discord as a positive, though perhaps painful step in the right direction. "We are in the middle of a revolution," she said of the aftermath of Hillary's run. Her organization, which encouraged women to seek elected office, had enjoyed a 61 percent increase in participation in 2008.

Dana Kennedy, a forty-year-old Clinton delegate from Arizona, was one of three hundred signers of a petition to get a roll call vote for Clinton. "My hope is that in the first round of voting I get to vote for her, and in the second round, I will vote for Obama," said Kennedy. "A vote for Hillary is a vote for history and *not* against him." Another Clinton delegate, Rosina Rubin from New York, said, "This is not about anger. We all want to elect a Democrat in November. But why wouldn't her name be placed in nomination? She is the only woman who has ever come this far. Her achievement represents a giant moment in American history. We just want to celebrate that." The women would have a chance to celebrate it later in the week, when Hillary walked onto the convention floor, straight into the New York delegation, and symbolically suspended the roll call by saying, "I move Senator Barack Obama of Illinois be selected by this convention by acclamation as the nominee of the Democratic Party for President of the United States." The Pepsi Center, which had been buzzing with midday convention chatter, fell dead silent, then erupted in applause on the word *Democratic*. It was, to my ear, the most unifying and moving moment of the convention—genuine, surprising, and a world away from the story of discord playing out on cable networks.

☆ ☆ ☆

In all this, too few women were considering the pressures going into Denver for the most important woman still in the presidential contest. "This black woman is wondering," Mary C. Curtis had written in the *Washington Post* in June, "where are [Michelle] Obama's feminist defenders? . . . Just as you didn't have to be for Clinton to decry the sexism in the coverage of her campaign, you don't have to be an Obama supporter to defend Michelle Obama against similar treatment." Michelle Obama, the reluctant political spouse and inheritor of Clinton's trouble-making first lady legacy, had had a treacherous ride along the campaign trail. At a February speech in Wisconsin she'd said that her husband's political successes had taught her, "People in this country are ready for change and hungry for a different kind of politics. . . . For the first time in my adult life I am proud of my country because it feels like hope is finally making a comeback."

The response was damning. The next day Cindy McCain gave a speech in which she said, "I am proud of my country. I don't know about you, if you heard those words earlier [but] I am very proud of my country." The conservative columnist Bill Kristol told Fox News, "[Michelle Obama] was an adult when we won the cold war without firing a shot. She was an adult for the last twenty-five years of economic progress, social progress. . . . I don't think the American people think on the whole that the last twenty-five years of American history is . . . nothing to be proud of." Many reactions revealed a virulent current of race and class condescension. Jim Geraghty wrote on the website of the *National Review,* "America hasn't been good to her? What, opportunities to go to Princeton, Harvard Law, working for top-shelf law firms and hospitals . . . that's not enough?" Apparently Michelle was supposed to be damn grateful for her hard-earned achievements.

Maureen Dowd's original portrayal of Michelle Obama as an emasculating nag had gained a purchase on the public imagination. As the facts of her life became more widely disseminated they were often cast in a precise light: she had been the hard-driving lawyer, Barack's boss; she had been resentful when the domestic chores had been dumped on her when he took to a political life; like Hillary, she exerted tremendous influence over her husband. Her critics began to spin an elaborate narrative in which that influence was going to be threatening, in part because Michelle was angry and in part because she was black.

If Barack Obama had done a masterful job of conveying that he and his campaign were beyond race, his wife provided a counterbalance. Writing for *Slate* Christopher Hitchens used twenty-two-year-old Michelle's senior thesis, a research paper about being black at Princeton, to link Barack to a series of controversial Black Power figures, from Louis Farrakhan to Malcolm X to Jeremiah Wright: "How is it that the loathsome Wright married him, baptized his children, and received donations from him? Could it possibly have anything, I wonder, to do with Mrs. Obama?" Hitchens's dun-dun-*dun* accusation was like a real-life version of Dana Carvey's Church Lady: Could it be . . . *Satan?* Claiming that Michelle's thesis had made reference to her being "much influenced" by the separatist politics of Stokely Carmichael, Hitchens casually recalled that Carmichael had taken the name Kwame Ture, and that Hitchens had last seen him speak before Farrakhan in 1985, on the night that Farrakhan "made himself famous by warning Jews, 'You can't say "Never Again" to God, because when he puts you in the ovens, you're there forever.'" Black Power, separatists, Louis Farrakhan, Jews in the ovens, Michelle Obama—all neatly tied together in a piece that cast both Obamas as members of a club that Hitchens knew made both conservatives and liberals nervous. Ta-Nehisi Coates pointed out on his blog at the *Atlantic* that Hitchens lied about what Michelle had actually written in her thesis, which was that Carmichael and Charles Hamilton had "developed definitions of separationism in their discussion of Black Power which guided me in the formulation and use of this concept in the study." As Coates noted, Michelle made no allusion to any influence they had over her personally or politically. But whatever Hitchens's moral or ethical lapses, they were moot. By midspring Michelle was widely caricatured as the paradigm of angry black femininity.

In April the *National Review* ran a cover story featuring a photograph of Michelle, brow furrowed in what could have been concern or enthusiasm, but frozen in a snapshot, her expression appeared to be fury; the cover line was "Mrs. Grievance: Michelle Obama and Her Discontent." In June, celebrating the clinching of the nomination, Michelle gave her husband a fist-bump, or dap. On Fox News E. D. Hill played the footage, teasing it with the query, "A fist bump? A pound? A terrorist fist jab?" (Hill was taken off the air soon thereafter.) Less than a week later *Salon*'s Alex Koppelman, following a reader's tip, caught Fox News running a banner below a story about Obama that read "Outraged Liberals: Stop Picking on Obama's Baby Mama." Appearing with Bill O'Reilly, NPR's Juan

Williams compared Michelle to a black separatist. "She's got this Stokely-Carmichael-in-a-designer-dress thing going." By the end of the primaries a rumor was running rampant: there was a tape floating around on which Michelle could be heard saying the word *whitey.*

So broad was the brush with which she was being painted that she got half of Barry Blitt's July cover caricature on the *New Yorker.* Titled "The Politics of Fear," it was a sendup of all the paranoid, racially inflected slander being applied to the Obamas. There was Barack in a turban terrorist-fist-jabbing his wife, who had an Angela Davis–style Afro and was carrying a machine gun.

The Obama campaign was desperate to counteract the vision. Appearing on *The View* in June Michelle gabbed about pantyhose and confessed to buying her dress at the mall store called White House Black Market; she won over daytime audiences by being as girly as girly could be. The *Daily News* headline read, "With the Help of Off-the-Rack Dress, Michelle Obama Eases Harsh Image," a good tip for anyone looking to rid themselves of that pesky black radical aura.

When I settled into the press seats at the Pepsi Center on the first night of the convention and received a printed copy of the speech Michelle was about to give, I shouldn't have been surprised by its content, but I was. I knew that making herself as unthreatening as possible was what she had to do, but as I scanned the pages, looking for the Michelle Obama I had seen ten months earlier, I could find barely a glimpse of her. What I found instead was a woman turning herself inside out to emphasize her identity as a wife, a mother, a sister, a daughter—anything but a lawyer, a thinker, a person in her own right. Her speech was so comforting, so just-folksy, so daughterly and wifely and motherly that it made Nancy Reagan seem like an ambitious hussy with a wandering eye.

She was introduced in a video by her mother, who referred to her as "my baby," and then by her older brother, the basketball coach Craig Robinson, who called her "my little sister." Robinson's role was to lay down the evening's theme ("Black Potential First Ladies: They're Just Like Us!") with anecdotes about how as a child Michelle memorized every episode of *The Brady Bunch*. He explained that, though she eventually quit her powerful law firm job, she did take something from it: "a young lawyer by the name of Barack Obama."

A gifted orator, Michelle delivered her milquetoast address with such charismatic force that it almost made me forget it was an act of partial self-erasure. If it was slightly dispiriting to hear this smart and accomplished woman sum herself up in relation to the other people in her life—"a wife who loves my husband" and "a mom whose girls are the heart of my heart and the center of my world"—it was leavened by the fact that she was using every bit of her personal power to wrap the crowd around her little finger. She reminded the audience that during the span of this convention we would celebrate the eighty-eighth anniversary of women's suffrage and the forty-fifth anniversary of "that hot summer day when Dr. King lifted our sights and our hearts with his dream for our nation."

"I stand here today at the crosscurrents of that history," said Michelle in the best part of her speech, "knowing that my piece of the American dream is a blessing hard won by those who came before me." When she put her daughters to sleep at night, she said, she thought about the families they themselves would one day have. "One day, they—and your sons and daughters—will tell their own children about what we did together in this election . . . how this time, in this great country—where a girl from the South Side of Chicago can go to college and law school, and the son of a single mother from Hawaii can go all the way to the White House—that we committed ourselves to building the world as it should be." It was powerful and beautifully executed. But the speech itself was a sad indication that no matter how much we had done together in this election, the world we were committed to building still was not as it should be. It apparently would not warmly welcome this ambitious and dynamic woman until she was willing to briefly dim her own bright lights, downplay her autonomy, and present herself as an unthreatening wifely and maternal ideal. We had not sufficiently protected Michelle Obama against the race and gender inflected attacks she was now dodging, nor from the rigid expectations of "wife-of" femininity that Hillary had encountered sixteen years before, nor from the style-over-substance fate to which she was about to be confined.

✳ ✳ ✳

On Tuesday, the night before she released her delegates, Clinton showed up at the Pepsi Center in a Phoenician orange pantsuit, appearing onstage after thunderous applause for the savviest ad she'd ever run, a video narrated by Chelsea, in which Hillary confessed her childhood dreams of being an astronaut while the Kinks blared "Girl, you really got me." "She was able to play with the boys, and yet sort of earn their respect," said Dorothy Rodham, identified as "Hillary's mom." "People who've worked with her feel I think a lot of respect and affection for her, and she unleashes people's energy," said Bill, identified as "Hillary's husband." In a photo negative of Michelle's speech on the previous night, everyone in the video was described in relation to Hillary. "It's so important for little girls to have someone to look up to," said a young woman in the video before a clip of Amy Poehler imitating Clinton's laugh. This was the message and the tone that her campaign had struggled and failed to achieve.

"It is time to take back the country we love, and whether you voted for me or whether you voted for Barack, the time is now to unite as a single party with a single purpose," said Clinton. Though some would accuse her of using her moment at the convention to fan the PUMA flames, she was in fact telling them to can it. She went on, "I want you to ask yourselves: Were you in this campaign just for me? Or were you in it for that young Marine and others like him? Were you in it for that mom struggling with cancer while raising her kids? . . . Were you in it for all the people in this country who feel invisible?"

"She went directly at the tension head-on," said Lissa Muscatine, who wrote the speech. "That was what Obama did so well throughout the campaign. He dealt with difficult issues by going straight into them."

"My mother was born before women could vote," Clinton bellowed one last time. "My daughter got to vote for her mother for president. This is the story of America." Later, outside the Pepsi Center, Clinton's former campaign chairman Terry McAuliffe stepped into the summer night, starry-eyed, smiling, shaking his head. "If she'd given speeches like that during the campaign, things would have turned out differently," he said.

McAuliffe wasn't the only one making this assertion. If she had appealed to people on an emotional level, presented herself as a candidate of change, been the feminist heroine so many had hoped she might have been, maybe it would have been different. Maybe, like Dorothy, she'd had to hustle all the way through Oz before realizing that she'd had the power all along.

Or maybe not. Had she taken the more emotive approach, let her feminist flag fly earlier, would she have made it to Texas and Ohio? More realistically, would she even have made it to Iowa?

It didn't matter now. For Hillary Clinton, the rousing speech in Denver was the end. Not the end of Hillary, but the end of her 2008 presidential story. What nobody knew, on that warm Denver night, was that from the ashes of her campaign, another woman, this one a Republican, would soon be rising.

9 ENTER PALIN

"McCain picked Palin." This was the urgent sentence that yanked me from sleep on a pull-out couch in the house *Salon* had rented in Denver. My colleague Alex Koppelman, conscious earlier than the rest of us the morning after Barack Obama's speech at Invesco Field, was standing above me, repeating, *"He picked Palin,"* as if, if he said it louder, I might better divine its meaning. On the AeroBed next to me, my colleague Caitlin sat up and started rubbing her eyes.

"Michael Palin?" I asked.

"No, *Sarah* Palin," said Alex, heading down the stairs to start writing, shouting over his shoulder, "She's the governor of Alaska. She's young and popular. Social conservatives love her because she kept her baby even though she knew he had Down syndrome. And oh," Alex turned around, "she's a woman."

The night before, America had witnessed Obama accept his party's nomination on the forty-fifth anniversary of Martin Luther King's "I Have a Dream" speech. The man had filled a stadium. It had felt like one of those rare occasions, ever rarer in the cable and Internet age, when the nation seemed, briefly, to be focused on the same thing. For an hour we were all looking in the same direction at the same time. Now the McCain team had dropped a bomb. In choosing Palin they had not only made a strategic appeal to disillusioned women in the Democratic Party; they had established their own claim to history. Palin was the first Republican woman ever selected as a vice-presidential nominee, and only the second woman in American history behind Geraldine Ferraro.

Later it would become clear that Palin's selection was not the carefully considered move it first appeared; it was in fact so impulsive a choice as to border on the accidental. John Heilemann and Mark Halperin reported in their book *Game Change* that the McCain campaign had been planning for most of the summer to make a splash by nominating former Democrat Joe Lieberman, the junior senator from Connecticut who had been Al Gore's running mate in 2000 and was buddies with McCain. The move would have been attention-getting, but Lieberman's pro-choice position and (tepid) support of gay rights would have imperiled Republican Party unity. The plan was scuttled at the last minute.

Former *Ms.* editor Elaine Lafferty, disgusted with the Democrats after Hillary's loss, was having meetings with Carly Fiorina, the former CEO of Hewlett-Packard then serving as an economic advisor to McCain. "She was encouraging me to get involved with the McCain campaign," Lafferty told me in 2009. Lafferty soon became part of a group that was pushing the Republican nominee to consider a woman as his running mate. Lafferty's friend John Coale, an attorney and the husband of Fox News host Greta Van Susteren, was also talking to McCain. "I went on his bus with him," Coale told me in 2010. Coale, a friend of the Clinton family, had campaigned for Hillary throughout Pennsylvania and had heard from many voters how much they wanted a woman to be president. "These were women with blue-collar jobs and they were passionate for Hillary," said Coale. "Time and again they told me it was because Hillary was a woman. I thought McCain could capture those voters." Coale brought some colleagues along with him to talk to McCain. "We urged him to pick a woman, big time," he said. "I always thought it would be Carly Fiorina or Meg Whitman. Carly and Meg were in the final running in his mind, as far as I could tell. He was talking about them."

But in the days leading up to the Republican convention in Minneapolis, before which McCain would be forced to select a running mate, his aides were not talking about Whitman or Fiorina. According to Heilemann and Halperin, McCain campaign manager Steve Schmidt and advisor Rick Davis had found a Charlie Rose interview with the forty-four-year-old governor of Alaska in July and had concluded that Sarah Palin was a star, and a socially conservative one to boot. As the Lieberman idea crumbled they began to fixate on the widely unknown governor, who could make their presidential ticket a history-making one. McCain spoke to her briefly by phone. The attorney A. B. Culvahouse, in charge of McCain's vetting process, asked another attorney, Ted Frank, to write up a report on Palin. The report, which came with a caveat that its hasty preparation meant that it might be incomplete, turned up criticisms of Palin's inexperience and an ongoing ethics investigation into accusations that as governor she fired Alaska's public safety commissioner after he'd refused to fire state trooper Mike Wooten, the estranged husband of her sister Molly. Schmidt and speechwriter Mark Salter met with Palin at the home of Bob Delgado, a McCain supporter in Flagstaff. Culvahouse spoke to Palin by phone, during which she told him that her sixteen-year-old daughter, Bristol, was pregnant. According to Heilemann and Halperin, Culvahouse responded by joking, "Is she getting married? . . . Is she getting married *tomorrow*?" Palin met with McCain in person at his ranch in Sedona; they took a walk by the creek and spoke for an hour. After conferring briefly with his advisors, McCain offered Palin the job.

As the reporter Anne Kornblut would point out in her book *Notes from the Cracked Ceiling,* there were very few women on McCain's lean staff to begin with, and none of them had been brought into conversations about having a woman on the ticket. No one asked campaign senior advisor Nicolle Wallace, a well-respected, savvy advisor who had most recently been a political analyst at CBS, working alongside Katie Couric, and who might have provided insight into the public presentation of powerful women. No one ran it by Fiorina, whose tenure at Hewlett-Packard had made her one of the world's best-known and most controversial businesswomen, and who might have had ideas about introducing Palin to the political spotlight. There were no women to mull in advance how voters regarded mothers of young children compared to fathers of young children (let alone how they might react to a mother whose young daughter was pregnant out of wedlock), no comprehension that Palin's beauty was anything other than an asset, no one to remind McCain that his new running mate would have to meet a higher bar of expectation than a man would, or to weigh whether or not she was strong enough to clear it.

Wallace would tell a 2010 panel convened by Kornblut that she learned about Palin only when her candidacy was already a done deal, late on the night before it was to be announced. "Were we ready for anything? No!" Wallace said. "I was the first woman I think to learn her identity, I think the fourth breathing human to learn her identity." Wallace remembered stressed-out speechwriter Mark Salter asking her if she thought it was a problem that Palin "sort of believes in Creationism." "I said, 'I don't know. I'll have to Google that,'" said Wallace. "Steve Schmidt said, 'And her daughter's pregnant, what do you think of that?' And I said, 'Um, I'll be right back.' . . . We were ready for nothing. . . . Three boys picked her. So they didn't ask, you know, girl questions." The biggest problem, Wallace told Kornblut's panel, was that "no one was prepared to defend her. . . . If you picked Jesus Christ, you have to be able to defend him. If your nominee is perfect and known and vetted, you have to be able to defend them. The early problems had less to do with her looks or her gender; it was that everyone was Googling her to find out who she was and what she believed in. Where she lived and how many kids she had."

In Denver we were Googling her too. Palin's gubernatorial campaign website advertised that she was pro-life and believed "that marriage should only be between a man and a woman." She belonged to a conservative women's group called Feminists for Life and had said in her campaign for governor that she was opposed to abortion even in cases of rape and incest, though she did believe in an exception for the life of the mother. She was a longtime member of the National Rifle Association, and when it came to health care she had said, "I support flexibility in government regulations that allow competition in health care that is needed." But there were other more unexpected things, like her reported willingness to stand up to crooked Alaska Senator Ted Stevens; the *Washing-*

ton Post's November 2007 report that outrage over Alaska's corrupt politics had "catapulted a reformer [Palin] into the governor's chair"; the catty political blog *Wonkette*'s post at the same time asserting, "We can never resist an opportunity to run a picture of the hottest Governor in all 50 states (and my total girl crush)." In the spring of 2008, Palin had enjoyed an 80 percent approval rating in Alaska. She had listed the state's private jet on eBay. A February 2008 *Vogue* profile had quoted an *Anchorage Daily News* reporter describing Palin's "small-town sincerity that voters found very appealing" alongside the editor of *Alaska* magazine, who said of Palin, "She really is a breath of fresh air. . . . It feels like a new era in Alaska." She appeared to be independent-minded and attention-getting, electrifying if combustible qualities on a national ticket.

In her introductory press conference Palin made it clear that she was not going to be bashful about celebrating her unprecedented place in presidential history. Noting—to big applause—that McCain had chosen her almost eighty-eight years to the day that women got the right to vote, she said, "I think as well today of two other women who came before me in national elections. I can't begin this great effort without honoring the achievements of Geraldine Ferraro in 1984 and of course Senator Hillary Clinton, who showed such determination and grace in her presidential campaign." Palin paused for the screeching affirmation of the crowd of fifteen thousand, the largest yet drawn by the McCain campaign, in Dayton, Ohio. My colleagues and I stared at each other dumbly in Denver; the Republican vice-presidential candidate was offering shout-outs to Democratic politicians in her first speech, and her Republican audience was eating it up. She wasn't finished. "It was rightly noted in Denver this week that Hillary left eighteen million cracks in the highest, hardest glass ceiling in America. But it turns out the women of America aren't finished yet, and we can shatter that glass ceiling once and for all!" The pinnacle of feminist self-congratulation to which Hillary had managed to ascend only in her losing moment was the place from which Palin launched her candidacy.

It was not crazy, in those days, to wonder if this scheme mightn't be a huge success. Though all of them would take it back within weeks, if not days, I knew women—Democratic women, liberal women—who told me that though they would never vote for Palin, they kind of liked her, and liked McCain for having put her on the ticket. It was a gesture that, at first, seemed to mean something. The actress and comedian Kristen Schaal, a devout Hillary supporter, would tell me in 2009, "I remember how when Palin first came on the scene I was so excited because there was a woman there, even if it was the worst woman I could imagine. It turned out she was a monster, but at first I was like, *Yes!*"

✳ ✳ ✳

Palin's approach to political power was very different from Hillary's, and from Geraldine Ferraro's, and, for that matter, from any of the other women—Dole, Moseley Braun, Schroeder, Chisholm—who had made modern runs for national executive office. Palin was a governor, and before that a mayor. Instead of having worked within larger male-controlled local, state, or national governing bodies, she had been a boss; she had executive experience she would tout throughout the campaign as being vaster than Barack Obama's.

As of 2009 according to the group Equal Representation in Government and Democracy, there had been only thirty-one female governors in U.S. history, and they'd come from only twenty-three states. Among those who studied women's increased political profile, governorships were often cited as the most promising route to the White House. Barbara Lee, a philanthropist and feminist long obsessed with putting more women in office, in 1999 founded the Barbara Lee Family Foundation, an organization jointly dedicated to art and getting more women into politics, with an eye to examining and evaluating the paths of women governors. In 2010 Lee told me that Sarah Palin fit a classic model of female gubernatorial success in that she had won her office by selling herself as a clean politician; voters, Lee said, are often willing to believe a female candidate is more honest than a male: "When women become governors, voters really trust them." She also pointed out that though women running in gubernatorial elections face resistance when it comes to getting elected, once they're in office people tend to like them more than male governors, and they often enjoy high approval ratings, just as Palin did when McCain selected her. "We're tougher on women before they're elected," Lee said, "but once [women] get into these positions, voters . . . find them more believable, honest and trustworthy." Many states, including Texas and Arizona, that have had one female governor go on to elect other women more easily. "Women executives are powerful role models," Lee continued. "So when John McCain picked Palin, a woman who was also a mother with young children, to run on a presidential ticket, it was a good example, and really quite amazing."

For generations, largely because of the comparative sluggishness with which domestic roles had been reimagined and maternal expectations readjusted, the majority of women who could freely enter politics in the wake of the second wave were those who were single or childless. Most women with kids had to wait until their children were teens before diving into the electoral fray, limiting their opportunities to build the experience and support necessary to be taken seriously in a run for the presidency. At forty-two Palin had been elected not only Alaska's first female governor but also its youngest. She had shot from city council member to mayor to governor to vice-presidential candidate in twelve years, a timeline comparable to Barack Obama's. Even more unusual was that she had given birth to her fifth child while governor; her son Trig was four months old when Palin became McCain's running mate. Alongside women like New York Senator Kristin Gillibrand, former Massachusetts governor Jane Swift and Arkansas Senator Blanche Lincoln, all of whom had young families, Palin represented a new generation of female political possibility.

Palin, who would etch herself into the American consciousness as "just another hockey mom" from Alaska, was one of those inheritors of feminist progress who had been taught to expect that she could do anything. She quickly shimmied up the professional pole while her husband, an oilfield production operator on Alaska's North Slope for part of the year, shouldered lots of the child rearing, with help from Palin's village of grandparents, aunts, and uncles who helped raise each other's children.

This was one of the most undeniably progressive things about Palin, perhaps most striking in the context of the hypereducated, prosperous segment of the left that was supporting Obama and in which the purported "Opt-out Revolution" was taking place. Predominantly liberal climes, in which privilege might ease the burdens of the work-life balance, had been the ones in which high-powered mothers had felt unable to escape old domestic responsibilities long enough to capitalize on or profit from their liberated and liberating career choices. But here was Palin, in her mid-forties, a baby on her hip, a seven-year-old at her side, and three more kids in various states of adolescent disarray; she was a governor, and now a vice-presidential candidate. Coale, the Democratic donor who had urged McCain to pick a woman, who would befriend Palin and go on to work with her after the election, told me in 2010, "I was around when the women's movement started in the early seventies, and if you take away the abortion issue, Palin is what everyone was fighting for, in the respect that she has a family and a husband who more than pulls his weight with the kids, the house. He is like the feminist dad that everyone hoped to achieve someday." Indeed in 2009 a profile of Todd Palin in *Esquire* included a scene in the hectic Palin family kitchen on an evening when he was about to sub for his wife at a corporate event and Sarah was teaching her daughter's then-fiancé Levi Johnston how to marinate and cook roast beef. This was the illustration of professional and domestic partnership, of household tasks freed from gendered expectations, of which feminists had long dreamed. The morning McCain announced her candidacy, Palin presented her oddly monikered brood—Track, Bristol, Willow, Piper, Trig, and First Dude Todd—to the nation as credentials, not liabilities. It was an instance in which it was impossible to ignore the social shifts that Palin represented.

Palin's arrival at McCain's side surprised everyone. As commenters began to parse the choice on CNN, John Roberts, who had previously held forth on how the major function of a vice president was "to go to funerals" and similarly untaxing ceremonial duties, changed his tune, telling correspondent Dana Bash, "Children with Down syndrome require an awful lot of attention. The role of vice president, it seems to me, would take up an awful lot of [Palin's] time. It raises the issue of how much time will she have to dedicate to her newborn child?" Bash sounded unmoved by Roberts's concern, countering with "If it were a man being picked who also had a baby four months ago with Down syndrome, would you also ask the same question?" Meanwhile at MSNBC Andrea Mitchell was consumed by the question of whether or not Palin would neuter big bad Joe Biden, an energetic debater. Apparently forgetting that the Delaware senator had not been paralyzed by chivalric courtesy while debating Hillary Clinton, Mitchell wondered whether Biden "can be tough against a woman. Doesn't it give her a gender advantage?" As I searched the web for further Palin information, I noticed that she had already been called a GILF (MILF—or "Mom I'd Like to Fuck"—for governors) and that the *Wall Street Journal* had quickly posted a piece about her workout routine and diet. "My ideal fantasy is to be running on a hot dusty road just wearing running shorts and some kind of top that wicks away sweat," she told the paper.

I didn't know which was worse: watching a grim cycle lurch once more into gear or acknowledging that the Republicans and John McCain, in their attempts to manipulate the female electorate, had walked through a door that had been left opened by my own party.

✳ ✳ ✳

Less than two weeks later Sarah Palin—The story! The phenomenon! The pit bull in lipstick! The political superstar!—was eclipsing every other political story that had come before her. Every day there was some new twist. Putting the words *Sarah, Palin,* or *Wasilla* in a headline guaranteed blockbuster traffic online. She had an equally hypnotic hold on those who loathed her and those who loved her. In my liberal world she had burrowed deep into the psyche of every woman I knew, all of whom talked in jittering staccato about their bad dreams and imagined arguments with her or her supporters. A line kept running through my brain, spoken in the mid-Atlantic clip of *All About Eve*'s Addison DeWitt about that movie's titular, parasitic ingénue: "There never was, and there never will be, another like you."

Palin was simultaneously seductive and seditious, the kind of woman who spoke on behalf of other women but appeared not to like them very much. The kind of woman who, as Jessica Grose at *Jezebel* eloquently noted, gained her power by doing everything modern women had believed they did not have to do: presenting herself as maternal and sexual, sucking up to men, evincing an aw-shucks lack of native ambition. She met with such adulation because her posture reinforced antiquated gender norms. Her success made her the object of obsession for the women whose gendered goodwill she was trying to co-opt, and who saw how well her retro version of femininity was going over.

Within days of the announcement of Palin's nomination, news of Bristol's pregnancy broke. The Palins released a statement saying they were "proud of Bristol's decision to have her baby and even prouder to become grandparents," a statement that Palin would later claim, in her memoir *Going Rogue*, was not an authentic expression of family pride, but a move forced by campaign advisors. In actuality, she wrote, the family had been anything but pleased to hear of Bristol's pregnancy. McCain camp aides reiterated that "Bristol Palin made the decision on her own to keep the baby." Not lost on pro-choice Democrats was the fact that this "decision" was one that neither McCain nor Palin wanted to allow other American women to make were they to find themselves in Bristol's position. A pre-Palin piece in *In These Times* reported that McCain, who supported overturning *Roe v. Wade*, had said during his 2000 primary run for president, "[If our daughter got pregnant,] the final decision would be made by Meghan with our advice and counsel." When reporters pointed out to him that he had just described a pro-choice situation, McCain replied, "I don't think it is the pro-choice position to say that my daughter and wife and I will discuss something that is a family matter that we have to decide."

On the right, the pregnancy merely affirmed Palin's place in the pantheon of socially conservative heroines. Religious conservatives used Bristol's uterine condition as a chance to move their football down the field. Tony Perkins of the Family Research Council made the public statement "[Teen pregnancy] is a problem that we remain committed to reducing through encouraging young people to practice abstinence." He congratulated Bristol on "following her mother and father's example of choosing life in the midst of a difficult situation." Focus on the Family's James Dobson announced that the Palins "should be commended once again for not just talking about their pro-life and pro-family values, but living them out even in the midst of trying circumstances."

I didn't have a problem with Sarah Palin accepting McCain's nomination knowing that her young daughter was pregnant, but I found considerably less defensible her choice to turn Bristol into a living tableau of pro-life politics, and then to make those pro-life politics the crux of an argument that she and her family represented a "real" America, in which Barack Obama apparently did not live. At the Palin-smitten Republican convention the trick of wringing patriotism from an unplanned pregnancy was performed over and over. According to delegates interviewed by CNN, Bristol's pregnancy made Palin "a real person like the rest of us." A Texas delegate told the network, "If anything, it shows the Republican Party is a real American party." South Carolina Governor Mark Sanford told the *New York Times*, "People are looking for real. Real means blemishes, real means warts, real means real. These family imperfections make people say, 'That family isn't so different from my family.'"

This wholly mystifying definition of authenticity was crafted by the morally and religiously self-righteous faction of the right that had held sway in the GOP since Ronald Reagan began cultivating their allegiance in the 1980s. However illogical their rhetoric, the praise of Palin's imagined American realness reverberated with blue-collar voters. The economic and class divide, about which John Edwards had been so adamant, which Hillary Clinton had so advantageously addressed, and about which Barack Obama had been perhaps a touch too laissez-faire—and which he may have nudged a little wider with his comments about guns, religion, and bitterness—was now being crowbarred open by Palin and McCain, regardless of the fact that every bit of their agenda worked against working-class and poor people and on behalf of the champagne-swilling populations they claimed to disdain.

Some on the left legitimately noted that Bristol's pregnancy was a visible ramification not of some extra-American America but of what happens when you restrict young women's freedom, fail to provide them with ample sex education, and make birth control difficult to get. A few vainly tried to point out the hypocrisy of a party that for decades had been portraying itself as an exemplar of straight and straitlaced family values. But most of the attacks on Palin wound up being personal, sudsy, and slightly delusional.

The revelation about the pregnancy had come only in the wake of rumors about the circumstances of Trig's birth. Palin hadn't publicly revealed her own pregnancy until practically the moment Trig came into the world; reportedly she had gone into labor in Texas, where her water had broken—though she later claimed that her amniotic fluid was merely leaking—and then taken a long plane ride back to Alaska to give birth. Now there was a widely disseminated conspiracy theory that the baby wasn't really hers, but Bristol's. The allegation had found traction on, yes, generally liberal, Obama-supporting, Palin-hating blogs, a truth that the McCain camp was already flogging as persecution of their working-class female candidate by the elite.

The focus on and fetishization of pregnancy from both left and right was dispiriting. I understood that it was way more fun to cook up theories about the Palin family's quirks than it was to talk about policy. But it firmly resituated women's political prospects back in the realms of sex, scandal, and maternity, in a year and a presidential campaign that had so far managed not to be about female fecundity, but competitive ferocity.

To his credit Barack Obama held a very firm position on Bristol Palin's pregnancy, noting that if anyone in his campaign were to push the story forward they would be fired. Obama said that the pregnancy "has no relevance to Governor Palin's performance as a governor or her potential performance as a vice president." He also pointed out that his own mother had been eighteen when she gave birth to him. "How a family deals with issues and teenage children, that shouldn't be the topic of our politics," he said. But it was.

☆ ☆ ☆

Palin's speech at the Republican convention was astonishingly good. She lionized McCain, pointedly calling him "a true profile in courage." "Our family has the same ups and downs as any other," she said, pressing home her dysfunctional bona fides, talking about her son and nephew serving in the Middle East, and promising families of special-needs children that if she and her running mate were elected they would "have a friend and advocate in the White House." She thanked small-town America and her parents, noting, "Among the many things I owe them is a simple lesson that I've learned: that this is America, and every woman can walk through every door of opportunity." Especially one that had been sledge-hammered open for her in advance. Then Palin got mean, discussing her own experience. "I guess a small-town mayor is sort of like a 'community organizer,'" she said with a sneer, "except that you have actual responsibilities. I might add that in small towns, we don't quite know what to make of a candidate who lavishes praise on working people when they're listening, and then talks about how bitterly they cling to their religion and guns when those people aren't listening."

Palin's speech was delivered with an appealing calm that made me wonder whether, when she was done, she might enjoy some fava beans and a nice Chianti. I feared that I had just seen the future of gender politics, and that its name was Sarah Palin. Staring at her on television, all I could think was, *This is it. She's going to be the first woman president.*

That was when I began to have a series of persistent nightmares. I wish I could claim that they were sophisticated ones in which Palin led troops into Vancouver or led children in a recitation of "Sinners in the Hands of an Angry God." Alas, they were juvenile fear fantasies in which she kidnapped my cats and enjoyed brunches with my girlfriends while I banged on the restaurant window; in one tour-de-force she was an actual witch leering at me from a windswept hill, a baby doll grasped menacingly in her hands.

As these night terrors demonstrated, Palin's candidacy was testing my own beliefs about how I respond to women in power. My reactions to her were all tied up in her gender, a factor that I had always believed, as a matter of course and principle, should neither bolster nor dim impressions of a person's goodness or badness, smartness or dumbness, substance or lack thereof. When it came to Palin, I worried that my rules were changing.

I was perfectly capable of picking out and objecting to the sexism being leveled against the governor by the press, her detractors, and her own party. The liberalish radio host Ed Schultz, who had said on air that Palin set off a "bimbo alert," also asked, in conversation with Larry King and Republican Susan Molinari, "What kind of mother is she? Is she prepared to be the vice president? Is she going to be totally focused on the issues?" The *Washington Post*'s Sally Quinn asked if Palin was "prepared for the all-consuming nature of the job. . . . Her first priority has to be her children. When the phone rings at three in the morning and one of her children is really sick what choice will she make?"

That stuff was all familiar and sickening, and plenty of people on the left said so, from the linguistics professor Deborah Tannen, who called questions about Palin's ability to mother sexist, to the former Clinton strategist Howard Wolfson, who said, "There's no way those questions would be asked of a male candidate." Kim Gandy of NOW released a statement making it clear that though she did not support Palin and though her organization would be working to help elect Barack Obama, they would "monitor the media and call them out for their sexism directed at Palin. A woman slurred, regardless of her party or stances, is a woman slurred." The feminist writer and lawyer Susan Estrich weighed in, remarking, "No one would be asking these questions if she were a man. No one asked whether Arnold Schwarzenegger should run for governor because he has four children. . . . This is how the double standard works. . . . I have no doubt that Barack Obama can count on his fingers the number of times he has been home in the last 19 months to put his two beautiful daughters to bed. . . . Does this make him a 'bad father'? Should it undercut his claim to the presidency? Of course not."

But all that stuff was clean-cut. I was torn about the more subtle ways in which Palin's gender had me all disoriented. The rhetorical ground had shifted so quickly beneath the feet of feminists, that I was left with only a tenuous grasp on even the basic vocabulary of my beat. Palin, who initially referred to herself as a feminist, was being written about as one, including in a piece in *Adweek,* which called her "a classic third-wave feminist." Serrin Foster, the president of Feminists for Life, was on NPR crowing about the fact that Palin was "proud to say she is a feminist and pro-life at the same time."

During a panel at *Newsweek*'s Women & Leadership Conference in March 2008 Karen Breslau had asked Palin what she saw in the coverage of Clinton. Palin replied, "I do think that it's a more concentrated criticism that Hillary gets on so many fronts; I think that's unfortunate. But . . . she does herself a disservice to even mention it, really. You have to plow through that and know what you're getting into. . . . When I hear a statement . . . coming from a woman candidate with any kind of perceived whine about that excess criticism or a sharper microscope put on her, I think, man, that doesn't do us any good. . . . Work harder, prove to yourself to an even greater degree that you're capable, that you're going to be the best candidate . . . [it bothers] me a little bit to hear her bring that attention to herself on that level." But now that it was Palin under the microscope, she and her allies were perfectly willing to "whine."

Republicans were eager to talk about the sexism Palin was facing. Former Pennsylvania senator Rick Santorum not only opposed the use of birth control but had compared legal abortion to the institution of slavery and believed that radical feminists had forced women into the workforce against their will. Now he was talking about Palin as the "Clarence Thomas for feminists," by which he meant that feminists had an obligation to support her, just as "the African-American community obviously should have rallied behind Clarence Thomas and his achievement." Rudy Giuliani, the former mayor of New York who had famously used a press conference to let his second wife know he was leaving her, asked delegates at the Republican convention, "How dare they question whether Sarah Palin has enough time to spend with her children and be vice president? How dare they do that! When do they ever ask a man that question? When?" That morning, he'd taken his consciousness-raising roadshow to television, asking on CBS, "Where are the feminists?" and telling Fox News, "I'm at the point of [being] really angry!" McCain's advisor Steve Schmidt was painting any questions about Palin's vetting, or really any criticism of her at all, as an attempt "to destroy the first female Republican nominee for vice president of the United States who has never been a part of the old boys' network that has come to dominate the news establishment in this country."

Some days it felt as if I was watching a civics filmstrip about how much progress women made on the presidential stage in 2008 burst into flames, while in the back of the room a substitute teacher was threading a new reel into the projector. It had the same message and some of the same signifiers—Glass ceilings broken! Girl Power! Old boys' clubs!—but its meaning had been distorted. Hillary Clinton's 18 million cracks had weakened not only the White House's glass ceiling, but the wall protecting *Roe v. Wade*. The potential first female vice president in American history described her early career as that of "your average hockey mom" who "never really set out to be involved in public affairs." Teen pregnancy, once an illustrative talisman for sex educators and contraception distributors, now served those who sought to eliminate sex education and contraception.

In this strange new pro-woman tableau, feminism meant voting for someone who would limit reproductive control, access to health care, and environmental protections. It meant cheering for someone who supported the teaching of creationism alongside evolution, who had reportedly inquired locally about the possibility of using her position to ban certain books from the public library. Palin was the kind of feminist who by dint of her large family and load-bearing husband managed to juggle family and a burgeoning political career, but who would support no medical, health care, family leave or labor policies that would make similar paths possible for other women. In this *Handmaid's Tale*–inflected universe, in which femininity was worshipped but females denied rights, the CNBC pundit Donny Deutsch told us that we were witnessing "a new creation . . . of the feminist ideal," appealing because instead of being voiced by hairy old bats with unattractive ideas about power, it was now embodied by a woman who did what Hillary Clinton did not: "put a skirt on." Deutsch went on to say, "I want her watching my kids, I want her laying next to me in bed."

What Palin so beguilingly represented, not only to Deutsch but to the general public, was a form of female power that was utterly digestible to those who had no intellectual or political use for actual women: feminism without the feminists.

Although the Republicans would have us believe that Palin could simply stand in for Hillary Clinton, there was nothing interchangeable about these politicians. We had begun the election with one kind of woman and had ended up being asked to accept her polar opposite as a (cuter and beskirted!) consolation prize. Clinton's femininity, based on competence and an assumption of authority that upended gender expectations, was the kind that remained slightly unpalatable in America. It was a kind of power that had nothing to do with the flirtatious or the traditionally feminine. It was authority that was threatening because it so closely and calmly resembled the kind of power that the guys on the presidential stage had never questioned their right to wield.

The pro-woman rhetoric surrounding Palin's nomination, on the other hand, was a crafty bastardization of everything feminism had stood for. More than any of the intergenerational pro- or anti-Hillary arguments that had provoked such consternation during the primaries, I feared that Palin's candidacy and the faux feminism in which it was wrapped would actually imperil women's progress rather than speed it. If adopted as a successful narrative by the nation and its women, Palin's story would not just subvert but erase the meaning of what real progress for women meant, what real gender bias consisted of, what real discrimination looked like. It would put us all in reverse.

Perhaps that's why my reaction to Palin was so bone-deep, and why she was shaking some of my convictions about how to approach gender. When, on an early September Sunday morning, I picked up the *New York Post* with its front-page headline "Lady Killer: Hill to Check Hockey Mom" next to photos of Palin in porno-librarian mode and Clinton with her teeth bared, I did not roll my eyes in disgust at the imagined cage match. Instead I envisioned it. More than that: I enjoyed it. I wanted more than a hockey metaphor, hoping instead for a cinematic showdown, in which Clinton showed up, guns blazing Ripley-style, to surprise the mother alien just as she is about to feast on independent voters, shouting, "Get away from them, you bitch!"

Everything about the narrative surrounding Palin (and my fantasies of her defeat) was hypercombative and hyperfeminized, including the emerging media line about how it was, of course, the fault of Hillary supporters that she existed in the first place. Those who had raised their voice about sexism, those who had expressed an interest in female leadership, those who had made a fuss—they were somehow to blame for Sarah Palin and were therefore being implicated in the distortion of a feminist project.

This was the claim. And there was a germ of truth in it. But one could lay just as much blame at the feet of those on the left who failed to speak out about sexism when Hillary was running. For while it chafed to hear Rudy Giuliani and John McCain hold forth on the injustice of gender bias, part of what their running commentary threw into stark relief for anyone paying attention was the fact that we had never heard a peep or squawk or gurgle of this nature from anyone in the Democratic Party during the entire time Hillary Clinton had been running for president. If any of the Democrats had taken to defending her with a fraction of the zeal and bluster the right was now applying to Palin's cause, there might not have been so many angry people in the Democratic Party for Republicans to prey on. If there hadn't been so much stone-cold silence, so much shoulder-shrugging "What, me sexist?" inertia from the left, if there had been a little more respect accorded to the unsubtle clues being transmitted by 18 million voters that maybe they were interested in this whole woman-in-the-White-House thing, then the right would not have had the juice to charge this particular device.

Which led straight to my greatest nightmare: that because my own party had not cared enough to lay its rightful claim to the language of women's rights, Sarah Palin would reach historic heights of power by conforming to every outdated notion of what it meant to be a woman. I feared that she would hit her marks by clambering over the backs, the bodies, the rights of the women on whose behalf she claimed to be working, and that she would do it all under the banner of feminism, a banner that had essentially been handed to her by a party that was not proud enough to march under it.

10   POP CULTURE WARRIORS

IN THE DAYS following her Twin Cities rollout Sarah Palin agreed to a lone sit-down interview with ABC's Charlie Gibson, a demoralizing affair in which Gibson failed to disguise his pleasure at catching her out on her lack of familiarity with the Bush Doctrine. Gibson's condescension garnered Palin enough sympathy to neutralize the potentially candidacy-killing effects of the interview, but the conversation had exposed serious gaps in Palin's ability to discuss policy. The McCain camp quickly cordoned Palin off from the talking press, parading her silently in front of cameras at the U.N. and cultivating an air of inaccessibility that provoked suspicion among the media and the public. Under pressure the campaign at last agreed to let Palin sit down with CBS anchor Katie Couric. In her book *Going Rogue* Palin would write that she believed the interview was supposed to be "pretty mellow . . . short and sweet, about balancing motherhood and [her] life as governor," a cushy arrangement brokered by Nicolle Wallace, Couric's former colleague and Palin's advisor. Everyone else involved in the negotiations, including Wallace, denied Palin's version of events. Whatever the terms, the

Couric-Palin conversations that took place over a few days in late September turned out to be some of the most devastating and gripping television in the history of presidential politics.

Palin came off as bewilderingly flat-footed, ill-equipped even to bullshit her way out of tight conversational spots, and prone to bizarre enunciations that verged on self-parody. Observations like "The bad guys are the ones who say Israel is a stinking corpse and should be wiped off the face of the earth. That's not a good guy who is saying that," and that Alaska's "narrow maritime border" with Russia afforded her foreign policy experience made Palin sound politically infantile. Most damning was her inability to express herself clearly: her sentences were knotted, labyrinthine thickets from which she could not cleanly emerge without simply trailing off.

The interviews, when they aired, could have been set to the music from *Jaws*. "I'm just going to ask you one more time," Couric said at one point, smiling almost apologetically: "Specific examples in [McCain's] twenty-six years of pushing for more regulation?" Palin could only chirrup lamely, "I'll try to find you some and I'll bring them to you!" *Chomp!* Just like that, Couric totaled Palin's reputation, at least for the 2008 race.

Inevitably both Palin's supporters and her critics began to emit a bleating sympathy. The conservative pundits Kathleen Parker and Kathryn Jean Lopez wrote of their shuddering realizations that Palin was not ready for the spotlight. *Salon*'s Glenn Greenwald watched the Couric segments and confessed that he "actually felt sorry" for Palin. Judith Warner wrote a column on her *New York Times* blog called "Poor Sarah," about the wave of "self-recognition and sympathy [that] washed over" her when she saw a photo of Palin talking to Henry Kissinger. Palin, "a woman fully aware that she was out of her league, scared out of her wits, hanging on for dear life," reminded Warner of herself, and of what she dubbed "Imposter Syndrome," a condition she imagined was shared by women who watched Palin and felt, "She *can't* possibly do it all—the kids, the special-needs baby, the big job, the big conversations with foreign leaders. And neither could they."

The spectacle was disquieting. As it became clear that McCain's team had elevated Palin to a presidential ticket not because she was a woman with the experience and credentials to be a vice president, but because she was a woman, Palin's personal and professional shortcomings were being fused to her gender so tightly that even a clever critic like Warner projected upon her a spectral embodiment of her own grim self-estimation, and worse, a manifestation of some universal condition of female inadequacy.

I understood how terrible it felt to have one hand over your eyes and the other on the mute button while watching the second female candidate for vice president speak. But this misery moved me to anger, not to sympathy: anger at Palin, at the crassness of the man who had selected her, and at the misogynistic mash that had been made of an otherwise groundbreaking year. Why, after 18 million people voted for Hillary Clinton, was I reading about ladies who just couldn't imagine having a "big job" and "big conversations"? Even if the McCain campaign had been craven and sexist in thinking it could pass Palin off as an anemic Hillary substitute, she was in fact a grown woman, governor of her state, a candidate who averred that she had not blinked when asked to run for the vice presidency. I was willing to talk about the gendered double binds Palin faced, but not to feel sorry for her because she could not get through a television interview intact. She had made the choice to go on television in the first place.

I knew women like Sarah Palin, suburban mothers of my childhood acquaintances, savvy broads whose ambitions had been circumscribed by fate or economic circumstance but who believed, perhaps rightly or perhaps not, that they had been built for loftier opportunities than their world had so far offered them. Smart or stupid, gifted or lacking talent, these were women possessed of self-certainty as much as of vulnerability; they were survivors, not snifflers. I refused to be manipulated into another stage of gendered regress based on the assumption that Palin could not withstand the criticism she was earning.

This was a woman who took the national stage and sneered at the work of community activists. She told Couric that she did not get a passport until 2007 because she hadn't come from a family that handed out backpacking trips, thereby passing off incuriosity and lassitude as "regular people" qualities and doing a disservice to plenty of Americans who didn't come from privilege yet still managed to learn about the larger world. I did not feel sorry for a woman who used her special-needs child to garner support from Americans in need of health care reform she didn't support. I did not feel sorry for anyone whose project was reliant on the support of women whose rights she would limit and whose civil liberties she would curtail. Pity for Sarah Palin seemed disrespectful of every woman who had ever been unfairly dismissed based on her gender, because Palin's was a fair dismissal based on her willingness to take on a job for which she was not qualified. It was disrespectful of minority populations of every stripe whose place in the political spectrum had been unfairly interpreted as tokenism, because in Palin's case her presence on the ticket was tokenism of the basest variety. And Palin was tough. She could bite the head off a moose and move on.

☆ ☆ ☆

What I did think was remarkable was that it had not been at the hands of Charlie Gibson—or Brian Williams, or Chris Matthews, or Tom Brokaw—that Palin had fallen, but at the hands of Katie Couric, who despite almost a decade as the highest-earning television journalist on the planet and a history-making arrival as the first solo female anchor of a nightly newscast, was still regarded as perky and unserious. And it wasn't just Couric who was turning in good work. Although the year in media bluster may have been owned by the frat boys at MSNBC, in those fall weeks the season's defining interviews, most fine-boned analysis, and buzziest commentary were coming from their newsroom sisters.

In her 2007 book *The Terror Dream* Susan Faludi points to the post-9/11 ardor for mission-accomplishin' masculinity as the cause of the decreasing frequency with which female journalists and pundits appeared on air and in print through the mid-aughts. Later in the decade, though, it was possible to detect an emergence from that gender depression, a shift surely catalyzed by the emergence of powerful female political players, including Condoleezza Rice, Nancy Pelosi, Hillary Clinton, and Sarah Palin. "You want African Americans around to talk about Barack Obama, right?" Couric said to me in a 2009 interview. "You want women around to reflect their experiences and see a female candidate through their particular prism."

To some small extent the media had to mirror the figures and stories it was covering. For generations politics had been male and white, and in turn the political media had been male and white. Frances Kissling, the former head of Catholics for a Free Choice, had often referred to *Meet the Press* as "Meet the Patriarchy." But the strides made by female political figures in the first decade of the twenty-first century created a corresponding appetite for female interlocutors who could make sense of their advancements. Female newscasters, long considered interlopers in the exclusively male domain of presidential politics, now had a choice perspective, not only on the women candidates, but on the world's reactions to them. By the blighted standards of its history, the American political media was crawling with women in 2008.

It would be reported in 2010 that NBC veteran Andrea Mitchell was the television reporter with the most evening airtime of the decade, clocking in at 2,416 minutes between 2000 and 2009. At CNN Candy Crowley was dominating coverage of Clinton's campaign, turning in such reliable reporting that Gloria Steinem wrote her a fan letter. Dana Bash admirably parried the sexist insinuations of John Roberts, and Gloria Borger and Donna Brazile were regular mainstays of the CNN politics panels. PBS's Gwen Ifill hosted the vice-presidential debate; 2004's most popular pundits, Arianna Huffington and Ana Marie Cox, remained a cable news presence, and a cast of new talking heads appeared, including Melissa Harris-Lacewell, Anne Kornblut, Leslie Sanchez and Joan Walsh, all of whom regularly duked it out on MSNBC and CNN. "It definitely had to do with there being a woman candidate," Walsh told me about her fast-multiplying invitations to be a cable guest in 2008.

Latoya Peterson, a writer at *Racialicious* who did some commentary on CNN, said, "The election allowed a lot of us to get a toe-hold where we wouldn't have before. . . . The need to have different types of people discussing these issues allowed so many more people [a] chance to be heard." Faludi herself was contributing op-eds about the gender politics of the election to a *New York Times* editorial page that now included not just the prose cartoons of Maureen Dowd, but also an incisive, funny political column by Gail Collins. In 2005 *Salon* had launched *Broadsheet,* a section of the magazine devoted to women's news, and during the election season *Slate* fol-

lowed suit with its blog (later a short-lived stand-alone website) the
XX Factor. Texas Monthly launched a political column called "In
the Pink," and the *Washington City Paper* debuted a section called
"The Sexist." At the same time, long-ghettoized girl zones like daytime television were providing political insight, and breakout stars
like Couric, Rachel Maddow and Campbell Brown were asserting
their perspectives on the unfolding election narrative and building
audiences.

☆ ☆ ☆

One of the canniest questions asked of Hillary Clinton in all of
2008 came from Couric, during a webcast following the final debate
between Barack Obama and John McCain: "Why do you think
Sarah Palin has an action figure and you have a nutcracker?" Couric would later tell me what she believed the answer was: "Sarah
Palin was less threatening than Hillary, it's pretty basic." But her
exchange with Clinton never got that far. Instead Clinton replied
with transparent insincerity, "I don't have any idea, Katie." Couric pushed her about whether she ever felt "the injustice of it all."
No, said Clinton, before turning mock-serious: "Maybe someday
I'll have an action figure. . . . I still have aspirations!" Couric flashed
a grin—gummy, leonine—and joked, "A girl can dream, can't she?"
    Apparently she could. Two years after having taken an inglo-
rious nose-dive from NBC morning to CBS prime time, Couric
found herself widely credited with having changed the course of a
presidential election. An advertising generator for NBC during her
Today tenure, Couric had been sold for years as America's sweet-
heart, at least when she wasn't in contract negotiations; then she
was splashed across tabloids as a hard-bargaining businesswoman
who chewed through producers. In 2006 she grabbed at the opportunity to become the first woman to sit alone at the nightly news
desk; CBS would pay her $15 million a year for it. The move caused
a media fracas about her lack of gravitas, in which critics emphasized that their qualms weren't about Couric being a *woman,* but
about her being a woman who had spent her mornings reporting
with gloss and bounce on fad diets and celebrity breakups. Few
seemed to recognize that being glossy and bouncy before noon was

one of the only avenues open to women in the television news business. The complaints were an early iteration of the "It's not any woman, it's *that* woman" line that would be deployed against Hillary Clinton by those who didn't stop to consider the factors that might lead a woman to become like *that*. The *Sturm und Drang* surrounding Couric's move might have been appropriate had it been 1943 and the Pentagon transferring stewardship of the Manhattan Project to Lassie. "The fact that networks seem willing to concede that the best man for the job is clearly a woman means that it just isn't the same job anymore," David Carr wrote in the *New York Times*.

After a nanosecond of boost upon its debut, Couric's nightly broadcast, indeed leavened with celebrity baby photos and chatty familiarity, plonked CBS right back into its long-held third-place berth. As Couric told me later, "People seemed to take some sort of perverse joy in it."

★ ★ ★

Even before the Palin interview Couric had been making election season noise: she was one of the only journalists to voice her dissatisfaction with her colleagues' treatment of Clinton during the race, asserting at a June 2008 speech, "Senator Clinton received some of the most unfair, hostile coverage I've ever seen." In a later segment she noted, "One of the great lessons of [Clinton's] campaign is the continued and accepted role of sexism in American life, particularly in the media." Accusing her male peers of misogyny was a bold move in those overheated, hyperdefensive days. Keith Olbermann responded by naming Couric a World's Worst Person, huffing and puffing, "It is sad that Ms. Couric could not have . . . separated the hype from the news in her own promulgation of the nonsense that Senator Clinton was a victim of pronounced sexism."

But according to the critics, Couric turned in the best network coverage of the political conventions. It was made of the same stuff that had long powered her career: intelligence, approachability, and journalistic instinct. One incident, in which she nabbed Michael Dukakis in a Denver security line and got an interview that ended with the former Democratic presidential candidate apologizing to the American people for the Bush dynasty, was part of what prompted *Times* critic Carr to point out "what has been apparent for the last two decades to anybody with a television: Ms. Couric is a highly skilled interviewer, and people tend to tell her stuff." With the poll-rattling Palin interview, which got more airtime than *It's a Wonderful Life* on Christmas Eve and burned its way across the Internet, Couric's provocative critiques about her colleagues' sexism were forgotten. Her success was in drawing out Palin's inchoate sputtering by asking mostly very direct and mild questions, an approach reminiscent of Roger Mudd's 1979 interview with presidential hopeful Ted Kennedy, who had drawn a rambling blank when Mudd had queried simply, "Why do you want to be president?" Couric's straightforward approach was the sort that she had honed on morning television, where the goal was not to skewer, but simply to engage. "During the course of the interview I made sure I was as nonjudgmental as possible," Couric told me, "that I had no facial affect, that I didn't even cock my head when I didn't understand what she was saying." When I asked her whether she felt her gender had any impact on the way she approached Palin, she suggested that perhaps it was less about her approach than viewers' responses. "Charlie was criticized for having his glasses and being overly avuncular and condescending, which I frankly didn't think he was. But people project into whatever situation they're looking at. Perhaps the fact that I was female [made] people [feel] that it was less threatening. I don't know."

In 2010 CBS News would receive two Alfred I. duPont–Columbia University Awards, one for Couric's Palin interviews. The award committee pointed out that Couric's approach "prompted the most revealing remarks and had the greatest impact on the presidential campaign. . . . These were the interviews heard around the world." True, most people didn't watch their news at six-thirty anymore, but Couric's impact was significant: she had pushed the role of network news anchor beyond the confines of a televised half-hour, proved that the job still had the power to alter political story lines, and opened a door that other women might walk though—without having to fit themselves into anchor chairs that had been built for men.

Couric's former *Today* colleague Campbell Brown was also carving out new space at CNN. Brown, who moved to cable after having been passed over for Couric's *Today* job, was a frank and amiable television presence. She began appearing on her nightly CNN show, *Election Center,* in March 2008 and by fall was an Internet sensation thanks to a series of interviews and commentaries in which she displayed a short-tempered impatience with the dishonesties of a manipulative election season. It started with her demanding straight answers about Palin's experience from McCain spokesman Tucker Bounds, whose clock she cleaned so efficiently that McCain canceled an appearance on CNN's *Larry King Live* in retaliation.

When Palin was kept hermetically sealed from reporters during her visit to the U.N. Brown took to her anchor desk and went *Network* on the McCain campaign. "I have had enough of the sexist treatment of Sarah Palin," she began. Calling on the McCain campaign to "stop treating Sarah Palin like she is a delicate flower that will wilt at any moment," she went on, "She is strong, she is tough, she is confident. And you claim she is ready to be one heartbeat away from the presidency. If that is the case, then end this chauvinistic treatment of her now. . . . Free Sarah Palin." Brown told me in 2008, "I was [simply trying to point to] a degree of hypocrisy in accusing those of us in the media of being tougher on her than we would have been on another candidate because she was a woman. We would have been just as tough on any presidential candidate we had so little information about."

In late October Brown again let loose, this time on Palin's behalf. The press had latched on to revelations that Palin had spent $150,000 of the Republican National Committee's money on clothes for her and her family to wear on the campaign trail. The disparagement this information inspired on the left reflected a major comprehension gap about how much it cost to keep a woman looking well-groomed, especially by the harsh aesthetic standards of the modern celebrity (and political) media and especially when her appearance was not only part of the campaign's investment, but destined to be scrutinized by fans and detractors alike. It escalated into a point-and-hoot festival of Palin hate that became quickly misogynistic. Brown said on air, "There is an incredible double standard here and we are ignoring a very simple reality: women are judged based on their appearance far, far more than men . . . and look, I speak from experience here. When I wear a bad outfit on the air, I get viewer e-mail complaining about it, a lot of e-mail, seriously. When Wolf Blitzer wears a not-so-great tie, how much e-mail do you think he gets?" Brown said. There has been plenty of talk and plenty written about Sarah Palin's jackets, her hair, her looks. . . . There was plenty of talk and plenty written about Hillary Clinton's looks, hair, pantsuits. Compare that to the attention given to Barack Obama's fifteen-hundred-dollar suits or John McCain's five-hundred-twenty-dollar Ferragamo shoes." These were not issues that had historically been brought to bear on presidential elections. Now a dustup about the budget of a vice-presidential campaign was allowing women in news rooms to communicate careers-worth of marginalization.

✳ ✳ ✳

Women were also shaking up election coverage in another under-valued genre: the daytime talk show. It wasn't unusual for political candidates to appear on chat shows, but in 2008 they weren't always there just to share recipes (except when John McCain cooked ribs with Rachael Ray) or accept moony compliments (except when Barbara Walters told Barack Obama he was "very sexy looking"). In the lead-up to primaries throughout the general election it also became increasingly possible to see politicians, especially conservatives like McCain, made uncomfortable by the informal assertiveness of daytime television.

Perhaps it was the product of a generation of post-second-wave female journalists, from Couric to Sawyer to Brown to Meredith Vieira, finding prime-time berths either unavailable or inhospitable and settling into female-friendly daytime slots. Or perhaps it was because daytime talk television had expanded to include women of different colors (Oprah Winfrey, Tyra Banks, Whoopi Goldberg, Sherri Shepherd), ages (Joy Behar, Barbara Walters), and sexualities (Rosie O'Donnell, Ellen DeGeneres) than the more straitlaced white guy nightly news, creating a more diverse platform on which to casually entertain socially progressive issues.

Most likely of all was that 2008's energetic daytime engagement with the presidential election was a side effect of Oprah Winfrey's engagement with Obama's campaign. Winfrey had leveraged decades of cultural capital to endorse Barack Obama, giving him a boost that may have helped put him over the top in Iowa. But unwilling to exploit her platform on Obama's behalf, Winfrey was clear that she would not invite him or the other candidates onto her show, as had been her custom in past election years. This sent presidential contenders scurrying to reach daytime audiences via other chatty outlets that did not adhere to traditional templates for political discourse. Thus were born some of the most weirdly sophisticated and direct exchanges of the season.

In the year preceding the election Ellen DeGeneres was talking a lot about her wedding to actress Portia de Rossi, a union that had especially sharp political implications thanks to California's Proposition 8, which would reverse the state's legalization of gay marriage. In September 2007, when Hillary Clinton told DeGeneres that she supported equal benefits for gay partners, a repeal of "don't ask, don't tell," and an end to discriminatory hiring practices—an exasperating everything-but-marriage response—DeGeneres cut to the political quick by asking, "Do you think it would be possible for someone to run and openly say 'I support gay marriage' and win?" In May 2008 she opened her interview with McCain by saying, "Let's talk about the big elephant in the room," in reference to her forthcoming nuptials. McCain responded, "I think that people should be able to enter into legal agreements. . . . I just believe in the unique status of marriage between man and woman." DeGeneres replied, "We are all the same people. You're no different than I am. Our love is the same. . . . When someone says, 'You can have a contract, and you'll still have insurance' . . . it sounds to me like saying, 'Well you can sit [here], you just can't sit there.'" McCain could only say, "I've heard you articulate that position in a very eloquent fashion. We just have a disagreement and I, along with many many others, wish you every happiness."

By October DeGeneres was discussing Sarah Palin's support of Proposition 8 and telling viewers, "Maybe it's because I'm gay that I think we should all be equal, but . . . we need to learn to love [people] for who they are and let them love who they want to love." These were glimpses of what a daytime cadence made possible: a faux-breezy exchange as vehicle for a larger, sometimes genuinely moving conversation about justice and equality within the democracy.

Over at *The View* Barbara Walters and company were, as the *New York Times* reported, making "a conscious effort . . . to insert their daytime talk show forcefully into the nation's political conversation." And they did it to occasionally impressive effect, such as on September 12, when John McCain sat down with Whoopi Goldberg, Joy Behar, Sherri Shepherd (who had previously admitted that she had never voted before 2008) and Elisabeth Hasselbeck. Presiding was Walters, who after decades of barreling away in legitimate journalism, in her later years had put herself to pasture in the daytime lineup.

Walters and her colleagues began to quiz McCain about campaign ads misleadingly suggesting that Obama had used the phrase "lipstick on a pig" in reference to Sarah Palin. "We know that those two ads are untrue, they're lies," said Behar, using words that the press had been too polite to utter. "Yet . . . at the end of it [you] say 'I approve these messages.' Do you really approve them?" In the next segment Goldberg jocularly asked McCain if she was allowed to call him J-Mac, and then asked, "Do you believe in the separation of church and state?" When McCain said that "sure," he believed in secularism, Goldberg asked whether he was troubled by the fact that his running mate did not share this view; she was referring to Palin's expressed belief that the Iraq war was God's will and to her Christian-inflected opposition to abortion even in cases of rape and incest. "Judeo-Christian values were the foundation of our nation," McCain responded. Goldberg retorted that the nation was made up not only of Judeo-Christian disciples but of "Muslims . . . Zoroastrians . . . [and] Wiccans." Even Hasselbeck, the program's conservative bugaboo, after assuring McCain that he had her vote, asked if he would overturn *Roe v. Wade*. McCain replied that while he wouldn't impose a litmus test on Supreme Court nominees, "they would have to have a clear record of strict interpretation," which Walters promptly translated as "another way of saying 'people who would want to overturn *Roe v. Wade*.'" When McCain again talked up a strict interpretation of the Constitution Goldberg asked, "Do I need to worry about becoming a slave again? . . . Because certain things . . . in the Constitution . . . had to change." To this, all McCain could say was, "That's an excellent point. I thank you."

It was not only great television, but great journalistic interrogation from people unafraid to ask combative questions of a presidential candidate. *The View*'s hosts appeared so roused by the pelts hanging from the edge of their coffee table that they spent the rest of the political season wallowing in debate about the Weather Underground and the Keating Five like a *MacNeil/Lehrer NewsHour* that also included interviews with the likes of "the fabulous Alec Baldwin!"

☆ ☆ ☆

All this paled in comparison to the year's most improbable news media juggernaut, MSNBC's Rachel Maddow, whose combination of relatable zeal and high-brow smarts made her a television anomaly. Maddow kicked off the election season with her impish revelation to Pat Buchanan and Chris Matthews that bloggers were blaming Clinton's New Hampshire victory on Matthews's overzealotry. "I didn't mean it in a mean way at all," Maddow told me in a summer 2008 interview. "But I knew that it was just going to blow his mind."

Matthews was far from the first talking head to get the Maddow treatment. Before primary season began, clips of Maddow, an Air America host often invited to cable news shows as a ballsy gremlin of the left, had flooded the Internet. Her specialty was making Tucker Carlson's head explode and getting under Buchanan's skin until all he could do was gibber at her about socialism. But the election klieg lights that transform character actors into media leading ladies had made Maddow, at thirty-five, with fewer than five years of national broadcast experience under her belt, the explosive newcomer of 2008, landing her own nightly hour-long show just after the political conventions concluded.

Air America had taken a chance on her (her prior broadcast experience was as a part-time "newsgirl" at a local radio station in western Massachusetts) when it launched in 2004. Four years later love was too weak a word to describe how some people felt about Rachel Maddow. They lurved her, loaved her, luffed her. *New York* magazine's online "Intelligencer" column ran an item headlined "Why We're Gay for Rachel Maddow," and the blogosphere was dotted with similarly besotted posts.

What was remarkable about Maddow's ascension was not its

velocity—Anderson Cooper's coverage of Hurricane Katrina had made him a household name in less than a week—but the shifts in media it seemed to demarcate. Maddow was one of the few left-liberal women to have busted open the world of TV punditry, which had previously made icons of right-wing commentators like Ann Coulter and Michelle Malkin. Unlike her pneumatic, bilious female counterparts on the right or her cocksure male colleagues, Maddow had succeeded not through bluster, but thanks to a combination of brisk thinking and galumphing good cheer. She was neither a shiny matinee idol nor a smooth-talking partisan hack. She was a Rhodes scholar, a lesbian, and a policy wonk with a Ph.D. who had started as an AIDS activist focused on prison reform. Her rise seemed to signal a hopeful move away from the thuggish and angry and toward the lucid and nuanced.

Part of the hypnotic hold Maddow had on her audience was that despite her place in the "liberal media's" firmament, her election commentary was, in a funny way, nonpartisan. During the incendiary primary season she maintained an almost maddening equilibrium, expressing dismay and appreciation for just about every candidate. Weeks after Clinton's concession Maddow called the New York senator's war vote "unforgivable." But Maddow had also risen to her defense, especially in moments when no one else was willing to. She found herself "frequently underwhelmed" by Obama, and would go on to remain a critic of his administration, especially his ramping up in Afghanistan. "He got it right in opposing the war," she said to me in the summer of 2008, "but his war policy stuff now is bullshit." It was ironic that Maddow, perhaps Air America's most successful product (besides future senator Al Franken), had traveled through the looking glass of partisan journalism and come out the other side an electoral agnostic, a liberal in the purest, almost mineral sense of the word.

During the election Maddow was very often the only girl in the room. "It means I get dumb questions that I wouldn't otherwise get," she told me. "Anything about gender, anything about women voters, even if I really obviously have no expertise in the subject or it's not my turn to talk. I get that question." She smiled. "I love the idea that I am the voice of woman. Look at me! It's like, really?

The one woman in the room is really mannish!" She gestured at her baseball T-shirt and baggy jeans.

The segments that got Maddow the most traction out of the gate were, unsurprisingly, her bits on Palin, especially one about Palin's bizarro-world insistence that a legislative report on the Alaskan ethics scandal Troopergate revealed that she did not abuse her authority, when in fact it had found the opposite to be true. Maddow's commentary was direct: "She is lying. This is a person running for office who's been confronted with an uncomfortable and inconvenient fact, and her response to that is to look into the camera and lie to you. Enthusiastically and repeatedly." Like the other journalists I spoke to, Maddow didn't believe that her gender made her a better critic of Palin than she was of McCain or Obama or Biden. But the viral attention she got was often amplified after she said something pithy and cutting about the Alaska governor.

It was telling that the enthusiasm surrounding television's newswomen came not during Clinton's candidacy, but during Palin's. The dispiriting interpretation was that the willingness on the part of Couric, Maddow, Brown and other women to be tough on Palin fed an appetite for girl-on-girl combat. When I wrote columns critical of Palin they got more traffic than any other in my career, furthering my suspicions that viewers prefer their female journalists attacking other females.

But Brown had also made a splash defending Palin, and *The View* women had gone after McCain, not his running mate. There was clearly something else empowering television's women to come out swinging. Maybe it was months of bitten tongues, of sitting through Matthews and Olbermann and Joe Scarborough and Christopher Hitchens trying to explain how women think and vote and what they sound like. Now they had something to say for themselves.

✵ ✵ ✵

A year after the election some of the media surges by women had receded. After a maternity leave in 2009 Campbell Brown returned to lower ratings, and in May 2010 again showed off her knack for candor by announcing that because "not enough people want to watch my program," she was leaving it. Postelection, the obses-sion with Maddow began to cool, though she often beat her rival, Larry King, among viewers twenty-five to fifty-four. Enthusiasm for Couric's renaissance subsided, but she remained in the CBS anchor chair, dire predictions to the contrary. In December 2009 Diane Sawyer took over the evening anchor desk at ABC. The hosts of *The View,* for their part, made health care reform, troop escala-tion in Afghanistan, and gay marriage regular topics of their morn-ing kaffeeklatsch. They had rediscovered what groundbreaking talk show host Phil Donahue had observed sixteen years earlier, when he explained his own success: "The usual idea of women's program-ming was a narrow, sexist view. . . . Women were interested in a lot more than covered dishes and needlepoint." According to the *Los Angeles Times* in February 2010 *The View*'s ratings were high, and producer Bill Geddie told the paper, "We realized [that political conversation] wasn't just for Sunday mornings anymore." Even Sun-day mornings, long populated by Beltway-bound white guys jaw-ing about the week's news, were changing. In 2010 Candy Crowley was named the host of CNN's Sunday show *State of the Union,* and ABC handed stewardship of *This Week* to the veteran CNN foreign correspondent Christiane Amanpour.

With the election over, female punditry became less ubiquitous, though MSNBC, and *The Rachel Maddow Show* in particular, con-tinued to feature regular commentary from Ana Marie Cox, Melissa Harris-Lacewell, Joan Walsh and others. For some reason Walsh got the brunt of some marked male aggression. In January 2009 she was on MSNBC debating former House majority leader Dick Armey about the economic stimulus plan when Armey announced, "I'm so damn glad that you can never be my wife because I surely wouldn't have to listen to that prattle from you every day." Three months later, after she debated G. Gordon Liddy on CNN over the release of the Bush torture memos, Liddy said almost the exact same thing when he rehashed the debate on his radio show.

"I'd rather have it out there," Walsh said of these incidents. "Moments like that actually represent progress, because it was so shocking to so many people. It showed people what we're up against. Women are still judged on marriageability, and marriage-ability has a lot to do with keeping your mouth shut."

At the start of *The Terror Dream* Susan Faludi recounts a prophetic nightmare she had on the night of September 10, 2001, in
which she was shot in the throat by a young man on a plane. She
recalled, "[In the dream] I noticed that I was still alive but unable
to speak"—an apt image for her argument about the silencing of the
female media in an age of terrorism. Not ten years later the election
allowed a lot of women to dislodge the metaphorical bullets from
their throats. There still was not parity, but by refusing to keep
their mouths shut women were regaining their voices and expanding their presence in the media.

☆ ☆ ☆

The increasing number of powerful women in politics and media
during the election meant extended opportunities for the women
who portrayed them in other pop culture venues. As Amy Poehler
told me in 2008, "There are so many women . . . in politics and
entertainment and in positions of power that you get to imperson-
ate. It's really cool."

Predictably, there was still resistance to women gaining ground
in terrain that had always been dominated by men. In a December
2006 *Vanity Fair* piece called "Why Women Aren't Funny," Christopher Hitchens offered not an argument so much as a provoca-
tion—a stew of Rudyard Kipling verse and some claptrap about how
women find neither their "physical decay" nor their future of episi-
otomies inherently funny—alongside a photo of a lumpen, mirth-
less female whom *Feministing*'s Ann Friedman correctly observed
resembled no one so much as Hitchens himself. It was the small and
grating death rattle of a Rat Pack–era sentiment.

In April 2008 *Vanity Fair* published a winking mea culpa, putting comedians Tina Fey, Amy Poehler, and Sarah Silverman on its
cover alongside an article by Alessandra Stanley asking, "Who Says
Women Aren't Funny?" Stanley quoted Nora Ephron, who sensibly
observed, "There is no question that there are a million more funny
women than there used to be, but . . . there are more women in a
whole bunch of places, and this is one of them." As Poehler told me,
"The struggle as a female comedian was done for me by the women
that were on *SNL* from the beginning, or the women who were on

SCTV, or the women in the films in the eighties when I was growing up."

The Hitchens flap was mostly a sideshow and a distraction from
the truly compelling story about women and laughter at the start of
the twenty-first century: the introduction of sometimes dry, occasionally side-splitting humor into what most would agree had not,
until now, been an uproarious social movement. The news was not
that women were funny; it was that they were making feminism
funny.

✫ ✫ ✫

It wasn't that women had never been witty about the oppressions
and restrictions of their gender. Jane Austen became wildly popular, even with men, by transforming tales of the torturous fiscal
and romantic constraints of Regency womanhood into social satire.
But a century after Austen's death, as suffragists clamored loudly
for greater liberties and extended rights, the weight of their project and the unlikelihood of its triumph did not lend themselves to
whimsy. Neither did the social agitation of the 1960s and 1970s
do anything to diminish feminism's prim reputation. In part that
was because language that was offensive to feminists was often the
sexualized language of objectification; any attempt to police it was
countered with aspersions of frigidity. Gloria Steinem told me in
2009, "We were objecting to . . . guys in the street saying things
like 'Why aren't you smiling, honey?' . . . When we objected, that
probably gave us the reputation for being humorless." Then there
was the practical reality that there were not many belly laughs to
be harvested from the fight to break down prohibitive economic,
social, and professional barriers. Talking with the thirty-year-old
comedian Sarah Haskins in 2009, I ventured that feminism might
be getting funnier than ever before. Haskins's initial response was
to object, but then she paused and said, "Okay, actually, it wasn't
ever funny. 'I want to work at your office.' 'Ha ha.' 'No, I'm not joking. I want to work at your office.'"

Certain individual feminists were funny, both in public and
private. Covering the women's movement for *Esquire,* Ephron
penned wry pieces about consciousness-raising and those parties

where women used hand mirrors to look at their cervices. Erica Jong wrote sometimes hilariously about liberated female sexuality. Gloria Steinem, who worked as a television comedy writer before becoming a movement leader, was, Ephron told me in 2010, "much funnier than anyone remembers." In 1973 *Ms.* magazine ran a cover illustration of a Lichtenstein-style cartoon in which a man asks, "Do you know the women's movement has no sense of humor?" and a woman responds, "No . . . but hum a few bars and I'll fake it!" By and large, though, these chuckles were aberrations; feminism's straitlaced reputation was not altogether without merit.

But as conditions for some women began to improve, when they did not have to hold so fiercely to their convictions or fight as hard to get heard, women became increasingly likely to have a few laughs at their own expense, though often literally at their own expense; Phyllis Diller and Joan Rivers both succeeded in comedy's boys' club with brutally self-lacerating acts. The 1980s saw improvements in Hollywood, thanks to feminist comedies like *9 to 5* and later the emergence of Roseanne Barr and what Barbara Ehrenreich would call her "special brand of proletarian feminism." At the turn of the millennium Sarah Silverman's dirty act obliterated the assumptions behind Friars Club director Jean-Pierre Trebot's 1983 comment (in response to Diller dressing in drag to infiltrate the roast of Sid Caesar) that the club did not allow women because "the language gets kind of graphic." A 2007 episode of Silverman's eponymous Comedy Central series includes a nostalgic montage of her entering the same abortion clinic during the Reagan, Clinton, and Bush administrations while Green Day's lyrics "I hope you had the time of your life" plays in the background. Silverman's slightly less outrageous contemporary, Margaret Cho, crowed to Jessica Valenti in the *Guardian,* "Everything I do is about feminism," though that assertion was hard to reconcile with her joke, "Laura Bush is pretty but you know her pussy tastes like Lysol."

Increasingly, women were applying profane humor to politics, relationships and sexism itself. In a 2006 interview with Amy Poehler for *Bust* magazine the television writer Jill Soloway compared the still meager roles for adult female comedians to "a tiny pubic mustache." Poehler replied that female comedies should "be like full, giant '70s bushes." Wanda Sykes opined in her 2006 HBO comedy series about how great it would be "if our pussies were detachable." "You could do anything. You could go visit a professional ball player's hotel room at two o'clock in the morning. Sex? My pussy's not even in the building!"

Sykes made the most of 2008's political season, noting to Jay Leno in the fall of 2008, "I'm a feminist, but I'm sorry . . . [Sarah Palin]'s crazy!" Complaining that "they don't let [Palin] talk," Sykes continued, "They say, 'Oh, she's meeting with the world leaders,' but there's no reporters. I'm like, 'Is she meeting with the world leaders, or did you take her to the Epcot Center [and] let her drink around the world? Because I've done that! Maybe I should be secretary of state!" Months later Sykes returned to Leno's couch, mocking the press covering the about-to-be-inaugurated Obamas as "trying to dance around the race issue because they don't know how to do it without sounding racist. . . . 'Who's the real Michelle Obama?' . . . You know what they're saying is, 'When are we gonna see *this*?'" Here Sykes waved her finger in imitation of a black female stereotype. "They're waiting for her to throw all his stuff out on the White House lawn and [say] 'You get the hell out of my house!'"

"The power to make people laugh is a really big power," Steinem told me. "To come into a position where you can make people laugh not out of hostility but out of revelation, because you make people recognize something, is really big-time important." By 2008 women were yukking it up with a gut-busting abandon never before associated with gender and its discontents. Making jokes not necessarily (though sometimes) at the expense of other women, comedy was for the first time not just being embraced by feminism, but was serving a feminist agenda: making the circumstances of both liberation and lingering double standards laughably clear.

* * *

If Katie Couric was the nail in Sarah Palin's vice-presidential coffin, the hammer was Tina Fey. Fey's deadly impression of Palin was played out over half a dozen sketches for which Fey returned to *Saturday Night Live,* where she had been the first female head writer and where, in February, she made news with her comedic defense of Hillary Clinton, "Bitch is the new black." Her impression of Palin synthesized all that was mind-blowing about the vice-presidential candidate, crystallizing the improbability of her existence on a presidential ticket—and the hyperfeminized role she was hired to play there—with a (barely) amplified portrait of Palin's winking flirtatiousness, her rambling sentences, her dropped-*g* gerunds, and her penchant for trailing off midargument.

The Palin sketches, largely written by *SNL*'s Seth Meyers, contained indelible one-liners that captured Palin's self-assured vacuity and cheerful malevolence. As Fey's Palin described herself in a scene with Will Ferrell's George W. Bush, "I'm one part practiced folksy, one part sassy, and a little dash of high school bitchy!" They also communicated the hypocrisies and inconsistencies of her religious social conservatism. "I believe that marriage is meant to be a sacred institution between two unwilling teenagers," said Fey, portraying Palin in the vice-presidential debate sketch. The genius of Fey's impressions, which gave *Saturday Night Live* its highest rating in fourteen years, was that they boiled the reality of Palin down into its undeniable "You betcha"–studded essence. In the parody of Palin's conversation with Couric, the *SNL* team even included verbatim sentences cribbed from the interviews. This was what the show had done to political candidates for years. Gerald Ford's clumsiness, Michael Dukakis's diminutive erudition, Al Gore's waxen obsession with a "lock box," George Bush's menacing snicker—these outsized versions of real-life characteristics were the meat of the show's political play. In a profile in *Vanity Fair* Fey responded to griping that she had been mean to Palin: "What made me super-mad about [that criticism] was that it seemed very sexist toward me and her. The implication was that she's so fragile, which she's not. She's a strong woman . . . also, it was sexist because, like, who would ever go on the news and say, 'Well, I thought it was sort of mean to Richard Nixon when Dan Aykroyd played him.'"

Fey's take on Palin was serendipitous, prompted by the strong resemblance between the two women. But that likeness was part of what made it groundbreaking: a vice-presidential candidate looked like a famous comedian. A female comedian. And on it went. Hillary Clinton had been played by Poehler for several years. The interview that brought Palin low had been administered by Couric, a woman also played by Poehler. The vice-presidential debate had been moderated by Gwen Ifill, prompting a guest appearance by the inimitable Queen Latifah. Inasmuch as each of the impersonations relied on the amplification of feminine traits—Poehler/Couric's heavily mascara'd and incessant blinking, Poehler/Hillary's hyenic laugh, Fey/Palin's sexy librarianism—in ways that might indeed be sexist or reductive, those characteristics were ripe for amplification only because the objects of political and media parody had high-pitched laughs and wore mascara and pencil skirts. The heightened femininity of Palin's political persona also came in for examination; during the Couric-Palin sketch, Couric pointed out to a stumped Palin, "It seems to me that when cornered you become increasingly adorable." That little one-liner, accompanied by Fey's inspired shooting of fake finger guns, distilled a gender dynamic—wherein women infantilize themselves as a defensive strategy—it might otherwise take thousands of words to unspool.

When it came to analysis of presidential gender dynamics in 2008, few could have touched the textured acuity of Fey and Poehler's first Palin-Clinton sketch, in which the candidates give a press conference about sexism in the media (during which Fey/Palin crows the enduring line, "I can see Russia from my house!") and provided not just the first glimpse of Fey's embodiment of the Alaska governor, but a new vision of Poehler's Clinton.

Poehler did not bear any resemblance to Clinton; neither was she the world's most skillful mimic. From the start she had relied on the broadest possible identifying attributes in her performance: the big laugh and ravenous hunger for the presidency. But in comedy, as in real life, the arrival of Palin on the scene threw Clinton into new focus. Next to Palin, Clinton's good qualities—her brains, competence, work ethic, her belief in secular government and reproductive freedoms, her ability to complete sentences—became far more evident than they had been before there was another potential "first woman" to compare her to. Nothing conveyed these haze-clearing realignments of perspective as quickly and as firmly as Fey and Poehler did in five and a half minutes. The parodic depiction of the two women side by side exposed the complex dynamics of Palin's parasitism, their unwilling symbiosis, and their stark differences.

In the sketch, when Palin speaks of the "ugly role sexism is playing in the campaign," Poehler's Clinton notes dryly, "[It's] an issue

which I am frankly surprised to hear people suddenly care about."
More deft even than Couric's unanswered question about the nutcracker and the action figure, these two performers laid out the variety of ways that women's bodies could be used against them:

> FEY/PALIN: *Stop photoshopping my head on sexy bikini
> pictures!*
>
> POEHLER/CLINTON: *And stop saying I have cankles. . . .*
>
> FEY/PALIN: *Reporters and commentators, stop using words
> that diminish us, like "pretty," "attractive," "beauti-
> ful" . . .*
>
> POEHLER/CLINTON: *"Harpy," "shrew," "boner-shrinker."*

Next came a vision of how these two candidates' fates were tied
together, as Fey/Palin chirps, "Look how far we've come: Hillary
Clinton, who came so close to the White House, and me, Sarah
Palin, who is even closer. Can you believe it, Hillary?" Poehler/
Clinton, her eyes bulging, shouts back in disbelief, "I can not!"
before elaborating, "I don't want to hear you compare your road to
the White House to *my* road to the White House. I scratched and
clawed through mud and barbed wire. And you just glided in on
a dog sled wearing your pageant sash and your Tina Fey glasses!"
When Fey's Palin responds that it just goes to show that anyone can
be president if they want it enough, Poehler/Clinton lets loose with
crazed laughter and says, "Yeah, you know, Sarah, looking back, if
I could change one thing, I probably should have *wanted* it more,"
before ripping a piece of wood from the podium. This was the story
of these two women, told as directly and almost as honestly as anyone else had managed it, crescendoing with Poehler's ability to say
what Hillary never could have: "I invite the media to grow a pair.
And if you can't, I will lend you mine."

While Fey got all the credit for her work on Palin, the harshest comedic blow to the Alaska governor came from Poehler, who
on a later episode sat at the "Weekend Update" desk with the vice-
presidential candidate herself. After the setup, in which Palin declined
to perform a rap about herself, Poehler launched into the fevered routine on her behalf, bellowing lyrics like "I'm Jeremiah Wright 'cause

tonight I'm the preacher / I got a bookish look and you're all hot for teacher," as the real Palin bopped gamely at the news desk. Backed by two Eskimos and Jason Sudeikis as the First Dude, Poehler's verse got harsher; she sang, with sing-songy patriotism, "My country 'tis of thee, from my porch I can see, Russia and such." Amping it up further, Poehler mimicked Palin's animal blood lust, peppering a guy in a moose costume with imagined bullets, and snarling, "Now you're dead, 'cause I'm an animal! And I'm bigger than you!" As the enormously pregnant Poehler made her exit, she stopped very close to Palin, leaned in, and growled, "I'm Palin, I'm out!"

Poehler seemed to me incandescent in her willingness to exhibit such raw aggression in front of her mark. Making the moment even more sublime was the fact that Poehler was dancing around just one week before giving birth to her son. The layers of the act were remarkable: here was a woman in the last days of pregnancy, doing her public and nationally visible job—precisely the behavior that had helped to distinguish Palin as an anomalous mother-governor—appearing on television just fifty-five years after Lucille Ball's pregnancy could not even be mentioned on the air. Poehler had spent years impersonating the first woman to run for president, and here she was, throwing herself around the stage in front of the woman who had been sent to capitalize on her gains. In Poehler's exertions the strides women had made in recent decades became blindingly apparent.

It was culture as politics as comedy as culture as politics. It was goofy and grand.

☆ ☆ ☆

The fusion of feminism and funny wasn't just happening on *Saturday Night Live*. Improbably, Comedy Central's male-hosted double-header of fake news shows, *The Daily Show* and *The Colbert Report,* had also expanded the feminist conversation. In the years since his 2005 launch as a faux right-wing airbag in the style of Fox's Bill O'Reilly, Stephen Colbert had been one of the most reliable hosts of feminist writers and activists and had offered a friendly place for political women to be funny. Ohio Representative Stephanie Tubbs Jones made an appearance as a character called "Judge Tubbs" in a send-up of daytime legal shows. And it was on *Colbert* that Donna Brazile said, "I'm a woman, so I like Hillary. I'm black, I like Obama. But I'm also grumpy, so I like John McCain."

Colbert's own routines touched frequently on issues of gender. A June 2007 segment of "The Word" was dedicated to "Rodham" and the news that Hillary would be dropping her maiden name to campaign for the presidency. "You don't see the other seventeen presidential candidates dropping their maiden names!" blustered Colbert, shining an exaggerated light on the double standards plaguing Clinton. "For too many years women in public life have had an unfair advantage when it comes to media attention. If Hillary has a bad hair day, that's front-page news!" Colbert would do a bit in 2009 about the passage of the Lilly Ledbetter Fair Pay Act, complaining, "If you can't discriminate against women, what is the point of hiring them?"

Colbert's benighted antifeminist persona allowed him to mock misogynistic attitudes by playing them off his many feminist guests. Linda Hirshman explained the domestic inequities chronicled in her manifesto *Get to Work* after Colbert promised to explain to her that "a woman needs a man like a fish needs to be cooked and served to me for dinner by a woman on a bicycle." When Jessica Valenti, who gave Colbert a T-shirt with the slogan "Feminist Chicks Dig Me," suggested that she wrote her first book, *Full Frontal Feminism,* to empower young women, Colbert asked, "Why not just get *The Secret*? Because then they can just visualize equality and it will come to them!" Colbert gave young feminists the opportunity to dodge the uptight stereotypes of their forebears, and the forebears themselves a chance to disprove them. When Jane Fonda and Gloria Steinem appeared to advertise their women's radio network, they cooked an apple pie with Colbert in a segment called "Cooking with Feminists." Colbert got to say, "Gloria, if you'll grab some of those Macintosh apples and explain to me, what is the state of American feminism?" and to wonder, "How can you tell if a woman is a feminist or just angry?" So it wasn't Catharine MacKinnon, and maybe Colbert was declawing feminists, making them playful when feminism should be taken seriously. But the show also made the women's movement, its leaders and its writers, available and visible, an approachable part of popular cultural discourse, rather than being cast only in opposition to it.

On Jon Stewart's *Daily Show* the feminist edge came from the correspondents, especially Samantha Bee. In September 2007 Bee did a *Sex and the City* parody in which she swanned around New York in a tutu pondering the fact that women could now be "doctresses, body-buildtrixes, and firemenwomen," as the onscreen text asked, "Is America ready . . . for a catty, stacked, whorish, menstruating . . ." woman president? In 2007 Bee did a segment on busty and lusty cable newswomen, calling them NILFs, or "news I'd like to fuck," in which she reported that one CNN anchor's "screen says Baghdad, but her open neckline says 'Bag these,'" while another reporter "interview[ed] someone just back from Iraq in a skirt that barely covers *her* Sunni Triangle." Katie Couric cited the skit to me in 2009, noting that it "was so funny and so true," but that it had also thrown into perspective her own confusion: "Are we supposed to be fetching or are we supposed to be smart?" Couric continued, "I do look at some of those anchors on cable and I think, 'God, did I encourage this?' Because sometimes I'd show my legs on the *Today* show. And sometimes I look back and think, 'God, that skirt was a little too short.'" Here were larger questions of gender and self-representation, summoned by a piece on a comedy show.

"Feminism is important to me, women's issues are important to me, reproductive issues are very important to me," Bee told me in 2009. The idea that there was pointed comedy to be made from these issues was revolutionary, and occasionally moving. Bee recalled a segment she did at the Republican convention in which she asked conventioneers to talk about Bristol Palin's pregnancy, getting them to call her decision to have her baby a "choice." She was nervous watching the segment screen during the show. "This was close to my heart. . . . I think I cried when it screened and the audience loved it." Bee said, "I don't really know how it's possible not to be [a feminist]. I think people are coming back to it. For a decade nobody would use the word *feminism*."

In a piece in the *Guardian* about feminist humor Jessica Valenti wrote, "Most feminists develop a strong sense of humor—they have to. How else would we survive the daily sexism, a political climate that's hostile to our rights, and the general discrimination that comes with being a woman? If we couldn't laugh until we cried, we would probably spend all of our time sobbing." Such a grim assessment was nowhere more applicable than in Bee's laugh-or-you'll-weep take-down of John McCain's statements about late-term abortion during the final presidential debate. McCain had put air quotes around the term "health of the mother," calling concern with women's health the "extreme pro-abortion position." "Let's face it," Bee said in her *Daily Show* commentary, "women love abortions and will do anything to get one. The later the better. . . . Enough with the whining about rape, incest, and incest-rape. We're on to you, ladies. Those aren't the golden ticket to the abortion factory, okay?" John McCain, Bee said, "has finally put the concerns of women where they belong: in derisive air quotes."

"This place is very interested in gender and politics," Bee told me of *The Daily Show.* "There's a lot of vaginas around here, and we make our presence known." Another came aboard in spring of 2008, when Kristen Schaal, a thirty-year-old comedian and actress, pitched a piece about Hillary Clinton. "I really wanted Hillary to win," Schaal told me in 2009, "and I realized that she just wouldn't, and I couldn't believe it. She had everything in place to do it." Schaal did a piece called "Dear Madame President," in which she filmed a video to the future first woman president and wondered, "How did you do it? Did you have to be assertive? Were you a total bitch? Does that word even exist anymore?" Schaal made further appearances as *The Daily Show*'s "senior women's issues commentator," including one in which she stripped down to her Wonder Woman Underoos to protest the media sexism aimed at Clinton, and another with Bee in which the women fought over who would take over Stewart's anchor desk. Schaal parodied Palin with a flurry of accusations and excuses: "You are so sexist! . . . I'm not taking any questions! I'm still learning! This is a gotcha conversation! From my apartment I can see where they tape *Letterman*! I'm a maverick! I don't need the approval of the elites!"

Many of these comedy clips gained traction in part because they were posted on *Jezebel,* the pop culture website for women. *Jezebel* was founded in 2007 by Nick Denton, the bloodless British owner of the media site Gawker, to address women's media. It was a high-low hybrid that jibed with the cheekiness of the feminist blogosphere and was just serious enough in its feminist and political leanings to set itself apart from the cadaverous cynics dominating most pop culture sites. *Jezebel* cultivated a fan base of readers who called themselves "Jezebelles" and had an insatiable appetite for things that were feminist, things that were funny, and most especially things that were feminist *and* funny. As readership climbed—from fewer than 300,000 a month in the first three months to 1.4 million a month by the end of 2009—*Jezebel* became one of the most useful ways to disseminate clips. "You can really tell when something resonates with people," Bee told me. "I'm always excited when something of mine ends up on *Jezebel*."

The feminist comedian Sarah Haskins practically credited the site for her career. The twenty-nine-year-old Chicago native and Harvard graduate was touring with Second City when she was hired as a writer for the Current TV show *Infomania*. At home watching TLC's *Secret Life of a Soccer Mom*, Haskins noticed that a lot of the commercials were for yogurt; she proposed a segment about the common tropes of yogurt commercials: the assumption of constant dieting, women in gray hoodies (an outfit Haskins said indicated "I have a master's, but then I got married"), and spontaneous dancing over the deliciousness of dessert-flavored yogurt ("It's not real food, it's *yogurt*!"). Haskins's segment, in which she called yogurt "the official food of women," was the kickoff to a series called "Target: Women," in which she picked apart advertising aimed at women. Meant to be a short cycle of spots, the series extended through 2008 and all of 2009, and went on to include Haskins's commentary on the cultural fascination with Barbie, princess stories, underage pop stars, and the portrayal of Hillary Clinton supporters as angry ("You know what makes me angry? Watching you talk about how angry I am!").

Haskins told me in 2009 that she was "totally shocked" by the popularity of "Target: Women." "Women's identities are [often] constructed in ways that feel false, whether it's a bunch of pundits on MSNBC talking about Hillary and Sarah Palin or commercials that say that when you're cleaning, you should be wearing a snazzy outfit."

Paying attention to how culture addresses and represents

women, said Haskins, "has certainly raised my consciousness of
the presence of a generation of women who are perhaps reclaiming the term. . . . There are all these sites on the Internet that I had
no idea about, having a conversation that I certainly wasn't a part
of when I was in school." Like me, Haskins described herself as a
product of the "I'm not a feminist, but . . ." generation of backlash
inheritors, and said her experience as an accidental feminist comic
included "an education in, 'Oh, is this not a bad word anymore?'"
and noted that that had a lot to do with the power of comedy to
relax strictures and loosen ingrained attitudes. "A good joke lets
you see things through a new lens without pushing you to do it,"
said Haskins, summing up many of the election year's lessons about
feminism, pop culture and politics.

11   THE NEXT WAVE IS HERE

BY MID-OCTOBER SARAH Palin was receiving blame for McCain's expected loss from both Democrats and Republicans, and most pointedly from the people running her own campaign. Some inside the McCain camp, divided over its strategic errors and Palin's egregious performance, had opened fire on her in the press, anonymously telling reporters that her own advisors thought her an inexperienced prima donna who was sinking the ticket.

Whatever tight control the campaign initially had exerted over Palin's self-presentation had unraveled in her post-Couric spiral, and the distance at which the Republican presidential ticket was holding its vice president was alarmingly clear. When, in early October, McCain pulled his resources out of Michigan, Palin told Fox News that she disagreed with the strategy and admitted that upon hearing of the plan, she'd sent advisors an email that read, "Oh come on . . . do we have to?" Palin had obviously not been consulted or even officially informed of the decision to back out of the state. Her critics on the left and right were fixated on stories like her wardrobe budget. Her status as a McCain prop, a stunt gone terribly wrong, was ever more evident. And yet on the campaign trail she was drawing bigger and more frenzied crowds than ever.

It was no wonder that Sarah Palin was going rogue. As one unnamed Palin aide told *Politico*'s Ben Smith, Palin felt "completely mismanaged and mishandled and ill-advised" and made a decision to start trusting her own instincts. In addition to criticizing her boss's decision not to slug it out in Michigan, she openly criticized his unwillingness to attack Obama hard about his relationship with Jeremiah Wright. Hired as the pretty lady by the macho and ill-tempered POW, Palin was turning the Republican campaign strategy on its head by presenting herself as the pugilist and casting her boss as something of a pansy.

At a campaign stop in Colorado Springs in late October, Palin slipped the bonds of her minders and ambled over to a television news crew without permission or supervision; the *New York Times* reported that when campaign staffers noticed her in casual conversation with the press, they began shouting for her spokeswoman, who hustled to cut the interview off, but to no avail. On the same trip a reporter noted in the day's pool report that in her "continuing evolution from the least accessible to the most accessible of the four candidates," Palin took questions at a Cold Stone Creamery ice cream shop. The governor hadn't said anything particularly notable, but her steely insistence on talking at all demonstrated her conviction that she knew, better than John McCain or his team, how to campaign for office.

Whether out of courage or stupidity, Palin was a determinedly independent candidate and one who could see which side her bread was buttered on. In the weeks since her nomination had been announced the Rudy Giulianis and Rick Santorums had piped down a bit about the sexist rhetoric being thrown at her. Now conservative guys, anxious to fob off blame for McCain's poor showing onto his running mate, were sniggering about her outfits and calling her a lightweight. The women of the right-wing media had backed away from their support of her. Kathleen Parker wrote in late September that Palin was "clearly out of her league" and that she was tired of holding her breath every time she watched Palin being interviewed. She added, "My cringe reflex is exhausted."

But on the road Palin was becoming an ever greater sensation, with massive crowds of jubilant Republicans, many of them female, who had found in her not only a candidate to cheer, but an icon of female political empowerment. As the male-run campaign began to abandon her Palin turned to the people who still considered her the party's newest rock star: Republican women. She was committed to addressing her place in history and saw herself as a feminist heroine, even if most feminists didn't agree.

Palin's effect on female Hillary holdouts was the opposite of what McCain strategists had hoped. Her marked differences from Clinton prompted most of Hillary's faithful to throw their Clinton bumper-stickered cars in reverse and back Obama with a panicked energy. The introduction of Palin probably did more for Democratic unity than a month of awkward Unity breakfasts. Kim Gandy said, "I am frequently asked whether NOW supports women candidates just because they are women. This gives me an opportunity to once again answer that question with an emphatic 'No.' We recognize the importance of having women's rights supporters at every level but, like Sarah Palin, not every woman supports women's rights." Feminist excoriations of Palin did not stop there. Suzanne Braun Levine, the first editor of *Ms.* magazine, wrote, "Even behind the reportedly clear glasses she wears to play down her beauty-queen credential . . . she can't disguise her inexperience." A spokeswoman for NOW told *Politico* that Palin was "more a conservative man than she is a woman on women's issues," a statement so troubling that Gandy would go to lengths to disown it and clarify that it did not represent her organization's attitude toward Palin. At *Salon* Cintra Wilson wrote that Palin was a "Christian Stepford wife in a sexy librarian costume" and the "hardcore pornographic centerfold spread" for Republicans.

Other critics noticed the pile-on and didn't hesitate to point to its hypocrisy. The Libertarian columnist Cathy Young wrote, "Left-wing feminists have a hard time dealing with strong, successful conservative women in politics. . . . Sarah Palin seems to have truly unhinged more than a few, eliciting a stream of vicious, often misogynist invective." *Jezebel*'s Megan Carpentier wrote a series of posts castigating feminists for their hypocritical fury; in one of them, plaintively headlined, "Please, People: Stop Making Me Defend Sarah Palin," she pointed out, "Sexism doesn't just hurt women when it's directed at liberal women. Being sexist to Sarah Palin hurts us by reinforcing stereotypes . . . and by allowing conservatives to point fingers at us and call us hypocrites." Melissa McEwan at *Shakesville* launched a Sarah Palin Sexism Watch with the tag line, "We defend Sarah Palin against misogynist smears not because we endorse her or her politics, but because that's how feminism works."

But there were still other Democratic women who believed that feminism worked differently, that it meant not just gamely defending Palin against sexist criticism, but supporting her full throttle. A small number of Democratic women, some livid about the florid ways the vice-presidential candidate was being dissed, some convinced that it was a feminist imperative to back any woman running for executive office, and a few still too sore to embrace Obama, were dissenting. They were angry at the national women's organizations for which some of them had worked and volunteered, and they wanted to make a public stand against them.

In early October Shelly Mandell, the president of Los Angeles NOW, a feminist organizer for more than three decades, and chief organizer of the March for Women's Lives in 2004, introduced Sarah Palin at a speech in California. Making clear that she was appearing personally, not on behalf of the National Organization for Women, Mandell told the crowd that she was there "as a woman's rights activist for thirty years who has worked for all those years to see this day." "I'm a life-long Democrat," said Mandell, "I don't agree with Governor Palin on several issues . . . [but] I know Sarah Palin cares about women's rights, she cares about equality, she cares about equal pay, and as vice president she will fight for it." Mandell did not mention that Palin's running mate had been vocal in his denunciation of the Lilly Ledbetter Fair Pay Act. "It is an honor to call her sister," Mandell said. "America, this is what a feminist looks like."

NOW's California president Patty Bellasalma hit back hard, issuing a statement that read in part, "The use of Shelly Mandell's Los Angeles NOW title was apparently intended to mislead the public, and indeed has resulted in local television outlets and internet reports misstating that LA NOW has 'endorsed' Sarah Palin or that she has a record of supporting women's rights. This in fact is not the case."

Mandell wasn't the only one to break with feminist opinion on Palin. Elaine Lafferty, the former editor of *Ms.* magazine who had volunteered for the Clinton campaign, officially signed on as a McCain consultant soon after he picked Palin. Lafferty, coauthor of a book with her friend and Fox News anchor Greta Van Susteren, had a complicated history with institutional feminism. Her two-year stint at *Ms.*, from 2003 to 2005, had been officially successful; under her stewardship the struggling magazine's circulation had jumped and she had published critically lauded stories. But behind the scenes there had been tension between Lafferty and the Feminist Majority Foundation, which had taken control of publishing *Ms.* in 2001, about her desire to move the magazine in a more broadly popular direction. At the time of her exit from *Ms.*, Lafferty told the *New York Observer,* "My vision of *Ms.* was that it would be a thinking woman's magazine—a feminist magazine for sure, but my vision of feminism is a big tent . . . as the original *Ms.* was; they didn't check membership cards at the door. I don't believe in dogma, in exclusion or rhetoric. I thought it could be a magazine that invites women into the conversation about how we live today."

Lafferty's words would resonate three years later, when criticism of feminism's exclusivity and elitism would be applied by people looking to stretch the movement's defining boundaries not simply outward, but rightward, and in doing so perhaps permanently explode them.

Lafferty came aboard the McCain campaign as Palin's unofficial *consigliere* on all matters feminist and began helping her with, as Lafferty would call it, "a speech that Palin had long wanted to give on women's rights." That speech took place on October 21 in Henderson, Nevada. Behind Palin stood Lafferty and NOW's Mandell, along with another NOW dissenter, former Oregon chapter president Linda Klinge, and Lynn Forester de Rothschild and Prameela Bartholomeusz, both vocal Hillary dead-enders and members of the Democratic National Platform Committee. Palin introduced and thanked the group for their bravery before asking the women in the audience, "Are you ready to break the highest hardest glass ceiling in America?" She next made a point lifted directly from the Obama-embittered PUMAs: "Somehow Barack Obama just couldn't bring himself to pick the woman who got eighteen million votes."

"American women, Democratic, Republican and Independent should not just let Barack Obama take their votes for granted," said Palin, sounding like the millions of Democratic women who had tried, with varying degrees of cogency or lunacy to express this very conviction to their own party peers. It would have been easy, in fact, to believe that Palin, a Republican hired by a Republican, was now doing the bidding of the knot of angry and unhealed Democratic women standing behind her, so closely was she adhering to what had been their own talking points during their party's nominating process.

Then came a part of the speech in which the interest of disenchanted Democratic women fused with what was unmistakably Palin's own experience of feminism. "When I was a kid Congress passed a law, that's come to be known as Title IX, and that law allowed millions of girls to play sports," she told the crowd. "Over time, that opened more than just the doors to the gymnasium. Along with other reforms, Title IX helped us to see ourselves and our futures [in] a different way. Women of my generation were allowed finally to make more of our own choices with education and with career and I have never forgotten that we owe that opportunity to women, to feminists who came before us. We were allowed to be participants instead of just spectators [of] the achievements of others." This was all pretty remarkable coming from a woman who opposed abortion even in cases of rape and incest. It was downright confounding given that she was running alongside a man who voted nineteen times against increasing the minimum wage, who voted against the Violence Against Women Act and against funding for the Office of Violence Against Women, who voted against expanding the Family and Medical Leave Act and to terminate funds for family planning. But she wasn't done.

Palin assured anyone surprised by her embrace of a feminist history that "equal opportunity is not just the cause of feminists. It's the creed of our country." Were she given the honor of serving, she said, "I intend to advance that creed in our own nation and beyond, because across the world there are still places where women are subjugated and persecuted as they were in Afghanistan, places where they're bullied and brutalized and murdered in honor killings. . . . No one leader can bring an end to all of those ills, but I can promise you this: these women too will have an advocate and a defender in the forty-seventh vice president of the United States." As her speech concluded, Shania Twain's power anthem "She's Not Just a Pretty Face" blared, and Palin embraced the rogue feminists standing behind her.

When I interviewed Lafferty in 2009 she said that just after the election, a teary-eyed Palin asked her, "Why does Gloria Steinem hate me? [She] was my hero. Why do they hate me? I'm a feminist." Lafferty was firm with me: "The woman I met during the campaign and that I was on the plane with was a feminist," meaning that she believed in the professional and economic potential of women, even if she didn't want to make policy to support it. She also believed in a redistribution of domestic work and had said, after giving birth to Trig, "To any critics who say a woman can't think and work and carry a baby at the same time, I'd just like to escort that Neanderthal back to the cave." Even I had to admit that the moment at the end of the vice-presidential debate at which she picked up her infant son had stunned me into silence. I knew the baby was there to advertise Palin's maternal allure, to protect her from criticism, to hammer home her anti-abortion bona fides, but still: seeing a vice-presidential debate in which one of the participants was holding her infant changed everything. As the feminist columnist Ellen Goodman wrote of Palin early on, "Mom to mayor to governor to veep nominee? There's one woman who didn't have trouble raising her hand in class. There's one woman who didn't think she had to be twice as good as a man to run. Be careful what you wish for." In many ways Palin embodied not only feminism's gains, but some of its still unmet aspirations.

The question of whether or not Palin "was a feminist" was one that obsessed and troubled lots of women. Katie Couric and I discussed it during our interview in 2009, during which Couric said, "I wrestle with this. . . . She's a successful woman. She's running the state of Alaska. She was a vice presidential candidate. Just because she doesn't believe in choice and she thinks abortion is tantamount to murder. . . . What is a feminist? Can you be a conservative feminist? I find this so interesting. . . . I think, 'Okay, maybe she is a feminist.' Then I think so many of her views indirectly or directly would hurt women. So I go around and around."

Some of the women associated with the earliest iterations of

American feminism had also been involved in the conservative Christian temperance battles. Gail Collins would remind readers in *When Everything Changed* that Republican women had been the strongest proponents of women's rights, while heavily Catholic working-class Democratic voters had been more reluctant to mess with gender roles. More recently those dynamics had been reversed by the liberal and radical Democratic women who led the midcentury social movements, and by Republican women who fought against modernization of the American family. Phyllis Schlafley opposed the ERA and pushed American women to stay home with their children, and Marilyn Quayle told the Republican convention in 1992, "Most women do not wish to be liberated from their essential natures as women."

Yet here was not just a candidate, but crowds of Republican women and a few Democratic ones, cheering on Palin's vision in which personal empowerment had no correlation to progressive policy, and beginning to agitate for a reevaluation of the meaning of feminism. On the day of Palin's speech about women, former Republican Massachusetts governor Jane Swift, the only woman before Palin to give birth while a sitting governor, told Greta Van Susteren, "There are some on the liberal left who believe that only they have . . . an ability to call themselves feminists. . . . I think a feminist is someone who believes that women should have equal opportunity to men. . . . It is someone like me, like Governor Palin, who hopes that our daughters, if they work hard and play by the rules, can do virtually anything they want to in their life."

When it came to bullying contests over language, it had never been difficult, historically, to get the feminist movement to hand over its lunch money. Perhaps in part because of its breadth and diversity, perhaps because of a lack of gumption that characterized many on the left in the fourth quarter of the twentieth century, perhaps simply because of the manipulative agility of the right, the women's movement lost almost every serious battle over words and imagery in the forty years following the second wave. The worst and most damaging defeats had come over the language of reproductive rights, in which abortion opponents had gobbled up the vocabulary of life, loss, morality, and emotion, while reproductive rights activists persisted with the limply fungible *choice*.

The word was meant to convey women's ability to make decisions regarding their own family and reproductive lives, but instead served most frequently as a baseball bat with which pro-lifers could hit feminism in its nuts. If *choice* was really the only word that feminists owned, then didn't that make every choice a feminist act? If the choice to have an abortion and the choice to continue a pregnancy were equally valid, then why, some women wondered, should the choice to give up a career, or stay in a bad relationship, or get breast implants be disparaged or dismaying? A year after Palin's appearance on the McCain ticket the conservative publication *Newsmax* ran a series of stories on "the newer feminism" that included one with the telling headline "Feminism Now Defined by Each and Every Woman." No one was quite sure how best to wrest stronger or more assertive language back from the other side.

The word *feminism* itself had not exactly inspired a ferocious defense by its own adherents. For decades the right had successfully demonized women who embraced the label as hirsute succubi, family-scorning and erotically disadvantaged old bags. In 2005 I wrote a story about old-school feminist organizations wondering whether to retire the much maligned word in favor of a new one, and a new generation of women determined to reclaim it. In recent years I had seen young women sporting "This is what a feminist looks like" shirts, and had read with surprise as teen and twentysomething celebrities identified themselves as feminists. Now that *feminist* was slowly clawing its way back to cool, Republicans wanted in. Sarah Palin, charismatic mascot of the you-go-girl spirit and the modern cross-party liberation she represented, had awakened in Republican women a desire to claim a piece of feminism as their own, but they were going to fight to remold it to suit their ideology.

Feminism's history of fluidity and combustibility, which originated with its impossible goal of adequately representing all of the interests of a population that came in innumerable shapes, sizes, colors, and identities, also made it legitimately vulnerable to incursions from those of a different ideological caste. The trouble here was that the intruding group was at odds with what was perhaps modern feminism's only truly immutable core value: a woman's right and ability to control her own reproduction.

Lafferty wrote in the *Daily Beast,* "Palin is being pilloried by the inside-the-Beltway Democratic feminist establishment. . . . Yes, she is anti-abortion. And yes, instead of buying organic New Zealand lamb at Whole Foods, she joins other Alaskans in hunting for food. That's it." Lines like this were practically enough to get thoughtful feminists—who, like Lafferty, *wanted* to expand the appeal of women's rights advocacy, who *wanted* more women to proudly celebrate equal opportunity, who *wanted* to move forward and away from the movement's reputation as exclusive, elite, white, and middle class—to say "Oh, that's it? Anti-abortion and no lamb from Whole Foods? Well, okay then, welcome!" before pausing to consider, "Wait, what was that first thing again?" That thing was at the heart of a very grave question for women's rights activists: could they work productively alongside women and men with anti-abortion stances? Could pro-lifers be feminists? As Couric wondered to me in 2009, "Should the feminist movement say, 'We have certain tenets but people who are pro-life, we can welcome them. Let's find our common ground to achieve things in other areas.'"

The trouble was that the goal of outlawing abortion (as well as desires to limit access to birth control and sex education)—not as a matter of personal belief, but as a legislative goal—was not compatible with feminism if feminism in fact meant supporting women's rights to pursue their life, liberty, and happiness on equal footing with men. Not believing in abortion personally was one thing. But preventing other women from exerting full control over their bodies and health, assessing their value as lesser than the value of the fetuses they carried, was, it seemed to me and many others, fundamentally antifeminist and antifemale.

Women like Lafferty, who had the stamp of being Democrats and professional women's rights advocates, were giving this effort a feminist, practically progressive imprimatur. And outside the feminist world they would fuel the assumption, so much in evidence with regard to Hillary, that female candidates appeal to female voters based only on sisterhood. In 2009, discussing her shock at seeing some NOW members support Palin after the struggles to communicate the fact that Clinton support and Obama support were *not* just about shared gender, NOW's Latifa Lyles told me, "Suddenly . . . everything [feminists had been saying] is out the window."

The hypercharged effect of this Woman Power fever, as well as the disjointed narrative in which Palin was the McCain campaign killer and also its biggest star, was obvious in Williamsport, Pennsylvania, on Mischief Night 2008. Five days before the general election, which she and her running mate looked increasingly likely to lose, Palin had drawn a crowd of thirteen thousand people to an outdoor baseball stadium in the near-freezing cold. How could she not have had supreme confidence in her future in politics when she was getting Lollapalooza-level turnout on an uncomfortably frosty night? On that same afternoon, in the same northern Pennsylvania town, her opponent, Joe Biden, the guy on the ticket that was lighting up polls around the country, managed to draw a crowd of only four hundred to a temperature-controlled school gymnasium.

People had been lined up since the morning at the site of the Sarah Palin rally; more than ten thousand tickets had already been distributed. There were hundreds of buttons for sale, reading "Read My Lipstick," "Hot Chicks Vote Republican," "We Love Sarah," and "Sarah-Licious." There were "You Go Girl" T-shirts and banners. As the line grew longer, eager attendees kibitzed and prepared for the big event. One woman held up an "I ♥ S & M" sign—for "Sarah" and "McCain"—and a man dressed up as Hillary Clinton explained why he/she was at the rally: "Obama ditched me."

"The media may not be portraying Sarah as popular," said Ellen Margraff as she waited in the line, "but look around." The polling on Palin was abysmal, but out in the world monster crowds with blankets and buttons, Christian literature and thundersticks in tow were willing to brave the cold for a glimpse of the woman they believed they would be cheering for well into the future. "I've come to see Sarah, our next vice president of the United States!" shouted Gloria Gordon, a sixty-four-year-old police officer. "Everything she says, I agree with one hundred percent of it." She added that should McCain and Palin fall short of their goals the next Tuesday, "she'll be president in 2012." On my way to report on Palin's last week of rallies I had been prepared to see Klannish, hate-spewing anti-Obama gatherings like the ones making the rounds on YouTube. But this crowd was not like that. These people were happy and pumped up, despite the fact that many of them knew Palin would most likely not be their vice president come January. They didn't care. Some of them were lifelong Republicans, some of them had found their enthusiasm for the right-wing ticket only through their enthusiasm for Palin. They believed that she would be president someday. And they really, really wanted a woman to be president.

"I'm a strong woman, and I really relate to strong women," said sixty-seven-year-old Gloria Stere, who wore a bright blue Palin Power T-shirt. Stere explained that she had just retired from running her own sewing machine business, and though a "dyed-in-the-wool Republican," she had considered voting for Hillary Clinton. But she was quick to add, "Palin is the one that absolutely made my mind up about supporting John McCain. I took one look at her, heard her speak, and thought, 'Oh my god, she is the one.'" Diane Ellis, a ninth-grade American history teacher, told me, "Even if they don't win the election I'll still be impressed by her. Hopefully in the next four years the Republican Party will realize what they have there, and maybe even bring her on as presidential candidate. She and Hillary going at it—that's what I'd like to see."

A security sniper ogled the crowd at Bowman Field with his night-vision glasses as a local minister took the stage to offer a benediction and pray for forgiveness "for so many [who] have shed innocent blood through the course of abortions, and so many [who] would stop the sanctity of marriage between a man and a woman." With these abominations in mind, he continued, "Thank you for raising up a woman like Governor Sarah Palin at a time like this. Bless her for standing against those who would remove the guns from our cabinets, and those who would want to remove the baby from the womb of her mother." In this version of the Newer Feminism the female heroine did not act on her own, but was raised up by God and selected by John McCain to work on behalf of enforced reproduction and restrictions on love. Before Palin took the stage the sound system blared Whitesnake singing "Here I go again / On my own" and "Like a drifter I was born to walk alone." The overture told the story: Sarah Palin was readying herself to ditch this suffocating campaign and assume her place as patron goddess of a socially conservative GOP faction and rebel feminist sect that worshipped women, at least from some angles, as vessels and caretakers. As the crowd got increasingly hot for Palin, I saw a sign that said, "Julianna's mommy is voting for Piper's mommy!"

When Palin walked onstage there was pushing and women

screaming, "Oh my god, Todd's so cute!" Palin gave a brief address. It resembled ingratiating vice-presidential boilerplate only in her assertion that the crowd must be "so doggone proud" of the local team and new World Champion Phillies. Palin wasn't in Pennsylvania to tell Pennsylvanians about themselves. She was there to tell them about herself, her husband, her family, and how she envisioned the country's future. She talked about the First Dude's snowmobile championships and made ample coded references to Ronald Reagan's 1964 speech endorsing Barry Goldwater, the white puffs of her breath in the cold night air making her repetition of the phrase "The time for choosin's comin' real soon" sound horror-movie eerie.

When I returned from Pennsylvania the weekend before the election I learned that Palin had been prank-called by a Quebec radio comedy team who had convinced her handlers that French President Nicolas Sarkozy wanted to speak with her. A recording of the embarrassing conversation was a big hit among Palin-haters, but it made me not just rationally defensive but viscerally angry on Palin's behalf. This wasn't political satire or parody or spoofing; it was a petty meanness that confirmed her admirers' worst assumptions: that the left applied the rules of civil discourse only to its own.

She was a bad vice-presidential candidate, like bad vice-presidential candidates before her, and her communications team had allowed a prank caller to get through. She was ill-prepared and inarticulate, and her chattiness about how much she liked Sarkozy's model wife, Carla Bruni, was cringey. But progress takes all sorts, and in the pantheon of political leadership there had been thousands of craven, ill-intentioned, pompous, and stupid men. There was no rule that said that in order to make history Palin had to be a decent, honest politician, nor that she be a rocket scientist. Were we to envision true equality in politics, it would involve as many Sarah Palins as it would Hillary Clintons. As Bella Abzug had said, "[The goal is not to see a] female Einstein become an assistant professor. We want a woman schlemiel to get promoted as quickly as a male schlemiel."

I had just witnessed Palin's power and the potential scope of her influence, and I thought it was a serious error to underestimate it, let alone mock it quite so cavalierly. As *Jezebel*'s Carpentier had pointed out, cruelty only made righteous the claims of conservatives that liberals did not respect them. On a June 2009 visit to Seneca Falls, New York, the birthplace of the suffrage movement, Palin would read aloud from the Declaration of Sentiments engraved on the monument, "We anticipate no small amount of ridicule." According to *Politico,* she then commented, "Some things never change."

My experience with Palin's supporters left me alert to the fact that she was building an army of followers—not just scared and angry xenophobes, as the press about anti-Obama voters would have us believe, but women (and men) who felt that their support for this candidate was about an expansion of opportunities for women. Ultimately Palin, like Clinton and Obama, was a candidate onto whom millions of voters, and millions of women, had projected their own hopes and dreams and identifications. The fever for Obama had demonstrated the emotional pull of history making. Now I felt a wave coming from the right, coming to wash over feminism.

I was not wrong. Nearly a year to the day that Hillary Rodham Clinton conceded the nomination for the presidency, an organization called the New Agenda would rally its troops in an art gallery in Manhattan for an event called "One for the Herstory Books." The organization's founder, forty-three-year-old former Wall Street trader Amy Siskind, had gained some notoriety in 2008 as one of the vocal Hillary dead-enders angrily pushing to count unofficial primary votes in Michigan and Florida. Though she never officially called herself a PUMA, in the months during which most Democrats had been rallying around Barack Obama in the general election she had worked to organize them, building a media presence for the New Agenda, which she called "a sisterhood of support." Siskind's sisterhood differed from the feminist organizations that had preceded it by not taking a position on abortion. As she explained on the group's website, "For women in this country to have power, we would need to focus on the issues that unite us, and put aside the issues that divide us. . . . When we come to the New Agenda we ask that you put that issue aside and work together on the 80% of issues that impact all women."

Siskind's Wall Street savvy helped to land her a platform. Within weeks of the official formation of the New Agenda she was speaking as "a feminist" on Fox and later on CNN and PBS; she was quoted in the *Boston Globe,* the *Los Angeles Times,* the *New Republic,* the *Wall Street* journal, and the *Washington Post,* and wrote columns for the *Daily Beast* and the *Huffington Post.* In these venues Siskind hammered home some fundamental feminist points about the continued wage gap and the toll it takes on both women and men. She assured readers, "The next wave is here. The players are different. The words are different." Perplexingly, she wrote, "Gone is 'equal rights.' . . . This wave is about reaching down beneath the surface to eradicate the roots of sexism that lie deeply buried in darkness, ignorance and bias. . . . Gone is 'feminism.' The word, hijacked by a few into an exclusive clique with liberal, pro-choice rites of entry, is being put to rest."

Siskind's feminism had been loosed from ideology, from policy investments that would otherwise tie it to the nominally more progressive party; it was antipathetic to a commitment to reproductive rights. It was supportive not just of Hillary Clinton and Sarah Palin, but of the burgeoning population of conservative female politicians—from Meg Whitman and Carly Fiorina (respectively running for governor and senator in California) to Minnesota Congresswoman Michele Bachmann—who did not support economic or social policies that helped women. And it would have an impact on institutional feminism and especially on those feminists whom Siskind believed had worked against either Clinton or Palin, like NOW's Kim Gandy. Siskind would claim that Gandy had secretly backed Obama in the primary. (Gandy campaigned for Hillary.) She would assert that Gandy had not defended Palin. (Gandy issued a statement condemning the "onslaught of double-standards and condescension" heaped on the Alaska governor.) At the annual NOW convention in the summer of 2009 some NOW members who had broken with the organization to support Palin campaigned against Latifa Lyles—the candidate whom Gandy had endorsed to succeed her as NOW president. Lyles lost the election by eight votes out of four hundred cast. Gandy told me, "I've probably been to thirty-four national conferences and . . . this was nasty and vicious and mean in a way I've never seen. I think it's going to be hard healing."

This was the energy I had first felt at the Palin rally in Pennsylvania. Something had been stirred up, not simply in the Republican

Party, but within feminism. It seemed to me that it was a mistake to ignore it. Palin's candidacy had empowered Republican women eager to claim their share of the feminist legacy and transform its institutions by making them more amenable to their anti-abortion positions and conservative policy positions. In light of the women's movement's history of losing battles over language and self-presentation, I feared that Elaine Lafferty might have been on to something beyond the candidate she was referring to when, in the days before the election knocked Palin off a presidential ticket but not out of the American consciousness, she wrote in the *Daily Beast,* "Will Palin's time come next week? I don't know. But her time *will* come."

12 THE AFTERMATH

IN HIS REMARKABLE victory speech on Election Night, Barack Obama addressed all those who had been driven apart by the election—not just right from left, but left from left, progressive from progressive, when he cited our sixteenth president: "As Lincoln said to a nation far more divided than ours: We are not enemies but friends. . . . Though passion may have strained, it must not break our bonds of affection." My colleagues and I watched with tears streaming down our faces.

On television it was the face of Jesse Jackson that provided the widest and most transparent window into the emotions of the night, the year, the new century, and the new America. In those first moments Jackson, who throughout the campaign had failed to hide his dissatisfactions with Obama, looked hardened, paralyzed by disbelief or regret or sadness or surprise or something that was certainly not yet fully realized joy. It was easy to project onto his closed face a million emotions, to imagine that his momentary reticence was born of the resentments built up during what had been, on generational and social and personal levels, for so many people a harrowing race for the American presidency.

In two years the eloquence and persuasive power of Barack Obama had steamrolled everything in its path, from racial bias to notions about how presidencies were won, to a Bradley tank of a primary opponent, to a long-held feminist fantasy, to the delicate reverence with which Jackson's generation of civil rights activism had been treated. But it was also true that Obama's win would likely not have been possible without the new and often uncomfortable dialogue about race, without the fire forging of the primary competition with Hillary Clinton, and certainly without the work and sacrifices of veteran activists, men and women who did not appear onstage with the president-elect, but who had sat in and marched and protested so that Americans like Obama might be treated as Americans. On Election Night Jackson was standing in for so many of his compatriots, a mere witness to the momentous history he'd devoted his life to making possible.

Twenty minutes after the news of Obama's victory had come the cameras again panned to Jackson, and this time his cheeks were wet with tears, his hand at his mouth. Now, among other things, he looked anxious, as if, like so many of the people wandering around him saucer-eyed and silent, he were still wound tight with fear: Is this happening? Is it real? But Obama's victory was real. In Brooklyn there were fireworks and people cheering as they ran along the sidewalk; from the roof of my building I could see that across the East River the Empire State Building had been lit up blue. On television, even Stephen Colbert was tearful. This was happening. America had cracked open.

Obama did not mention Jackson or Shirley Chisholm or Hillary Clinton in his Election Night speech. Instead he talked about someone whose name most of us had never heard before: Ann Nixon Cooper, a 106-year-old black woman who had voted for him and who would pass away almost exactly a year later. Obama told her story, a story that encompassed more than a century of American history and included in its sight line all the history makers who had preceded him. As Ta-Nehisi Coates later wrote, "He presented her not just as someone who'd been born a generation after slavery and had seen segregation, but as a woman who'd seen the women's-suffrage movement, the dawn of aviation and the automobile, the Depression and the Dust Bowl, and Pearl Harbor. He presented Nixon Cooper as an African American who was not doubly conscious, just conscious."

The America that Obama addressed on November 4 was one with shared rather than competing histories. And if everyone woke up on the morning of November 5 and headed once more into battles of perspectives and priorities, then fair enough. For a few minutes at least we had a spectacular view of the great American mash-up, in which mixed people of mixed experience and mixed ideologies were for an instant united in their difference, bound not by commonalities but by their participation in struggles that were often at cross-purposes but were ultimately in service of further perfecting our union.

What had revealed itself in Jesse Jackson's face was the rocky march to progress and its attendant trade-offs. When radical ideas about justice are presented to a society built on fundamental inequalities but masquerading as a harmonious union, the clash has the force necessary to break down brick walls, as Jackson's generation of civil rights and women's leaders had. But when those radical ideas take hold they become less radical, and get handed down to the next generation as assumptions. The fortunes of that generation rise and the purity of their convictions becomes diluted. They accept some things, both good and bad, from their forebears; they leave other things behind. Often we cannot predict what will remain and get passed on and what will get tossed overboard, which slights will reinflame resistance and which will pass. For a long period during my adolescence and early adulthood it seemed that I would not live to hear the word *feminist* uttered in earnest by anyone my age or younger. Just a decade into the new century it was back, embraced in a manner that broadened its reach, relaxed the rules about how it might be deployed, extended it so far outward that, yes, it became imperiled again. But its return also meant that someday feminism's legacy would bear fruit with regard to the presidency, even if it's not as sweet as many of us might have hoped.

In Arizona, where John McCain was conceding the election, Sarah Palin was hoping to give a speech of her own. She would not be allowed to do so, but her remarks would later be published.

Whether she won or lost, Palin planned to tell the nation and the world, "I will remember all the young girls who came up to me at our rallies . . . just to see only the second woman ever nominated by a major party in a national election. They know that in America there should be no ceilings on achievement, glass or otherwise."

In 2009 Palin quit partway through her term as governor of Alaska but remained a sensation. Her memoir, *Going Rogue,* was a best-seller, and John Coale, who had urged McCain to pick a woman and who later helped Palin with business dealings, told me in 2010, "I went to one of the book signings in Fairfax, Virginia. There was wet snow, but still, four thousand people lined up in the parking lot in this snow to wait to buy the book and have it signed. It's a phenomenon that I have never seen."

After the election Palin's politics moved increasingly rightward. "You go where it's warm," Elaine Lafferty told me in 2009. "Sadly, and I think mistakenly . . . Palin [is] more right wing today than she was. . . . I don't know how she feels about feminism these days, but I will always believe that she was the kind of woman who should have been on our side on a number of issues, and might have been."

In the spring of 2010 Palin returned to the work of co-opting and redefining "feminism" for the right. In a speech in May to the anti-abortion organization the Susan B. Anthony List, Palin deployed the f-word several times while arguing that antiabortion women hewed closer to first-wave feminist ideology than their pro-choice counterparts. She also began to speak often of a "Mama Grizzly" model of female Republican candidate, claiming that there was an "emerging feminist coalition" of conservative women on the rise.

And indeed, the consequences of Palin's appearance on the political stage became increasingly evident: the excitement she had generated on the right raised the profiles of other right-wing women, like Carly Fiorina, Meg Whitman and Michele Bachmann, who in a fundraising letter begged her supporters, "Don't let them Palinize me!" About Fiorina and Whitman, along with increasingly visible Republican offspring Meghan McCain and Liz Cheney, conservative columnist Kathleen Parker wrote, "This doesn't sound like your daddy's Republican Party, but it could be your daughter's."

* * *

Choosing presidential candidates is a funny business. Ideally, loyalty might be born of careful consideration of each contender's policy stances and voting records. But in a political system that rewards those politicians willing to dull their colors until they meld into one dingy, centrist gray it's rare to find anyone who mirrors our most heartfelt beliefs. If the liberal Democrats who split so passionately over Clinton and Obama had initially supported the candidate who, like many of them, believed that universal single-payer health care was the humane and practical course, that the Patriot Act eroded the basic civil liberties on which the nation was built, that gay people should have the same rights as straight people, that America should rejoin the Kyoto Protocol, that we should invest in alternative fuel sources, that the government should cut the money it spends on war and invest instead in education, that going to war in Iraq was a tragic mistake, then the Democratic nominee for president would have been Dennis Kucinich, a man who perhaps not coincidentally admitted during one presidential debate that he once saw a UFO at Shirley MacLaine's house.

In reality our presidential choices are based on factors less lofty than candidates' positions on emissions standards. We're looking for the pols who make practical mates, who can best provide for us in terms of fund raising and charisma, whom we like enough to give money to, to whose fortunes our moods, to say nothing of the well-being of our party and our nation, will be tied, someone we will be able to defend (at least to the point of indefensibility), someone who, in those final fretting weeks, will be the last person we think of before we go to sleep at night and the first person we think of when we get up in the morning. If we've chosen wisely, and often even if we've chosen poorly, we develop an intense bond with this famous stranger. His or her successes become our triumphs; his or her failures bring us low.

I originally chose to support John Edwards, who turned out to be a bad and stupid man. Elaine Lafferty, experiencing some post-election buyer's remorse of her own for having worked for Palin, teased during one of our interviews, "Compared to John Edwards, Sarah Palin was [Liberian president] Ellen Johnson Sirleaf!"

In the postgame analysis of Edwards's venal flame-out, an enormous amount of blame would be heaped at the feet of his wife, Elizabeth, for having been less saintly than her fans might have hoped, for having been nasty to and demanding of her husband's campaign staff, for having made disparaging remarks about John's intellect, for having been ambitious, short-tempered, and suspicious of John's aides. The unpleasant characterizations of Elizabeth made me sad. I believed them. But I was not sure that they actually contradicted my longtime beliefs about her: that she was aggressive, smarter than her husband, and usually right about stuff. I had never considered her saintly; I had thought her steely and formidable. I was not surprised that she was paranoid, controlling, and grumpy; it seemed to me that this kind of behavior might well have been exacerbated by the fact that, at the time she was exhibiting it, she was terminally ill with cancer, her husband was having sex with his videographer, and his staff was covering it up for him.

What was altered was my vision of Elizabeth as sensible, forthright, and honest. It turned out that she had enabled her husband's deception, that she had supported his decision to stay in the race and perhaps encouraged it even though she knew that he had had an affair that would make him unelectable if ever it were exposed. She had not let him take the obvious excuse—the return of her cancer—to bow out. And she had thus taken an enormous risk with the well-being of the nation she claimed to want to help through better health care and economic policy. She may not have believed that a marital transgression of the sort committed by so many politicians before him should bar her husband from highest office; I could even reach back far enough into my idealized view of her priorities and imagine that perhaps she believed so firmly in the work she could do for the country that she stormed forward, believing that that work superseded the dopey choices of her dopey husband. I had always believed that it was Elizabeth who truly wanted to be the president. Unlike Hillary, she would never even get close.

* * *

For the wife who was actually living in the White House, life was happily less tawdry, but under just as much scrutiny. Michelle Obama, whose image had been scrupulously reshaped in the final months of the campaign to emphasize her roles as mother, wife and fashion plate, was a sensation. In the period between the election and her husband's inauguration, the press went bananas for Michelle, while her team broadcast as loudly as possible that there would be nothing Hillaryish about her stay on Pennsylvania Avenue: she wanted naught to do with policymaking, she said again and again. Michelle dubbed herself "mom-in-chief," a sobriquet comforting enough to have been conjured by the editors of *Good Housekeeping* in 1956. In her first year in the White House she dedicated herself most publicly to advocacy of healthier eating, planting a vegetable garden on the White House lawn; she worked on behalf of military families and visited bases regularly; she invited local schoolchildren into the White House, reminding everyone that it was "the people's house"; and she spent time in her new city, at soup kitchens and homeless shelters, doing what she had been committed to in Chicago: working to weave together disparate communities in shared neighborhoods.

All of her tasks were authentically Michelle: from fitness to community relations, from Jimmy Choo to J. Crew, there had been traces of all her identifying first-lady characteristics back when I met her in Iowa in 2007. But it did seem that her public presentation was a bit muffled. Michelle was undeniably appealing in her first year in the White House. She was also a little bit Stepfordized, missing some of the cool self-assurance, the fiercely held and candid views on American history and economic injustice, the biting humor, and the dauntless energy that had motored her through her high-powered career and juiced her introduction to America as an outspoken independent thinker.

On some level, to be sure, my dismay was rooted in my white-lady perspective, which perhaps did not account for the ways in which adoration of Michelle as a maternal, sartorial, and physical ideal were themselves progressive in a culture that mostly still saw black women as caretakers of other people's children and that rarely celebrated nonwhite female bodies. Melissa Harris-Lacewell wrote that Michelle was crucial to broadening and correcting the distorted caricatures of black women "as crack mothers, welfare queens, and matriarchs." The *Nation*'s Patricia Williams argued that we had long been missing a discussion of black women as "loving mothers, beloved wives, valued partners, cherished daughters,"

and that "Michelle Obama represents a more comprehensive identity for all women, but particularly for black women."

It was all true. But it didn't take away from the fact that the popular vision of Michelle as beautiful, well-dressed mother and wife
seemed to include no room for the other aspects of her personality
and life, from personal ambitions to independent identity outside her
family. Michelle Obama had been described by her first boss as the
most ambitious associate he'd ever seen. In *The Audacity of Hope*
her husband had written of first meeting his wife, "Michelle was . . .
full of plans . . . on the fast track, with no time, she told me, for dis-
tractions—especially men." Michelle had gone on to enjoy a career
to which she had been committed, her own substantial paycheck,
and a rich, independent life in a city in which she was entrenched.
Now all of that was temporarily, or perhaps permanently, on hold.

In its postelection piece about the adjustments faced by the
Obama family, the *New York Times* did not mention the presumed
end of Michelle's job at the University of Chicago Medical Center. It did suggest that, once she had settled her children into the
White House, she would have to figure out "exactly what sort of
first lady she wants to be." The *Times* noted, "Although she dresses
with unusual care . . . friends say she has only a certain amount
of patience for the domestic arts. She is a get-it-done efficiently
Rachael Ray type, they say, not given to elaborate Martha Stewart–
like efforts." In *New York* magazine David Samuels wrote admir-
ingly, "She went to excellent schools, got decent grades, stayed away
from too much intellectual heavy lifting, and held a series of practical, modestly salaried jobs while accommodating her husband's
wilder dreams and raising two lovely daughters. In this, she is a
more practical role model for young women than Hillary Clinton,
blending her calculations about family and career with an expectation of normal personal happiness."

There was very little media recognition of the fact that Michelle
was a woman whose lifetime of personal success had had nothing
to do with Rachael Ray, Martha Stewart or the crafts they plied.
Instead most of the coverage affirmed the satisfaction America had
taken in successfully recasting this complicated, outspoken, queru-
lous and ambitious woman as a more digestible sort. Erased was the
woman whose robust energies and domestic disclosures laid bare

her dissatisfactions and disappointments with having to accommodate "her husband's wilder dreams"; in her place was one who could comfortably serve as inspiration to the next generation of women who apparently should not yearn to exceed expectations, but instead satisfy themselves with middling success and a more successful spouse, the more attainable form of female happiness.

Toward the end of Obama's first year in office there were some in the media, admirers of the more complicated vision of Michelle, who were getting itchy. Noting the impossibly high expectations that greeted the first lady when she entered the White House, *Newsweek*'s Allison Samuels wrote that she was now hoping for more from her. The first lady's solid approval ratings gave her "an opportunity to plug both the president's agenda . . . and her own. . . . Imagine turning her healthy-eating quest into a full-blown anti-obesity campaign that takes on the junk-food lobby. Or making AIDS prevention and condom use a part of the national healthcare debate." Samuels acknowledged that taking a stand would mean that Michelle would "risk controversy and maybe even failure. But if she doesn't use this chance to take on the issues that really matter, that's just a failure of another kind."

Michelle Obama remained, as she had been from the start, in an uncomfortable bind.

*　*　*

In January 2009 Hillary Clinton was sworn in as Barack Obama's secretary of state. Zipping around the world, keeping her head down and her nose to the State Department grindstone, she worked so quietly in her first year on the job that some pundits assumed that she had had her wings clipped. After all, the notion of Hillary as unmanned by her new boss and former adversary was gratifying; it kept alive the rivalry that had so titillated us; it perpetuated the vision of Hillary as villain, as irritant and player. As it turned out, even those who didn't much like Hillary didn't want her to disappear. Describing what was missing from New York City in the fall of 2009, journalist Peter Kaplan wrote wistfully in *New York* magazine, "The one-woman ambition generator named Hillary R. Clinton is exporting her Lucy Van Pelt–like certitude to other nations."

Clinton had settled into one of the stages that always seemed to surprise people, no matter how regularly she entered them: she was wonking out, delegating work to competent colleagues, and strengthening her own position within the company, in this case Barack Obama's administration. It seemed to be going very well, actually. Hillary Clinton had managed a phoenix flight out of the ruins of her presidential campaign and out of the opprobrium in which she had been held by Democrats and Republicans, in varying degrees, for so long.

In 2009 her favorability ratings rose above Obama's, both among Democrats, 91 percent of whom believed she was doing a good job at the State Department, and among Republicans, who in October told pollsters that they approved of her over Obama by a margin of 16 percent. An annual Gallup poll at the end of 2009 found Hillary the most admired woman in America; it was the fourteenth time since 1993 that she had secured the top spot (though in 2009 Sarah Palin was behind her by just one percentage point).

At a March 2010 Women of Courage Awards presentation, Michelle Obama thanked her "dear friend" Hillary, accidentally referring to her as "Senator" instead of "Secretary." Obama recovered by joking, very warmly, "I almost said *President* Clinton."

On Clinton's first day at Foggy Bottom, State Department employees gathered to greet and applaud her like trilling munchkins after Dorothy dropped a house on the Wicked Witch of the East. In a profile in *Vogue* Jonathan Van Meter described her joint interview, alongside Secretary of Defense Bob Gates, in front of students at George Washington University: "She is a rock star. Students camped out in line for hours to get tickets to the event, which sold out in minutes. When she first appeared onstage the audience leaped to their feet, and the applause was deafening. . . . And despite the gravity of the occasion, a young woman bellowed at the top of her lungs, '*I love you, Hillllary!!!!*,' as if she were at a Lady Gaga concert." Van Meter went on to describe how capably Clinton played the crowd, cracking jokes about herself and earning big laughs, and in a later letter to *Vogue,* a young man would write to kvell about Clinton and take credit for having been the bellower.

The funniest thing had happened, after all the ugly, all the crazy, all the compromise and slippery politics and game playing and backbiting: Hillary Rodham had returned, at least briefly. And this time she was popular, cool, beloved, competent, maternal, warm, and even funny. More remarkable was that she was unafraid to be the woman who had gone to Beijing in 1995 and made a resounding feminist statement, the woman whose nuanced pro-woman politics had been muffled, if not squelched, during her campaign for political currency and on the road to the Oval Office. "Of particular concern to me is the plight of women and girls, who comprise the majority of the world's unhealthy, unschooled, unfed, and unpaid," said Clinton in her statement to the Senate Foreign Relations Committee on January 13, 2009. "If half of the world's population remains vulnerable to economic, political, legal and social marginalization, our hope of advancing democracy and prosperity is in serious jeopardy. The United States must be an unequivocal and unwavering voice in support of women's rights in every country on every continent." When questioned about her commitment to women's issues by committeewoman Barbara Boxer, Clinton replied, "I want to pledge to you that as secretary of state I view these issues as central to our foreign policy, not as adjunct or auxiliary or in any way lesser than all of the other issues that we have to confront."

In April 2009, when Afghanistan made moves to allow the government to legislate the frequency of sexual congress within marriage, Clinton stepped in and challenged President Hamid Karzai, who agreed to review the law. At a press conference, alongside Karzai and President Asif Ali Zardari of Pakistan, Clinton spoke about the necessity of women's rights under their oppressive regimes: "I will also reinforce, as I have on many occasions that this is not just me speaking, but this is the American government speaking. That we do not believe either Afghanistan or Pakistan can achieve lasting progress without the full participation of all of your citizens, including women and girls." During a House Foreign Relations Committee hearing, Clinton tussled with Chris Smith, a pro-life representative from New Jersey, who asked her whether the Obama administration included abortion in its definition of reproductive health, and if there were plans to undermine anti-abortion legislation in Africa or Latin America. Clinton unblinkingly responded, "When I think about the suffering I have seen, of women around the world—I've been in hospitals in Brazil, where half the women were enthusiastically and joyfully greeting new babies, and the other half were fighting for their lives against botched abortions. I've been in African countries where twelve- and thirteen-year-old girls are bearing children. I have been in Asian countries where the denial of family planning consigns women to lives of oppression and hardship. . . . We happen to think that family planning is an important part of women's health, and reproductive health includes access to abortion." Michelle Goldberg would later write of Clinton's remark, "[It] stands as the strongest defense of reproductive rights worldwide ever to issue from the lips of a senior government official."

Gloria Feldt speculated to me in 2009 that Clinton's dedication to women's issues had been reawakened by her presidential odyssey. "I think she's more authentic and that her inner feminist has come out much more," she said. "She's always had a strong sense of justice about feminism, about women, but I think the campaign forced her to just go ahead and be it." Latoya Peterson agreed: "[She] was able to say that one of the key state strategies is women and the economic security of women around the globe, and that it's a key component of our diplomatic strategy. That's huge! We would never have been able to do that before." The fact that Clinton was emphasizing the importance of women in society, and that international success depends in part on the economic stability and education of women around the world, said Peterson, was "an amazing, revolutionary thing to say. . . . And it would not have happened if things didn't shake out the way they did. . . . All the backlash against gender has opened up a very unique position for the Obama administration to actually verbalize a lot of things that I think would not have been acceptable beforehand."

In trips to South Korea and Turkey Clinton was treated like royalty, swamped by crowds in much the way her husband was received abroad. In fact it was astounding that not two years after the Clinton campaign had relied on—and worried about—her husband's epically persuasive charms, Hillary, as *Double X*'s Dayo Olopade noted in her response to a profile of Bill in the *New York Times Magazine,* had wound up "with an ability to barn-burn and kiss babies and rile a political base of her own, bigger (or, in the Internet age, at least more quantifiable) than her husband's." It was impossible not to notice how unfettered she appeared—free, now, to be unflinching about the terms of her independent success. When, on a trip to Africa in the summer of 2009, she was asked by a Congolese student to relay her husband's opinion on an international economic issue, she shot back, "You want me to tell you what my husband thinks? My husband is not secretary of state. I am."

Michelle Goldberg had fought fiercely on behalf of Barack Obama and against the older women who called Clinton's campaign a feminist imperative. Marking the anniversary of Clinton's concession with a piece for the *Daily Beast,* she admitted that when she listened to the "rousing and gracious" speech now she couldn't "help but tear up." Still glad she supported Obama, Goldberg nonetheless wrote, "Hillary Clinton has been the feminist hero of this administration." Gore Vidal, who had switched his allegiance from Clinton to Obama during the primaries, said in a September interview that he regretted the choice: "Hillary knows more about the world and what to do with the generals. History has proven when the girls get involved, they're good at it."

As the Obama administration made its inevitable compromises, especially in the months before passage of health-care reform, there were occasional rumblings of retrospective reconsideration, what the writer Linda Hirshman and I took to calling WWHHDs ("What would Hillary have done?"). Of course many of Obama's fiercest supporters still took comfort, especially when they felt most dubious about whether or not he was doing a great job, in asserting that Hillary would have been much, much worse.

Me, I was glad that Hillary was not the president. Not because I didn't think she'd be good. I thought, as I'd always thought, that her presidency would have looked very much like Obama's. As someone who had never entertained many progressive fantasies about an Obama presidency, it was easier for me to be generally satisfied with his administration. I also knew that if she had made all of the same decisions that he had—sending more troops to Afghanistan, passing a too-small stimulus, bailing out the banks without any strings attached, not getting out of Iraq within the year, forsaking a public option in the health care bill—the loathing and censure of her, the projections of how much finer a leader Obama would have been, would have driven me mad. I thought frequently of Gloria

Steinem's answer to the question of what she felt when Clinton conceded: relief. Yes, there was relief. I was so relieved that I didn't have to defend her, and more than that, that now there seemed to be so many others who were cheering her.

But perhaps all the bonhomie surrounding Clinton reflected a depressing truth: that it was easier to embrace this woman in a state of diminished power, once she had lost the big prize, when she was no longer threatening the chances of the cool guy. In February 2009 Chris Matthews bestowed a "Hardball Award" on Clinton; it was the first he'd ever given to a woman. Though it was meant to reward "personal moxie, savvy, [and] basic street smarts," Matthews made clear what had earned Clinton her mention; showing clips of her Denver speech urging her voters to back Obama, he said, "[This award is] for a bit of timely humility, for . . . a willingness to serve our country over self. We salute you. I salute you."

Steinem saw the change in attitude toward Clinton as quite predictable. "It's always been okay for women to sing the blues," she told me. "Just not so good for us to win. We all know deep in our hearts if we want to be loved we have to lose." But when I told her that the directness of this equation, like so many of the ways in which people had behaved toward Clinton, startled me, she replied that that in itself was a hopeful sign: "I'm glad it surprised you because that means you have higher standards, as you should. I devoutly want you to be surprised."

It was in this same interview that Steinem first told me that she voted for Clinton because she did not believe she could win her party's nomination. Believing Steinem to have misspoken, I interrupted her. "Because you knew she *couldn't* win?" I prompted, waiting for the correction. "Right," she said gently. "I've always known she couldn't win."

Our conversation took place on the afternoon before Steinem's seventy-fifth birthday and six weeks before my thirty-fourth. Only forty-one years separated us, but her statement left me pole-axed. Whatever my doubts about Hillary, it had never crossed my mind that she couldn't win. I had always believed, with varying degrees of dismay and hope, that she *might* win. There were days that I believed that she *would* win. In truth, she almost did win. The difference between Steinem's and my perspective on possibility demonstrated the changes in four decades in America.

The standards would be even higher for the children who had watched this story unfold, like one girl George Packer described in New Hampshire, who had held aloft a placard that read, "Hillary 2008, Sophia 2040," or my friend Geraldine's seven-year-old niece Libby, whose mother had taken her to the polls on election day to vote for Barack Obama only to discover, as she joked to Geraldine, that Libby was a PUMA, still too indignant over Hillary's defeat to fully embrace Obama. My memory of voting for Geraldine Ferraro had stuck; I imagined that these girls would not easily forget their early political attachment to a female candidate.

Many convictions were shaken and strengthened in the tumult of 2008. But the important part, no matter how tempered by imperfection and regret, rebellion and rapprochement, fury and hurt feelings, was that the raising of American expectations would not end with Gloria Steinem or Jesse Jackson or Hillary Clinton or Barack Obama or Sarah Palin, any more than it had with Frederick Douglass or Elizabeth Cady Stanton. That was the often maddening path of progress: moving forward despite or in reaction to setbacks, sometimes in circles, sometimes in great leaps; occasionally—terrifyingly—falling backward. The road was circuitous and rough, but in 2008 we had inched further toward ensuring that the inequities of the present will surprise the inheritors of the future.

ACKNOWLEDGMENTS

I'D LIKE TO express deep gratitude to my exceptional agent, Linda Loewenthal, and terrific editor, Wylie O'Sullivan, as well as to everyone at Free Press, especially Martha Levin, Dominick Anfuso, Sydney Tanigawa, Jill Siegel and Christine Donnelly.

Thanks to the colleagues alongside whom I reported on women in politics and pop culture, especially Caitlin Shamberg, Alex Koppelman, Mike Madden, Kerry Lauerman, Walter Shapiro, Lynn Harris, Judy Berman, Tracy Clark-Flory, Kate Harding, Hillary Frey, Ruth Henrich and Katharine Mieszkowski. And also to the editors for whom I wrote the stories that eventually became this book, including Lori Leibovich, Mark Schone, Kevin Berger, Jeanne Carstensen, Joy Press and Sarah Hepola at *Salon*, Richard Kim at the *Nation* and Lisa Chase at *Elle*. Special gratitude to Lori and to Lisa, who have been editors and friends as long as I have been in journalism, and to Joy, whose wise early edits were fundamental to the shape of this book. Extra thanks also to my friend and boss Joan Walsh for sending me to cover the election and then giving me time to write a book about it.

Thank you to everyone who spoke with me on and off the record and to the friends and family members who permitted me to recount their experiences here, including Geraldine Sealey, Merideth Finn, Becca O'Brien and especially Barbara and Daniel Traister, who remain remarkably sanguine about my cannibalizing their life for my work.

To Anna Holmes, Jean Howard, Lynda Obst, Nora Ephron, Colin Robinson, Linda Hirshman, Caitlin Klevorick, Paul Starr, Alex Rossmiller and Katha Pollitt for ideas, advice and bracing disagreement. To Katherine Lanpher for the title, Joan Leibovich for a kick in the pants, Nancy Rathbun for swift transcription, Bradley Rife for aggressive fact-checking, Sara Culley for going to Africa with me, Laura Miller for the Scrivener tip, Bonnie Berger for more video clips than I could watch in a lifetime and Sarah Karnasiewicz for the photographs. Thanks to the late Mary Parvin, who thought I was a writer before I did.

I am grateful to the several people who read portions of the manuscript as I worked, including Katie Baker, Elisabeth Franck-Dumas, Heather McPherson and Aaron Traister. I simply could not have written this book without the editing, counsel and friendship of Zoë Heller.

Thanks to my family: Barbara and Daniel Traister, Aaron and Karel Traister, the Howard-Bakers, Howard-Twitchells, Traister-Nobles, Judy and Pheroze Wadia and the Wadia-Haackes.

My most profound thanks go to Darius Wadia, who doesn't really think that gender is that big a deal, and with whom I have more fun than I knew possible.

NOTE ON THE AUTHOR'S
USE OF HER PREVIOUSLY
PUBLISHED WORK

A NOTE ABOUT reporting: Throughout this book, I have drawn on my reporting, and in some instances my own writing, about women and politics and the 2008 elections. Though in most cases I have rewritten and reworked the material, there are some sentences, paragraphs and ideas that I have stolen from myself. I thank *Salon, Elle* and *The Nation* for the opportunities to report and publish the following pieces, to which I have returned in this volume.

FROM *SALON*

"Stand By Your Man '04," January 23, 2004

"Is America Ready for the Wild Kerry Family?," February 4, 2004

"Behind the Scenes at the March for Women's Lives," April 26, 2004

"Vote Your Vagina!" June 11, 2004

"W is for Women?," August 30, 2004

"Teresa, Full of Grace," July 28, 2004

"Morality Play," February 9, 2005

"Thelma for President!," September 29, 2005

"Obama on Tour," November 11, 2005

"Putting Out for Women," March 16, 2006

"Hillary Is Us," October 16, 2006

"The Ladies' Man," January 29, 2007

"Hillary's Chest War," July 30, 2007

"The 9/11 Backlash against Women," October 3, 2007

"Stop Lying to Yourself. You Love Dennis Kucinich," November 5, 2007

"America's Next Top Spouse," November 13, 2007

"Michelle Obama Gets Real," November 28, 2007

"Campaigning While Female," December 19, 2007

"The Witch Ain't Dead and Chris Matthews Is a Ding-Dong," January 9, 2008

"Undecided 08: Should I Vote for Clinton or Obama?," February 4, 2008

"Big Blue (State)," February 5, 2008

"Yentas for Obama!," February 5, 2008

"Clinton Gets Her Party Started," February 6, 2008

"Hey Obama Boys: Back Off Already!," April 14, 2008

"Attention, Pundits: It Ain't Over," April 22, 2008

"Hillary Clinton's Bionic Quest Continues," April 23, 2008

"Feminism Is the New Funny," April 25, 2008

"What's So Bad about Sweetie, Anyway?," May 16, 2008

"Hillary's Final Curtain," June 8, 2008

"Why Clinton Voters Say They Won't Support Obama," June 23, 2008

"Angry PUMAs on the Prowl in Denver," August 26, 2008

"Isn't She Lovely," August 26, 2008

"Palin, Pregnancy and the Presidency," September 1, 2008

"Zombie Feminists of the RNC," September 11, 2008

"McCain Skewered on 'The View,'" September 12, 2008

"The Sarah Palin Pity Party," September 30, 2008

"How the Election Ate Daytime Television," October 9, 2008.

"Ladies of the Nightly News," October 30, 2008

"Sarah Palin: 'The Time for Choosin's Comin' Real Soon,'" October 31, 2008

"A Scary Halloween with Sarah Palin," November 1, 2008

"America Has Cracked Open," November 5, 2008

"The Momification of Michelle Obama," November 12, 2008

FROM *ELLE*

"The Second Coming: Can the Most Alpha of Males Comfortably Morph into a First Lady?," December 2007

"Our Favorite Female Comedians: They've Made Feminism Funny," March 2009

"Katie Couric: Reports of Her Demise Were Greatly Exaggerated," April 2009

FROM *THE NATION*

"Rachel Maddow's Life and Career," July 30, 2008

SELECTED BIBLIOGRAPHY

SO MUCH RESEARCH for this book happened years before I knew it was research. In some ways I have been reading for the twenty years since I began high school about the events, and some of the characters, that shaped this story. The list below (organized by chapter, and in the order in which I used them as reference) is my attempt to catalogue the published sources on which I drew directly in the course of reporting and writing this book, but I'm afraid that it is probably incomplete.

I have not, for reasons having to do with time and resources, included in this bibliography the hundreds of television clips to which I make reference in the previous pages. But I'd like to extend my profound thanks to the many websites—most notably Media Matters, The Huffington Post and Jezebel—that kept their thousand eyes on what seemed like a thousand channels, and in doing so created a video record of a couple of crazy years in media.

INTRODUCTION

"Taking Sexism Seriously." Third Estate Sunday Review blog.

Seigel, Deborah. *Sisterhood Interrupted: From Radical Women to Girls Gone Wild.* New York: Palgrave Macmillan, 2007.

Hirshman, Linda. *Get to Work: A Manifesto for Women of the World.* New York: Viking Adult, 2006.

Bennetts, Leslie. *The Feminine Mistake: Are We Giving Up Too Much?* New York: Voice, 2008.

Levy, Ariel. *Female Chauvinist Pigs: Women and the Rise of Raunch Culture.* New York: Free Press, 2005.

CHAPTER 1

Bernstein, Carl. *A Woman in Charge: The Life of Hillary Rodham Clinton.* New York: Knopf, 2007.

Steinem, Gloria. "Right Candidates, Wrong Question." Op-ed. *New York Times,* February 7, 2007.

Douglas, Susan J. "Why Women Hate Hillary." *In These Times,* April 26, 2007.

Douglas, Ann. "The Extraordinary Hillary Clinton." *Vogue,* December 1998.

Lewis, Judith. "Do the Jane Fonda." *LA Weekly,* May 3, 2007.

Wilentz, Amy. "Yellow Pantsuit." In *Thirty Ways of Looking at Hillary: Reflections by Women Writers,* edited by Susan Morrison, 1–8. New York: HarperCollins, 2008.

Clinton, Hillary Rodham. *Living History.* New York: Simon & Schuster, 2003.

Balterman, Lee. "Class Leader Hillary Rodham of Wellesley College." *Life,* June 11, 1969.

Rodham, Hillary D. "1969 Student Commencement Speech." Wellesley College. May 31, 1969. Wellesley College website.

Mundy, Liza. "The Hillary Dilemma." *Washington Post Magazine,* March 21, 1999.

LiCari, Jonnel. "Molly Ivins: She Did Say That." *Wisconsin State Journal,* May 20, 1992.

Wills, Garry. "H. R. Clinton's Case." *New York Review of Books* 30, no. 5 (1992).

Ungles, Janet. "I'm Not a Romantic, I'm an Ironic." *Newsday,* June 24, 1993.

Ephron, Nora. "Remarks to Wellesley College Class of 1996." Wellesley College. 1996. Wellesley College website.

Packer, George. "The Choice." *The New Yorker,* January 28, 2008.

Starr, Paul. "The Hillarycare Mythology." *American Prospect,* September 14, 2007.

Clinton, Hillary Rodham. "Remarks by First Lady Hillary Rodham Clinton." United Nations Economic and Social Council. December 10, 1997.

Furchgott-Roth, Diana, and Christine Stolba. *The Feminist Dilemma: When Success Is Not Enough.* Washington, DC: AEI Press, 2001.

Green, Joshua. "Hillary's Choice." *The Atlantic,* November 2006.

Ivins, Molly. "I Will Not Support Hillary Clinton for President." *Columbus Free Press,* January 20, 2006.

Ephron, Nora. "But Who's the Candidate?," *Huffington Post,* April 18, 2006.

Chaudhry, Lakshmi. "What Women See When They See Hillary." *The Nation,* June 14, 2007.

Quindlen, Anna. "The Brand New and Same Old." *Newsweek,* May 28, 2007.

Hantschel, Allison. "I Won't Support Hillary Just Because She's a Woman." *Sirens Magazine,* October 19, 2006.

CHAPTER 2

Edwards, Elizabeth. *Saving Graces: Finding Solace and Strength from Friends and Strangers.* New York: Broadway, 2006.

Goldfarb, Zachary A. "Edwards Takes Heat over Quotations about Hillary." *Washington Post,* October 22, 2006.

Hirshman, Linda. "Homeward Bound." *American Prospect,* November 21, 2005.

Brooks, David. "The Year of Domesticity." *New York Times,* January 1, 2005.

Flanagan, Caitlin. *To Hell with All That: Loving and Loathing Our Inner Housewife.* Boston: Little, Brown, 2006.

Bennetts, Leslie. *The Feminine Mistake: Are We Giving Up Too Much?* New York: Voice, 2007.

Hawkes, Ellen. "Elizabeth Edwards, the Strategist." *Ms. Magazine,* spring 2004.

Koppelman, Alex, and Rebecca Traister. "Edwards Campaign Fires Bloggers." Salon, February 7, 2007.

Marcotte, Amanda. "Why I Had to Quit the John Edwards Campaign." *Salon,* February 16, 2007.

Broder, John M. "Edwards's Bloggers Cross the Line, Critic Says." *New York Times,* February 7, 2007.

Shark-Fu. "My People Call It Accurate." *Angry Black Bitch,* February 7, 2007.

Zuzu. "This Is Really Getting Out of Hand." *Feministe,* February 7, 2007.

Klein, Ezra. "Edwards, Marcotte, and McEwan." Tapped blog. *American Prospect,* February 7, 2007.

Schachner, Judith. *Skippyjon Jones.* New York: Dutton Juvenile, 2003.

Kantor, Jodi, and Jeff Zeleny. "Michelle Obama Adds New Role to Balancing Act." *New York Times,* May 18, 2007.

Lee, Tonya Lewis. "Your Next First Lady?" *Glamour,* September 3, 2007.

Dowd, Maureen. "She's Not Buttering Him Up." *New York Times,* April 25, 2007.

Collins, Lauren. "The Other Obama." *The New Yorker,* March 10, 2008.

Tkacik, Moe. "Maybe It's Just Us, but Michelle Obama Seems Pissed about Something Other Than Never Having to Work Again." *Jezebel,* May 21, 2007.

Glover, Mike. "Michelle Obama Goes Solo in Iowa." *Chicago Sun Times,* April 1, 2007.

Mundy, Liza. *Michelle: A Biography.* New York: Simon & Schuster, 2008.

Amusa, Malena. "Michelle Obama for President." *RaceWire,* May 22, 2007.

Giddings, Paula J. "The Woman beside Him." *Essence,* January 2009.

Dickerson, Debra. "Michelle Obama's Sacrifice." *Salon,* May 21, 2007.

CHAPTER 3

Sullivan, Ronald. "Dakotan Beats Humphrey by a Big Margin in Jersey." *New York Times,* June 7, 1972.

Santora, Marc. "Pointed Question Puts McCain in a Tight Spot." *New York Times,* November 14, 2007.

Green, Joshua. "The Front-Runner's Fall." *The Atlantic,* September 2008.

Green, Joshua. "The Hillary Clinton Memos." *The Atlantic,* September 2008.

Kornblut, Anne E. *Notes from the Cracked Ceiling: Hillary Clinton, Sarah Palin, and What It Will Take for a Woman to Win.* New York: Crown, 2009.

Lowy, Joan A. *Pat Schroeder: A Woman of the House.* Albuquerque: University of New Mexico Press, 2003.

Walsh, Joan. "Elizabeth Edwards Didn't Call Hillary Clinton a Man." *Salon,* July 17, 2007.

Scherer, Michael. "Hillary Is from Mars, Obama Is from Venus." *Salon,* July 12, 2007.

Abcarian, Robin. "Clinton Not an Easy Sell to All Women." *Los Angeles Times,* December 7, 2007.

Kissling, Frances. "Why I'm Still Not for Hillary." *Salon,* January 10, 2008.

Givhan, Robin. "Hillary Clinton's Tentative Dip into New Neckline Territory." *Washington Post,* July 20, 2007.

Chisholm '72: Unbought and Unbossed. Dir. Shola Lynch. 20th Century Fox, 2005.

Healy, Patrick. "For Clintons, Delicate Dance of Married and Public Lives." *New York Times,* May 23, 2006.

Simon, Roger. "Edwards Is Mad and Won't Take It Anymore." *Politico,* July 23, 2007.

Andrews, Helena. "Hillary and the Giant Peach." *Politico,* July 24, 2007.

"The Most Significant Photo of 2007 . . ." *Immodest Proposals,* December 17, 2007.

Althouse, Ann. "That Picture of Hillary on Drudge Right Now." *Althouse,* December 17, 2007.

Rich, Frank. "Is Hillary Clinton the New Old Al Gore?" *New York Times,* September 30, 2007.

Bumiller, Elisabeth. "Clinton and Obama Clash on 'Piling on' Remarks." *New York Times,* November 2, 2007.

CHAPTER 4

"Clinton Campaign Memo in Iowa." *New York Times,* May 23, 2007.

Klein, Ezra. "The Press Corps." *American Prospect,* January 6, 2008.

Packer, George. "The Choice." *The New Yorker,* January 28, 2008.

Alter, Jonathan. "How Tomorrow Became Yesterday." *Newsweek,* January 14, 2008.

Tapper, Jake. "Hillary's Debate Moment." Political Punch blog. ABC.com, January 5, 2008.

Steinem, Gloria. "Women Are Never Front-Runners." Op-ed. *New York Times,* January 8, 2008.

O'Rourke, Meghan. "Hillary's Moment, and the Problem of 'Seeming' Sexism." XX Factor blog. *Slate,* January 8, 2008.

Valenti, Jessica. "Hillary Tears Up on Campaign Trail, Edwards Attacks." *Feministing,* January 7, 2008.

Valenti, Jessica. "Hillary Sexism Watch: If a Woman Is President, Who Will Iron the Shirts?" *Feministing,* January 8, 2008.

Warner, Judith. "Emotion without Thought in New Hampshire." Opinionator blog. *New York Times,* January 10, 2008.

Tkacik, Moe. "So Basically, Women Voters Just Chose the 'Crying Will Get You What You Want' Candidate. Awesome." *Jezebel,* January 9, 2008.

Kornblut, Anne E. *Notes from the Cracked Ceiling: Hillary Clinton, Sarah Palin, and What It Will Take for a Woman to Win.* New York: Crown, 2009.

Grose, Jessica. "What Were New Hampshire Women Thinking When They Picked Hillary? Who Knows?" *Jezebel,* January 9, 2008.

Spaulding, Pam. "New Hampshire Primary Open Thread." *Pam's House Blend,* January 8, 2008.

Yglesias, Matt. "The Clinton Comeback." *The Atlantic,* January 9, 2008.

Healy, Patrick, and Michael Cooper. "Clinton Is Victor, Turning Back Obama; McCain Also Triumphs." *New York Times,* January 9, 2008.

CHAPTER 5

Steinem, Gloria. "Right Candidates, Wrong Question." Op-ed. *New York Times,* February 7, 2007.

Woolf, Virginia. *A Room of One's Own.* 1929. New York: Mariner, 2005.

Democracy Now! PBS, January 14, 2008.

Foner, Eric. *A Short History of Reconstruction.* New York: Harper Perennial, 1990.

Petty, Leslie. *Romancing the Vote: Feminist Activism in American Fiction, 1870–1920.* Athens: University of Georgia Press, 2006.

Douglass, Frederick. *Frederick Douglass on Women's Rights.* Edited by Philip S. Foner. Cambridge, MA: Da Capo, 1992.

Stanton, Elizabeth Cady, Susan B. Anthony, and Matilda Joslyn Gage, eds. *The History of Woman Suffrage.* Vol. 2, *1861–1876.* New York: Fowler and Wells, 1881.

Fang, Jennifer. "Gloria Steinem: Pitting Race against Gender." *Racialicious,* January 9, 2008.

Harris-Lacewell, Melissa. "Rally for Him Now: How Black America Can Revive Obama's Campaign." *Slate,* January 9, 2008.

The Education of Shelby Knox. Dir. Rose Rosenblatt and Maion Lipschutz. Incite Pictures, 2005.

Packer, George. "The Choice." *The New Yorker,* January 28, 2008.

"Unite, Not Divide, Really This Time." Editorial. *New York Times,* January 9, 2008.

Brown, Carrie Budoff. "Obama 'Unhappy' with Racial Memo." *Politico,* January 16, 2008.

Crenshaw, Kimberle, and Eve Ensler. "Feminist Ultimatums: Not in Our Name." *Huffington Post.* February 5, 2008.

Murray, Shailagh. "For Black Superdelegates, Pressure to Back Obama." *Washington Post.* March 3, 2008.

Seeley, Katharine Q. "Jackson: Not Upset by Clinton Remarks." *New York Times,* January 28, 2008.

Belton, Danielle. "Most Overhyped 'Obama' Fight: Poor Pitiful Politicians and the Black Blogger Revolt." *Black Snob,* April 9, 2008.

Jenkins, Carol. "The Invisible Majority." Women's Media Center. 2008.

Samuels, Allison. "The Legacy of My Grandmother." *Newsweek,* March 17, 2008.

Reed, Adolph, Jr. "Obama No." *The Progressive,* May 2008.

Smith, Ben. "A Ferraro Flashback." *Politico,* March 11, 2008.

"Morning in America: A Letter from Feminists on the Election." *The Nation,* February 27, 2008.

CHAPTER 6

Rush, George, and Joanna Molloy. "Obama Girl Has Hil Thrill." *New York Daily News,* August 23, 2007.

Kantor, Jodi. "Chelsea Clinton Talks Policy in Obama Territory." *New York Times,* February 16, 2008.

Wheaton, Sarah. "Obama's the Big Man on Campus." Opinionator blog. *New York Times,* February 2, 2007.

Steinem, Gloria. "Women Are Never Front-Runners." Op-ed. *New York Times,* January 8, 2008.

Morgan, Robin. "Good-bye to All That." Reprinted in *Dear Sisters: Dispatches from the Women's Liberation Movement,* edited by Rosalyn Baxendall and Linda Gordon. New York: Basic, 2001.

Morgan, Robin. "Good-bye to All That #2." *The Guardian,* February 14, 2008.

Levy, Ariel. "Goodbye Again." *The New Yorker,* April 21, 2008.

Friedman, Ann. "Goodbye Indeed." *Feministing,* February 5, 2008.

Goldberg, Michelle. "Hell Hath No Fury." *The Guardian,* March 13, 2008.

Dominus, Susan. "Feminists Find Unity Is Elusive." *New York Times,* February 1, 2008.

Collins, Gail. *When Everything Changed: The Amazing Journey of American Women from 1960 to the Present.* Boston: Little, Brown, 2009.

Bennetts, Leslie. "Go Away? Why Should She?" *Los Angeles Times,* March 9, 2008.

Hirshman, Linda. "Yo Mamma." *Slate,* April 18, 2008.

Martin, Courtney. "The Emotional Voter." Glamocracy blog. *Glamour,* April 3, 2008.

Hirshman, Linda. "The Trouble with Jezebel." *Double X,* May 12, 2009.

Dickerson, Debra J. "The Future of Abortion Providers." Mojo blog. *Mother Jones,* March 10, 2009.

Dickerson, Debra J. "Throwing Clinton under the Bus to Spite Mom." Mojo blog. *Mother Jones,* April 21, 2008.

Fortini, Amanda. "The Feminist Reawakening." *New York Magazine,* April 13, 2008.

Hirshman, Linda. "Looking to the Future, Feminism Has to Focus." *Washington Post,* June 8, 2008.

Powell, Kevin. "Time for New Black Leaders." *Huffington Post,* July 15, 2008.

Harris, Mark. "The Gay Generation Gap." *New York Magazine,* June 21, 2009.

Martin, Courtney E. "Generation Y Refuses Race-Gender Dichotomy." *Alternet,* June 18, 2008.

Valenti, Jessica. "The Sisterhood Split." *The Nation,* March 6, 2008.

Grose, Jessica. "*Ms.* Matriarch to Daughter: 'When Push Comes to Shove [Why] Can't You Vote for a Woman?" *Jezebel,* March 12, 2008.

Dickerson, Debra J. "Don't Trust Any Feminists under 30." Mojo blog. *Mother Jones,* March 16, 2009.

Martin, Courtney E.. "More Than a Mother-Daughter Debate." *American Prospect,* April 21, 2008.

CHAPTER 7

Pollitt, Katha. "Iron My Skirt." *The Nation,* June 5, 2008.

Wakeman, Jessica. "On Sexist Media Coverage of Hillary Clinton." *Huffington Post,* April 27, 2008.

Rosen, Ruth. *The World Split Open: How the Modern Women's Movement Changed America.* Revised edition. New York: Penguin, 2006.

Keetley, Dawn. *Public Women, Public Words: A Documentary History of American Feminism.* Madison, WI: Madison House Publishers, 2003.

DuPlessis, Rachel B., and Ann Snitow, eds. *The Feminist Memoir Project: Voices from Women's Liberation.* New Brunswick, NJ: Rutgers University Press, 2007.

Barber, David. *A Hard Rain Fell: SDS and Why It Failed.* Jackson: University of Mississippi Press, 2008.

Chafe, William H. *The Paradox of Change: American Women in the 20th Century.* New York: Oxford University Press, 1991.

Morgan, Robin. "Good-bye to All That." Reprinted in *Dear Sisters: Dispatches from the Women's Liberation Movement,* ed. Rosalyn Baxendall and Linda Gordon. New York: Basic, 2001.

Moulitsas, Markos. "Pie Fight Ad." *Daily Kos,* June 5, 2005.

Moulitsas, Markos. "The Curse of the Single Issue Groups." *Daily Kos,* May 23, 2005.

Harding, Kate. "Stupak: Two More Years?!?" *Salon,* January 14, 2010.

Harding, Kate. "Female 'Person of the Year.'" *Salon,* December 17, 2009.

Moulitsas, Markos. "Ditch the DCCC." *Daily Kos,* November 9, 2009.

Moulitsas, Markos. "Clinton's License to Do Harm." *Daily Kos,* April 17, 2008.

Packer, George. "The Choice." *The New Yorker,* January 28, 2008.

Hill, John. "Crash Course Looks to Super Tuesday." *Sacramento Bee,* January 21, 2008.

Geier, Kathleen. "Barack Obama Is Not Jesus." TPM Café blog. *Talking Points Memo,* February 5, 2008.

Hayden, Tom, Bill Fletcher Jr., Danny Glover and Barbara Ehrenreich. "Progressives for Obama." *The Nation,* March 24, 2008.

Fortini, Amanda. "The Feminist Reawakening." *New York Magazine,* April 13, 2008.

Kantor, Jodi. "The First Marriage." *New York Times Magazine,* November 1, 2009.

Alter, Jonathan. "Hillary Should Get Out Now." *Newsweek,* March 3, 2008.

Goldberg, Michelle. "Three A.M. for Feminism." *New Republic,* June 25, 2008.

Reed, Adolph, Jr. "Obama No." *The Progressive,* May 2008.

Spaulding, Pam. "Hillary Invokes RFK Assassination." *Pam's House Blend,* May 23, 2008.

Green, Joshua. "The Hillary Clinton Memos." *The Atlantic,* September 2008.

Shark-Fu. "A Toast from This Hard-Working American." *Angry Black Bitch,* May 8, 2008.

Krugman, Paul. "Sexism? Who Us?" *New York Times,* June 13, 2008.

Tannen, Deborah. "I'm Sorry, I Won't Apologize." *New York Times Magazine,* July 21, 1996.

Krugman, Paul. "Obama Does Harry and Louise, Again." The Conscience of a Liberal blog. *New York Times,* February 1, 2008.

Klein, Ezra. "Obama's 'Harry and Louise' Ad." Tapped blog. *American Prospect,* February 1, 2008.

Leibovich, Mark. "Man's World at the White House? No Harm, No Foul, Aides Say." *New York Times,* October 24, 2009.

Thurston, Baratunde. "This Primary Campaign Has Brought Out the Best and Worst in Me." *Huffington Post,* June 3, 2008.

Klein, Joe. "The Incredible Shrinking Democrats." *Time,* April 24, 2008.

"The Low Road to Victory." Editorial. *New York Times,* April 23, 2008.

Dowd, Maureen. "Wilting over Waffles." *New York Times,* April 23, 2008.

Sklar, Rachel. "Olbermann's Idea for Beating Hillary: Literally Beating Hillary." *Huffington Post,* May 2, 2008.

Boehlert, Eric. "So Now the Press Tells Candidates When to Quit?" *Media Matters,* April 30, 2008.

CHAPTER 8

Ephron, Nora. *Crazy Salad: Some Things about Women.* New York: Knopf, 1975.

Kantor, Jodi. "Clinton Bloc Becomes the Prize for Election Day." *New York Times,* June 7, 2008.

Boyer, Peter J. "One Angry Man." *The New Yorker,* June 23, 2008.

Horowitz, Jason. "Clinton Bundler on Obama's Doyle Pick: The Biggest 'Fuck You' Ever." *New York Observer,* June 16, 2008.

Heilemann, John, and Mark Halperin. *Game Change: Obama and the Clintons, McCain and Palin, and the Race of a Lifetime.* New York: HarperCollins, 2010.

Curtis, Mary C. "The Loud Silence of the Feminists." *Washington Post,* June 21, 2008.

Geraghty, Jim. "Contrasting John McCain and Michelle Obama." *National Review Online,* February 19, 2008.

Hitchens, Christopher. "Are We Getting Two for One?" *Slate,* May 5, 2008.

Coates, Ta-Nehisi. "Christopher Hitchens on Obama and Rev. Wright: When All Else Fails Blame Women." *The Atlantic,* May 6, 2008.

Koppelman, Alex. "Fox News Calls Michelle Obama 'Obama's Baby Mama.'" *Salon,* June 12, 2008.

Saul, Michael. "With the Help of Off-the-rack Dress, Michelle Obama Eases Harsh Image." *New York Daily News,* June 19, 2008.

CHAPTER 9

Heilemann, John, and Mark Halperin. *Game Change: Obama and the Clintons, McCain and Palin, and the Race of a Lifetime.* New York: HarperCollins, 2010.

Draper, Robert. "John McCain—The Making (and Remaking and Remaking) of the Candidate." *New York Times Magazine,* October 22, 2008.

Kornblut, Anne E. *Notes from the Cracked Ceiling: Hillary Clinton, Sarah Palin, and What It Will Take for a Woman to Win.* New York: Crown, 2009.

Vick, Karl. "'I'll Sell My Soul to the Devil'; Corruption Scandals Involve Alaska's Biggest Political Names." *Washington Post,* November 12, 2007.

Carpentier, Megan. "Any Excuse to Run a Picture of Sarah Palin." *Wonkette,* November 12, 2007.

Johnson, Rebecca. "Altered State." *Vogue,* February 2008.

Dittrich, Luke. "Todd Palin Is the Man for America Now." *Esquire,* May 2009.

Murphy, Jen. "Running Alaska: Sarah Palin." *Wall Street Journal Magazine,* September 2008.

Grose, Jessica. "Why Sarah Palin Incites Near-Violent Rage in Normally Reasonable Women." *Jezebel,* September 5, 2008.

Palin, Sarah. *Going Rogue.* New York: HarperCollins, 2009.

Sheppard, Kate. "McSexist." *In These Times,* July 21, 2008.

Seelye, Katharine Q. "Palin's 17-Year-Old Daughter Is Pregnant." The Caucus blog. *New York Times,* September 1, 2008.

Sullivan, Andrew. "Things That Make You Go Hmmm." The Daily Dish blog. *The Atlantic,* August 31, 2008.

Seelye, Katharine Q. "Palin's Teen Daughter Is Pregnant; New G.O.P. Tumult." *New York Times,* September 1, 2007.

Quinn, Sally. "Palin's Pregnancy Problem." On Faith blog. *Washington Post,* August 29, 2009.

Estrich, Susan. "Sarah Palin and the Double Standard." Fox News, September 3, 2008.

Lippert, Barbara. "Analysis: Feminism's Next Wave." *Adweek,* September 8, 2008.

CHAPTER 10

Palin, Sarah. *Going Rogue.* New York: HarperCollins, 2009.

Greenwald, Glenn. "Correction on Sarah Palin." *Salon,* September 25, 2009.

Warner, Judith. "Poor Sarah." Opinionator blog. *New York Times,* September 25, 2009.

Faludi, Susan. *The Terror Dream: Fear and Fantasy in Post 9/11 America.* New York: Metropolitan, 2007.

Carr, David. "A Ship Leaks, but She Wants to Anchor It." *New York Times,* March 13, 2006.

Carr, David. "The Media Equation: An Anchor Lets Down Her Hair." *New York Times,* September 14, 2008.

Steinberg, Jacques. "'The View' Has Its Eye on Politics This Year." *New York Times,* September 23, 2008.

Hall, Jane. "Q&A with Phil Donahue: Breaking a News 'Chokehold.'" *Los Angeles Times,* November 12, 1992.

Gold, Matea. "'The View' Gets Political: Viewers Love It (and So Does D.C.)." *Los Angeles Times,* February 8, 2010.

Hitchens, Christopher. "Why Women Aren't Funny." *Vanity Fair,* January 2007.

Stanley, Alessandra. "Who Says Women Aren't Funny?" *Vanity Fair,* April 2008.

Unterbrink, Mary. *Funny Women: American Comediennes, 1860–1985.* Jefferson, NC: McFarland, 1987.

Valenti, Jessica. "Sense and Humour." *The Guardian,* November 19, 2008.

Dowd, Maureen. "What Tina Fey Wants." *Vanity Fair,* January 2009.

Heffernan, Virginia. "Annals of Entertainment: Anchor Woman." *The New Yorker,* November 11, 2003.

CHAPTER 11

Smith, Ben. "Palin Allies Report Rising Camp Tension." *Politico,* October 25, 2008.

Kristol, William. "The Wright Stuff." *New York Times,* October 5, 2008.

Bosmon, Julie. "Palin Speaking Up for Herself." *New York Times,* October 21, 2008.

Parker, Kathleen. "Palin Problem." *National Review,* September 26, 2008.

Levine, Suzanne Braun. "Having It All." *Huffington Post,* October 1, 2008.

Harris, John F., and Beth Frerking. "Clinton Aides: Palin Treatment Sexist." *Politico,* September 3, 2008.

Wilson, Cintra. "Pissed about Palin." *Salon,* September 10, 2008.

Young, Cathy. "Why Feminists Hate Sarah Palin." *Wall Street Journal,* September 15, 2008.

Carpentier, Megan. "Please, People: Stop Making Me Defend Sarah Palin—Girl on Girl Crime." *Jezebel,* September 10, 2008.

Kolhatkar, Sheelah. "Les Ms.-erables Bust Cover." *New York Observer,* April 3, 2005.

Goodman, Ellen. "Sarah Palin Could Be a 'Bridge to Nowhere' for Women." *Boston Globe,* September 3, 2008.

Collins, Gail. *When Everything Changed: The Amazing Journey of American Women from 1960 to the Present.* Boston: Little, Brown, 2009.

Lafferty, Elaine. "Sarah Palin's a Brainiac." *Daily Beast,* October 27, 2008.

Smith, Ben. "Sarah Palin Takes Low-Key Return to the Road." *Politico,* June 6, 2009.

Siskind, Amy. "Letterman Quietly Ushers In the Next Wave of Feminism." *Huffington Post,* June 15, 2009.

CHAPTER 12

Coates, Ta-Nehisi. "American Girl." *The Atlantic,* January 2009.

Walshe, Shushannah. "Sarah Palin's Lost Speeches." *Daily Beast,* November 3, 2009.

Thrush, Glenn. "Bachmann: 'Don't Let Them Palinize Me!'" *Politico,* August 13, 2009.

Parker, Kathleen. "Republican Women: Hear Them Roar." *Washington Post,* October 15, 2009.

Heilemann, John, and Mark Halperin. *Game Change: Obama and the Clintons, McCain and Palin, and the Race of a Lifetime.* New York: HarperCollins, 2010.

Harris-Lacewell, Melissa. "Michelle Obama: Mom in Chief." *The Nation,* May 5, 2009.

Williams, Patricia. "Mrs. Obama Meets Mrs. Windsor." *The Nation,* April 8, 2009.

Obama, Barack. *The Audacity of Hope.* New York: Crown, 2006.

Kantor, Jodi. "Striking a Balance While Becoming a First Family." *New York Times,* November 6, 2008.

Samuels, David. "Regarding Michelle Obama: Normalizing the President." *New York Magazine,* March 15, 2009.

Samuels, Allison. "What Michelle Obama Must Do Now." *Newsweek,* October 24, 2009.

Kaplan, Peter W. "Couch Warfare." *New York Magazine,* September 6, 2009.

Landler, Mark. "Secretary of State Clinton Arrives at Foggy Bottom." The Caucus blog. *New York Times,* January 22, 2009.

Carpentier, Megan. "Hillary Clinton Taled the (Girl) Talk at Senate Confirmation." *Jezebel,* January 14, 2009.

Van Meter, Jonathan. "Her Brilliant Career." *Vogue,* December 2009.

Goldberg, Michelle. "Hillary's New Crusade." *Daily Beast,* June 7, 2009.

Olopade, Dayo. "Bill Clinton Has Finally Figured Out First Dudeship." *Double X,* May 27, 2009.

Teeman, Tim. "Gore Vidal: 'We'll Have a Dictatorship Soon in the U.S.'" *The Times (London),* September 30, 2009.

INDEX

ABOUT THE AUTHOR

Rebecca Traister is senior writer for *Salon,* where she has written about women in politics, media, and entertainment since 2003, and where she covered the 2008 presidential campaign from a feminist perspective. She has also written for *Elle,* the *Nation,* the *New York Observer, Vogue* and the *New York Times,* among other publications. She lives in Brooklyn with her husband.